*MIGUEL DE UNAMUNO*

# *MIGUEL DE UNAMUNO*

*Julián Marías*

translated by Frances M. López-Morillas

*HARVARD UNIVERSITY PRESS • Cambridge, Massachusetts • 1966*

Distributed in Great Britain by Oxford University Press, London

Library of Congress Catalog Card Number 66–18251
Printed in the United States of America

*Uxori dilectissimae*

## *PREFACE TO THE FIRST EDITION*

The need for a philosophical review of Unamuno's thought has been urgently felt for a long time. The disquieting and ambiguous bulk of his work has been impressing itself on the Spanish mind for many years, but as yet no one has been able to take a sufficiently clear position in regard to it. Unamuno has been a disturbing thinker, difficult to grasp, replete with intimate difficulties, disparate, crisscrossed by philosophical and religious errors and, specifically, by an unnecessary heterodoxy which, far from rising out of the deepest springs of his thought, diminishes and blunts his most perspicacious findings. But, at the same time there exist in his work brilliant guesses and inspirations which we cannot do without. This is why I have felt it worth while to make the effort to penetrate the meaning of Don Miguel de Unamuno's work, which is, strictly speaking, a problem of philosophy.

J.M.

Madrid
October 1942

## *PREFACE TO THE AMERICAN EDITION*

Whenever one of my books crosses a language boundary I have a sensation of anxiety and apprehension; for, whether I like it or not, it is going to turn into a different book, and is going to say to its readers something other than what I wrote. In fact, the written words are all that is necessary for the Spanish reader; the rest of what I want to say need not be expressed because it is too well-known; the reader, who belongs to the same society as the author, knows it already. But, when the book is translated into another language, when it speaks to those who do not share so many "family secrets," it cannot count on this context; the text must fall back on itself. Nor is this the worst of it. The foreign reader puts the text into his own context; that is, he receives and understands it out of certain assumptions which the author had not taken into account when he wrote. So the writer finds that he is saying both more and less than what he originally wrote.

The same words and turns of expression have different connotations, arouse different associations. I have occasionally made the experiment of reading one of my pages in the original and then in two or three foreign translations: it sounds in as many different ways as there are translations, has a diverse emotional tone, even a differing intellectual meaning.

One of my first books, *Miguel de Unamuno,* is now appearing in English in the United States. It is one of my most intensely written books (and by this I mean most deeply thought out and lived within the context of the Spanish language.) Therefore the hazard is greater when it transmigrates into another living body, that of the English language. Its rhythm, its pace, its tone, all change. Its "neighbors" also change: while my words have affinities with Ortega, Antonio Machado, Quevedo, and Cervantes, the words which now invest my book are nearer to Hemingway, Faulkner, Emerson, Poe, John Donne, or Shakespeare. What it now says it says with them—with their words, their turns of phrase, their voices. And it is all so different!

But the book is also about Unamuno. It may be argued that he has been translated into English many times and that American readers are familiar with his work. However, we are not dealing here with one of Unamuno's books, but a book *on* Unamuno: Unamuno *whole* and Unamuno *interpreted*. How can this view of Unamuno penetrate the mind—perhaps even the life—of a man or a woman of the United States?

The admirable translation of this book will allow the reader to slip very smoothly into its prose; but I should like this entrance into another world to be distinctly felt even though it be with velvety softness—even though the transition be, as Unamuno says of death's approach, "the velvet step of a naked foot." For what is involved, what should be involved for the reader, is to progress as far as possible, to achieve maximum enrichment, to stretch to the utmost his way of seeing and feeling things.

This is what Unamuno stands for, seen from an American perspective: the highest degree of the Other. His perspective, the order and disposition which the things of this world—and the next—assumed in his tormented heart, represent something irreconcilable to all the modes of installation in life which have ever existed in the United States. This does not mean that the American is incapable of understanding the Other; on the contrary, I believe that when he confronts it he will understand it very well—after having made the transition to which I referred.

I am particularly hopeful about the fate of this book in the United States. I feel that it expresses rather forcefully one form of looking at reality, of understanding life, of expecting death and trying to understand it. And that form is conditioned by what Spain has been for centuries, precipitated and distilled in the fierce personality of Unamuno, now interpreted from a different attitude and placed in a different context. Whatever the value of this form of living and thinking may be—not to say the value of this book—it represents something new for American readers. Since man is a spiritual cannibal and feeds on other lives, it is essential that occasionally something truly Other should be placed within our reach for us to devour, and thereby expand our personalities.

For good or ill, the world is becoming too homogeneous. We look alike, we understand each other easily—or think we do. Will this not end by producing a spiritual entropy? I remember the strong stimulus the United States gave me when I first discovered the country some fifteen years ago. All of it was profoundly different, strictly speaking another world. I took in everything voraciously, feeling that my soul was expanding, that I was beginning to be something more than I had been up till then. When I opened my eyes wide, not letting any synthesizing interpretation get between me and the things I saw, somthing new and irreducible came into me: I felt that from then on I was not going to be wholly the same person.

And now I wonder if I can give back to the United States some of the sense of newness I had then, with this vision of Unamuno, this tremendous fragment of Spain.

J.M.

Madrid
March 1966

*CONTENTS*

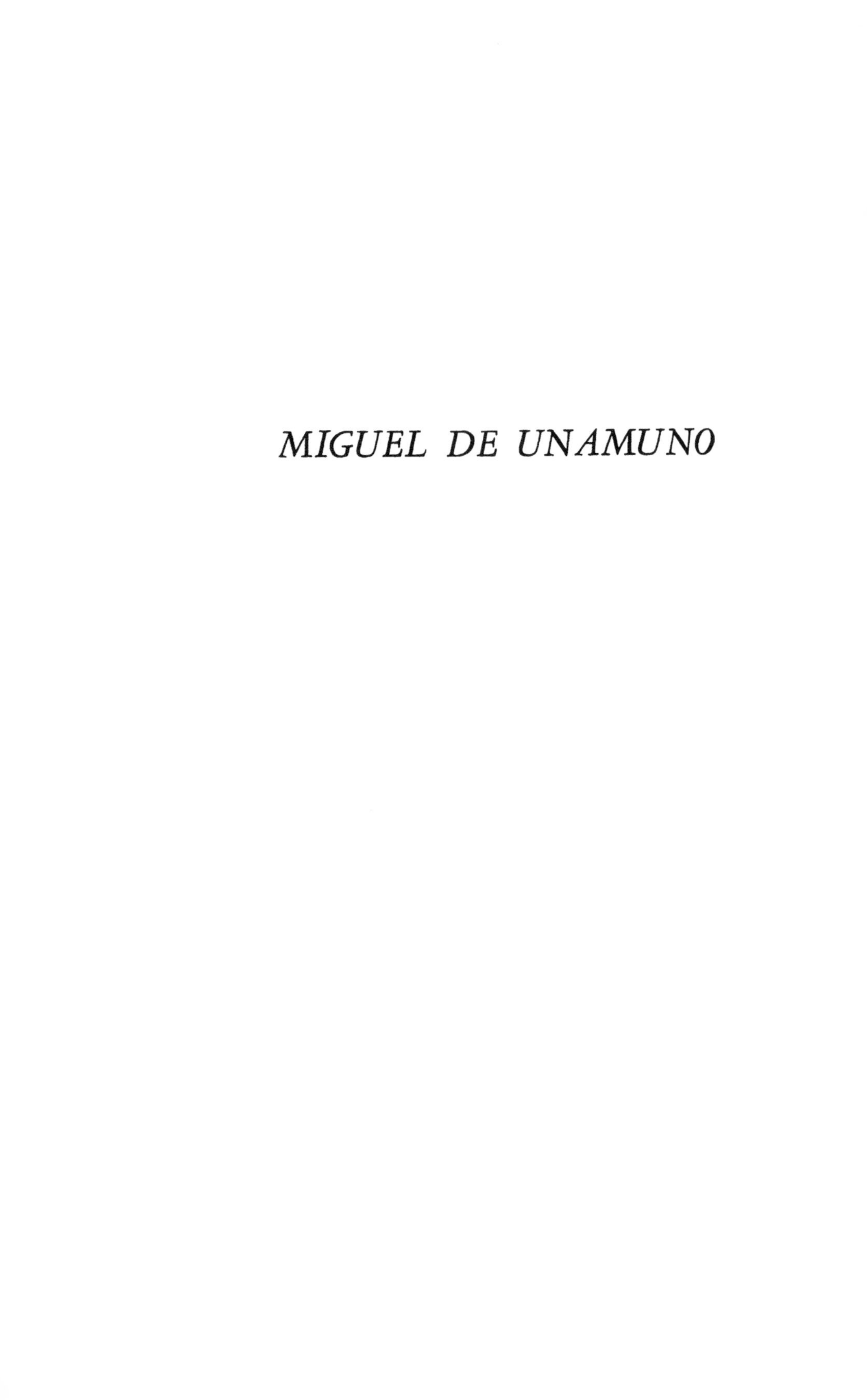

*MIGUEL DE UNAMUNO*

# I.

# THE PROBLEM

When we read Unamuno, especially when we peruse several of his books one after the other, we receive a strange and disquieting impression. On every page there are insights of great accuracy and precision, which spur our desire for further acquaintance and arouse impassioned curiosity. We embark on the reading of Unamuno with minds tense and alert, in the expectation of discovering deep and intimate truths; at every moment we seem to find what we are looking for, or at least the promise of its imminent appearance. No single page disappoints us, but as we turn the last one we feel overwhelmed with uncertainty. When we finish reading and hold the closed book in our hands, it seems to have become alien. We feel that we have not read aright, that its meaning escapes us, that maybe we ought to begin all over again. Perhaps a similar feeling came over Don Miguel de Unamuno when he finished writing a book, and impelled him to start over; but since a book cannot be written twice he created another, which really was always in some sense the same one. And this may have been the way in which all of Unamuno's work was born, in an anguished and very personal process whose meaning we shall discover later.

It is difficult to state explicitly what he is saying in his work; even more, it is equally difficult to know exactly what he is dealing with in it. It is generally conceded that all of his writings are splendid literature. Again, considering the fact that in many of his books Unamuno speaks only of philosophers and philosophical problems, it is said that his work is philosophy, though in a somewhat vague and unsatisfactory sense. But sufficient justification is not given for either of these views, and we do not discern very clearly either the reason for the presence of philosophical themes in Unamuno's literary work or the absence in it of the characteristics which we commonly demand, and find, in what is traditionally understood as philosophy. It is therefore important to learn just what the meaning of Unamuno's work is, what we can look for and find in it, to discover what he is telling us in his disturbing and enigmatic language. Above all, we must shed light on the relation in which his work stands to philosophy, and find out to what degree the one and the other are linked.

This point may seem to be of little value. It is customary to consider—and this based on Unamuno's own words—that his work is paradoxical and tortured, full of contradictions. The reader can take an almost sensuous pleasure in following the mental oscillation of an agony which he needs only to observe, a gratifying vision which does not require the painful effort of interpretation. Looked at in this way, it is quite possible to believe that Unamuno's work is and is not all things, or that it is all things at once. According to this idea, philosophy, literature, poetry, and religion would be battling and contradicting each other in every book and even in every sentence; to try to classify Unamuno would be as absurd as useless. Actually, these two adjectives would fit admirably if we were dealing with a classification or process of pigeonholing. But to understand the question we have formulated in that light is what is totally absurd.

This was also a problem for Unamuno himself. He constantly insists that he has never written a strictly scientific work, nor does he intend to write one. Just as he is about to speak most specifically of metaphysical questions, in chapter VI of his book *Del sentimiento trágico de la vida* [The Tragic Sense of Life], he seems to vacillate and feel doubt, and tells us, "I have no desire to deceive anyone nor to give the name of philosophy to what may, perhaps, be only poetry or phantasmagoria, mythology in any case." But neither was he convinced that it was no more than poetry, as is shown by that "perhaps," which he leaves dangling in the sentence as if his conscience bothered him. In many other places Unamuno emphasizes the points of scientific knowledge, or at least those of true scholarship, in his writings, and contemplates this duality of his with a kind of ironic melancholy which barely conceals an extreme sense of discomfort in the face of the problem. "I shall never be," he says, "more than a poor writer, regarded as an intruder and an outsider in the republic of letters because of certain scientific pretensions, and as an intruder in the realm of science because of my literary pretensions. This is my reward for trying to mix the two." * And in his essay "Sobre la erudición y la crítica" [On Erudition and Criticism] † he writes, "My enthusiasms were at that time, and continue to be today, all-embracing, but directed most especially to those twin sisters, philosophy and poetry." In another place he reminds us that Faith does not feel sure of herself and "seeks the support of her enemy, Reason." This dualism results in the "agony" about which so much has been said, perhaps to avoid dealing with it. But it is not enough simply to take notice of the agony and marvel at it. It is necessary to live it, or at least to attempt to find the basis of it, which is after all one way, maybe the most intimate way, of reliving it. Let us try to define the extent and meaning of the question.

## DISPERSION AND UNITY

It is impossible to find a system, much less a body of congruent doctrine, in Unamuno. He leaps constantly from one theme to another and shows only a flash of each. It is as if a collection of precious stones were revolving before our eyes, touched by the light at one instant only to be in shadow the next, with the initial gleam immediately replaced by another. Unamuno's assertions are never related to each other, nor is one supported by another in order to strengthen it and give mutual justification to the two. Each assertion remains shut up inside itself; it appears isolated and alone, and this, rather than its content, constitutes what has been vaguely called its arbitrariness. In the works of Unamuno, even in those which have the greatest intel-

* *Amor y pedagogía,* epilogue.
† *Ensayos,* volume VI.

lectual pretensions, one seeks in vain for a coherent logical process, a foundation for each assertion which would permit it to be used in its turn to achieve a new truth.

This description brings the aphorism to mind, yet it would be a serious error to consider Unamuno an aphoristic writer. Fortunately, this is not the case at all. The aphorism demands a pause in the process of thought, causing it to alight on a certain assertion not in order to pass on to another, but to let it stand and take pleasure in it. This shade of satisfaction is characteristic of the aphorism; the aphoristic writer deliberately cuts off the roots from which his thought has sprung in order to show it in an isolated, cut-off form, abruptly, like a flower broken from its stem and placed in a vase. The aphorism is always exhibitionism, and has an obvious aesthetic purpose; therefore its goal is the surprise provoked by the very abruptness of its isolation. When one reads an aphorism one does not see directly "what it is all about"; one does not know on what the author has based his assertion, nor even—this is essential—what his mind was concerned with when he wrote it. The aphorism artificially cuts off the necessary supports of interpretation; consequently, direct and complete intellection of it is impossible. By means of this procedure, both artificial and artful, I repeat, the aphorism surrounds itself with an aura of mystery and enigma which arises not from its mere meaning but from its unexplained presence. It is the strangeness of the unaccustomed. The aphorism gives us the same sense of surprise as would an isolated human footprint which apparently comes from nowhere and goes nowhere. Think of Schopenhauer's *Aphorismen zur Lebensweisheit,* or even more of Nietzsche—especially in *Jenseits von Gut und Böse* —and compare the sense of these with Pascal's *Pensées,* for example, or, if you wish, with the fragments of the majority of the pre-Socratics. In the former the assertions are set forth with pretensions of validity in themselves, and of essential sufficiency; their substance lies in their isolation, their lack of attachment. It is not so much what they say as the fact that they are surrounded by silence. In Pascal or Parmenides, however, the circumstances are very different. Their sentences are not flowers cut by the gardener's aesthetic hand, but plants pulled up bodily from the ground, still showing the root or the broken stem and demanding completion. Their fragmentary and incomplete character is not deliberate but accidental, and is an echo of a "not yet" of immaturity, or of the destructive action of time and the vicissitudes of transmission. The fragment of Parmenides or Anaxagoras is like the stump of a limb which demands to be made whole; the Pascalian thought is a preliminary and immature jotting which is presented as provisional and private and which also leads back to the spiritual and mental concern from which it springs. It is entirely opposite, then, to an aphorism.

Very well; aphorisms are by definition false, since nothing is true of and by itself; they constitute a radical inversion of the philosophical mode of thought. They are also the opposite of those propositions which condense the ultimate essence of a philosophy. Each of the latter is constantly sustained by all the other propositions in the system; it takes them into account and brings them into play. In other words, the proposition is sustained by the movement of the philosophical process of thinking itself, and this is what furnishes its essential truth. Expressions like the Aristotelian "Being is one and multiple," the Cartesian "cogito, ergo sum," Hegel's assertion that "the Idea is the absolute," or Ortega's "I am I and my circumstance" summarize a whole philosophy; without that philosophy they are not intelligible nor do they have meaning, nor in the last instance are they even true. It can therefore be said that the most precise philosophical thesis, formulated as an aphorism, would of necessity be false.

However, in Unamuno there is no question of all this. The isolation of his sentences is discontinuity but not pause. His thought does not stay quiet; on the contrary, it moves incessantly from one intuition to another, but progresses by leaps, conveyed this way and that by the demands of his intimate problems, his anguish, and his own contradictions. In Unamuno nothing appears conclusive and finished, but, instead, fragmentary and problematical; and, far from demonstrating a statement in definite and perfect isolation as an aphoristic writer does, Unamuno emphasizes the vital and impassioned source from which all his words have sprung. The reference to personal preoccupation is constant and explicit, and this last factor is what constitutes, in Unamuno's eyes, the true substance of his work, much more than the formulas in which he expresses himself.

Yet, on the other hand, there is a profound unity in all of Unamuno's work, diffuse as it is, a unity which reaches the point of monotony, as he himself admits. Unamuno has but one theme—as we shall soon see. No matter where we open one of his books, no matter what its genre, we find the same ambit of thought and of anxieties, much more clearly defined than in other authors whose work has more congruence and cohesion. How is this extraordinary unity achieved? Lacking any systematic connection of affirmations, one possibility remains: reiteration. And in fact repetition is the form in which Unamuno's thought is made unified. This characteristic of his style is by no means fortuitous; we shall soon see that it responds to a profound demand of the style's significance. Unamuno leaps from one theme to another, but repeating himself constantly; he darts away from a question, only to return to it a moment later. On whatever page we open one of his writings we find an identical atmosphere, a permanent and invariable note, forced into use with equal passion on the most widely differing instruments: the poem, the drama, the novel, the essay, the commentary on some book or event; and this is true throughout all of his volumes and all of his life. Not system, then, nor aphorism, but reiteration of many scattered moments: this is what constitutes the dynamic and permanent unity of Don Miguel de Unamuno's thought.

## PHILOSOPHICAL CONCERN

These repeated themes coincide with some of the most essential themes of philosophy. This is not to say anything about the treatment of the themes but about their content. And this fact means an initial contact with philosophy. At least it places Unamuno's thought inside an intellectual ambit coincident with that of metaphysics, and gives him a community of aims with some forms of it. There are even books of Unamuno's in which he speaks of nothing but philosophical problems, and allusions to such problems are frequent even in his lyrical poetry. Further, Unamuno turns repeatedly to the works of other men who have grappled with the same themes, and who are sometimes religious men, sometimes theologians, but principally philosophers. St. Augustine, St. Paul, Descartes, Spinoza, Pascal, Kant, Hegel, Bergson, Kierkegaard, William James, and numerous others constantly appear in his pages. Exegesis or commentary on them and their works was a necessity for him, and therefore Unamuno finds himself immersed in the problems of the history of philosophy—though in a very peculiar sense which we shall examine later—and consequently in philosophy itself.

But this alone would not be enough. It might have been that those references and quotations were only a subject of erudition, a simple catalogue of opinions, or that they were merely an example of intellectual curiosity, of an acute historical sense, of the pure pleasure of exploring the modes of thinking or the life histories of the best philosophical minds. But Unamuno is very far from either of these attitudes. Mere erudition and the sheer pleasure of historicism were always equally foreign to him; rather, he was distinguished by a deep-seated aversion to the first and a certain incapacity for the second. This does not imply that he did not possess a voluminous body of knowledge, including factual information, which was far superior to that of the vast majority of professional scholars; but it seemed to him that this knowledge had to be justified vitally, and he was repelled by any degree of the "erudite use" of knowledge; he felt that sometimes, even often, the erudite attitude is founded on a very limited store of knowledge. On the other hand, his historical sense was both one-sided and deficient, and this for two decisive reasons: his all-absorbing interest in individuality and his overweening desire to find in everything, even in the course of historical events, what he called the "eternal tradition," the intrahistorical and permanent element which defies the change and evanescence of temporal things.

Unamuno seizes upon the great figures of philosophy because he is motivated by a serious and very personal interest: that of the problems themselves. It must be repeated yet again—this is essential—that the themes of philosophy were also a *problem* for Unamuno. Whatever the intellectual fate of these questions in his thought, what is important is that they appear in the dimension of their aspect as problems. We might say that philosophy in and of itself, that is, the problem of philosophy, existed for Unamuno; but this is not necessarily to say that the result of his intellectual activity strictly deserves the name of philosophy. What I have just stated is by no means unimportant. For the majority of men philosophical questions do not exist, at least they do not exist as problems. At most they may be subjects of information, of curiosity or edification, but no more. In some cases there exists, in addition, comprehension of philosophical problems; that is, knowledge of their correct meaning. Most good professors of philosophy have this attitude. In Unamuno, apart from this and in even greater measure, there was a real and personal concern for these questions, a concern necessary to his life. Nevertheless, this is not enough: it is possible to feel the problems of philosophy very strongly and accurately and to be unable, in spite of this, to arrive at a true philosophical action. Philosophy is a strict mode of knowing, though of a peculiar kind, and cannot be confused in any way with anything else, not even with the liveliest and most authentic sensitivity to its problems.

This can all be summed up by saying that Unamuno's work is inevitably linked to philosophy, and that this relation is, naturally, a philosophical problem on which light must be cast.

## LITERATURE AND PHILOSOPHY

But it must not be forgotten that Unamuno's books belong to literature in their own right. To begin with, above all they are literary works, and are justifiably regarded as such. Together with the essay, his principal literary genres are poetry, the novel, and also drama. This is a fact important enough not to be passed over lightly. We are talking about odes, sonnets, dramas, and novels which are just that in the fullest possible sense. And it should not be thought that they make up Unamuno's purely literary work, as opposed to another body of work that could be called, for example, philosophical; for there is perfect unity among them all. For this reason it has been said, with full justification, that everything in Unamuno is poetry and that there is a profound relation between *Del sentimiento trágico de la vida* and his poem *El Cristo de Velázquez* [The Christ of Velasquez]. It would not be an exaggeration to consider the former as a poem also, in spite of its constant references to philosophical and theological thought and its quotations in several languages; but perhaps it could be said with equal justice that all of Unamuno's work exceeds and transcends poetry and literature in general. Our first glance tells us that it does not have a merely aesthetic purpose. Unamuno's verses or novels "have something to say"; this is the impression that the most naïve reader receives. But neither can this literature be regarded as "thesis literature," in which the author clothes certain of his opinions in the garb of poetic or lyric or novelistic or dramatic fiction so as to slip them into the reader's mind in a persuasive rather than a didactic way. Unamuno had too great a sense of the artistic and the literary —in the strictest and most authentic sense—to wander into any such tortuous byways. We are not dealing with works that are *apparently* literary, nor with the possibility that outside elements have been introduced into them artificially. What Unamuno wishes to say in these writings he says by using poetic, novelistic, and dramatic means; literary means, in short, although what he says may have a dimension which transcends the sphere in which literature moves. Later we shall see the importance of this point, and how the fact that it has not been clearly seen has often clouded a complete comprehension of Unamuno. He himself frequently referred to this question, which tormented him, for he realized, though somewhat vaguely, that, in spite of its apparently trivial and marginal nature, it was the key to his problematical and agonized personality.

We have, then, a body of work written in a reiteratively diffuse style, with a total lack of system, cast into strictly literary molds and yet full of philosophical problematism and concern, of metaphysical statements, of profound insights related to philosophy. What is the ultimate meaning of Unamuno's work? What forms the foundation for the single connection between these disparate elements? What sort of philosophy is it? Is it an incomplete kind, or a simple preliminary attempt? Is it an actual exclusion of philosophy? This is the problem.

Or rather it is the first problem, the fundamental question on which we must try to shed light. Afterward we shall have to confront another, still more serious and of consummate interest, which it is very necessary to pose if we are to deal with all the possibilities of philosophy in Spain. Throughout the length and breadth of his work Unamuno has left many pages filled with penetrating insights, acute and accurate assertions about philosophical themes. Unquestionably he at least guessed and glimpsed many essential things which may well be fruitful. He certainly anticipated a number of decisive points of present-day philosophy. His very point of view, which was not strictly philosophical, helped him to perceive areas of these problems which have remained on the margins of strict metaphysical speculation. These are truths which cry out to be gathered and incorporated into a higher unity from which they can give momentum to a useful intellectual movement; ideas which are waiting to be realized philosophically, which are urging and pressing to be so realized. And yet, as we shall see, Unamuno created, perhaps without consciously being aware of it, a method of knowledge which is put into practice in his writings; even, though this may seem paradoxical, in his most purely literary work. What are the discoveries of Unamuno? How far did he progress in his attempt to find out about the ultimate truths? What are the possibilities of the paths he explored, gropingly perhaps, but guided by an unerring instinct? We must also try to answer these questions.

# II.

# *UNAMUNO'S THEME*

## THE SOLE QUESTION

We spoke before of the unity, or rather the unitary quality, of Unamuno's thought, of the constant reiteration of the same theme. What is this theme? is the question that must be answered first of all. In an essay entitled "Soledad" [Solitude], published as early as 1905, Unamuno answers it specifically. "I am convinced," he says, "that there is only one burning concern, one and the same for all men. . ., the human question, which is mine, and yours, and every other man's, and all men's." "The human question," he adds, "is the question of knowing what is to become of my consciousness, and yours, and every other man's, and all men's, after each one of us dies." And this, which he also calls "the secret of human life," he defines elsewhere as "the appetite for divinity, the hunger for God." *

But this is not all. At the beginning of *Del sentimiento trágico de la vida* we find a few sentences whose meaning is crystal-clear. He says, "The man of flesh and bone, who is born, suffers, and dies—above all dies—he who eats and drinks and plays and sleeps and thinks and wills, the man one sees and hears, the brother, the true brother." And then he adds, "And this concrete man, of flesh and bone, is at once the subject and the supreme object of all philosophy, whether certain so-called philosophers like it or not."

These quotations could be multiplied a hundredfold, but there is no need to do so. It is more useful to pause for a moment on the

* "El secreto de la vida," *Ensayos,* I, 830.

last one, where this sole theme of man who dies is related to philosophy. Nor is it some vague relation, but one of making this theme *the* theme of philosophy. With this statement Unamuno affirms a total correspondence of the object of philosophy with that of his intimate preoccupation, and leaves them fundamentally linked. His problem is, therefore, that of philosophy as he understands it; it remains to be seen what is to be done in the face of this question.

And Unamuno continues to ask himself the motives for his burning desire to know. "Why do I want to know whence I come and whither I go, whence everything that surrounds me comes and whither it goes, and what all this means? For I do not want to die altogether, and I want to know definitively whether I am to die or not. And if I do not die, what will become of me? And if I do die, then nothing makes any sense." And shortly after this he asks himself whether the hunger for immortality is not perhaps "the true point of departure of all philosophy." *

To be sure, it is strange that Unamuno, who repeatedly quotes Kant, especially his *Critique of Practical Reason,* never reflected upon that passage in his *Logic* in which Kant defines the mundane concept of philosophy, that which is of interest to everybody, as opposed to the scholastic concept, which is of interest only to a particular school, and says that the former is the authentic and important one. Kant sums up the themes of philosophy in four capital questions: What can I know? What should I do? What can I hope for? What is man? The answers to these questions can be given by metaphysics, ethics, religion, and anthropology. And Kant adds this phrase, with which Unamuno would have agreed: "But in the last analysis all this could be said to be the concern of anthropology, because the first three questions refer to the last." †

The problem, therefore, is that of man, of the human person, and of his survival. And it is death which poses this question: it is a matter of discovering what dying is, if it means annihilation or not, whether dying is something that happens to man so that he can enter

* *Del sentimiento trágico de la vida,* chapter II.

† *Vorlesungen über Logik,* ed. G. B. Jäsche, Einleitung, III. See also translation by Julián Marías, in *Sobre el saber filosófico,* (Madrid, 1943), p. 45.

into everlasting life, or whether it means that he ceases to be, that *nothing happens to him*. For this is the agonizing and intolerable thing, as Unamuno realized very well: that nothing may happen. Man can gather unto himself his most fundamental energies, his "forces of being," and draw strength from the deepest bases of his soul to confront any thing: but to confront nothing, or, rather, not to confront anything? Unamuno has felt and has made to be felt, perhaps more than anyone else, the imminence of this problem, and in him it has had life and fullness of meaning. Leaving aside what Unamuno may have done to try to resolve it intellectually, and even to formulate it—this is another matter—what must be considered is the extremely acute and radical way in which he has discovered it, how he has sensed it in all its tremendous dimension as a problem.

But in order to throw light on the question of death, one must first learn about life. Death is always the death of something which lives; this is not accidental but occurs precisely because it lives; and this being alive is, in its turn, what constitutes the being of the living creature. This is so elementary that it almost seems a tautology; neverthless, it is not idle to recall it. The survival of man—resurrection of the flesh after the Judaic tradition or immortality of the soul after the Hellenic, Unamuno says—supposes death, because man dies, and death can be understood only from the point of view of the life of which it is a deprivation. Two living beings differ insofar as the life which is in them is different, and, as living is not the same for both, dying—which, for the moment, means ceasing to live—does not mean the same either. The death of a tree is not the same as that of an animal or a man, for their lives are very different; and even among men, historically, the meaning of death varies from one people to another and one epoch to another, because the verb "to live" is very far from having a single meaning; and even individually, deaths differ according to the lives which they conclude. The attempt to know human destiny after death obliges us to examine the problem of death beforehand; and, as man exists from the beginning and for the time being in life, Unamuno's sole question encompasses the questions of the being, the life, and the death of man, in an essential unity. The theme of Unamuno, therefore, stated with more precision, is man in his entirety, man who goes from his birth to his death, with his flesh, his life, his personality, and above all his desire never to die completely.

Upon this hypothesis, and moved by his anguish toward a desperate search for the truth, believing that this and no other is the object of philosophy, one would expect Unamuno to fling himself into the metaphysical study of living and mortal man. But instead of this he says that his affirmations are "poetry or phantasmagoria," and he writes poems, some dramas, and especially novels. What does this mean? Does Unamuno turn his back on his sole question? Does he renounce the attempt to know if he must die entirely?

## REASON AND LIFE

The fact is that Unamuno believes reason does not serve to solve his problem. "Reason is the enemy of life," he writes. He believes that the feeling and the passion for life come into irremediable conflict with reason and are in direct contradiction to it. And as he cannot do without either of the two, there must be struggle and agony. What is Unamuno's idea of reason? We have to examine this in some detail. His thought moves more or less within the compass of the philosophical ideas of the beginning of this century, when James and Bergson are coming to grips with the traditional idea of rationality, decisively influenced—let us not forget this—by positivism, and still more by positivist science. Furthermore, Unamuno was deeply indebted to the thinker Sören Kierkegaard, and this debt must be considered later on.

In the middle of the nineteenth century William James's pragmatism had already begun to note a serious problem in the relation of life to reason and truth, in the manner in which they were usually understood. James's solution, as is well known, consisted in giving a pragmatic sense, that is, one useful for life, to truth: the true would be that which is vitally effective; a belief which makes us act unerringly is a true one. With this, obviously, James makes truth relative and alters its precise meaning. His attempt to unite it with life is not fully realized, for the attempt is made at the expense of truth without achieving an idea superior to both which will permit their reconciliation. Unamuno breathed this pragmatist atmosphere, which influenced him decisively, especially in the way in which he understood religion. On the other hand, and in spite of his theoretical statements, he retained a root of authentic Christianity, greatly modified, but nevertheless alive, which always kept him from falling completely into the trivial interpretations of religion current in his time.

Bergson represents another, more important step in this question of reason and life. He distinguishes between two modes of knowing: on the one hand, what is properly called "intelligence," conceptual thought, reason; and on the other, "instinct," which vitally guides the animal, and in a certain sense man, in a blind and infallible way. Bergson believes that intelligence is designed to contemplate purely spatial things; it tends to consider everything as a solid body, fixed, measurable, rigid, invariable. In addition, it seeks out what is common to and typical of different individuals: intelligence is a generalizer. This explains the efficacy of reason, of conceptual thought, in dealing with knowledge of the physical and of mathematical objects, which by their very nature lend themselves to its essential possibilities. But with life, something else occurs. Life—meaning biological life, which is what Bergson deals with primarily—is not above all spatial, but temporal; it moves in a strange ambit, which is that of time, and not the inert time of a clock, computable and translatable into linear or angular measures—the hands moving over the face of the clock—but living time, what Bergson calls "real duration." This unitary, indivisible time acquires its maximum density, to the point of anguish, when we are waiting, when it reveals itself to us as something resistant, like vital reality itself. Very well then; intelligence diagrams this time, confines it to fixed concepts, stops its motion, and consequently destroys it in its temporality. Furthermore, life is always individual, and conceptual thought with its generalizing tendency passes over life's intimate and distinctive character. Intelligence, then, when it tries to think about life, kills it and can only come to know its inert cadaver. Only intuition, so close to instinct, can capture the reality of life, which is fluid, plastic, temporal, and individual. "Our intelligence," writes Bergson, "as it exists when it emerges from the hands of nature, has as its principal object the solid unorganized mass." He adds that intelligence can grasp clearly only that which is discontinuous and immobile. And he concludes with this radical and far-reaching affirmation: *Intelligence is characterized by a natural incomprehension of life.**

This philosophy, founded on intuition and on proximity to vital reality, has been extraordinarily fruitful for contemporary thought, but it has been affected since its beginnings by a danger of irrationalism. Intuition, in order to become authentic knowing, must be conceptualized and become reason in its strict sense; and Bergsonian thought does not reach this point.

But long before Bergson, and in a dimension much closer to the center of Unamuno's preoccupation, Kierkegaard had posed the problem. This tormented religious thinker, anguished and ironical, who lived in Copenhagen from 1813 to 1855, striding through its foggy streets and squares like a Nordic Socrates, raises primarily the question of individual and personal existence, rather than that of life in the biological sense. And Kierkegaard compares this reality of existence with rational and abstract thought. "In the language of abstraction," he writes, "what constitutes the difficulty of existence and of the existent being, far from being made clear, never appears at all, to tell the truth. This is precisely because abstract thought is *sub specie aeterni;* it makes an abstraction of the concrete, of the temporal, of the process of existence, of the misery of man, who has come into existence by means of a reunion of the eternal and the temporal. If it is admitted that abstract thought is the highest, it follows from this that science and the great thinkers proudly withdraw from existence and leave us simple mortals to put up with the worst of it." Further on he adds this paragraph, in which the difficulty that afflicts all these thinkers is expressed in the clearest and most peremptory manner. "To think of existence abstractly and *sub specie aeterni* means essentially to suppress it, and this is analogous to the highly touted

* Henri Bergson, *L'évolution créatrice,* 12th ed. (Paris: Félix Alcan, 1913), pp. 169–179; and see Bergson's work in general.

feat of suppressing the principle of contradiction. Existence cannot be thought of without movement, and movement cannot be thought of *sub specie aeterni*. To ignore movement is not precisely a master stroke, and to introduce it as a step in logic, and with it time and space, only causes a new confusion. However, in the measure in which all thought is eternal, there is a difficulty for existing things. With existence the same thing happens as with movement, and it is very difficult to come to grips with it. If I think about them, I annul them, and consequently I do not think about them. From this it would seem correct to say that there is something which does not permit itself to be thought about: existence. But then the difficulty remains that, since the man who thinks exists, existence coincides with thought." And finally, in another passage, he radically eliminates temporality from the sphere of pure thought: "Time does not permit itself any place in pure thought." *

Kierkegaard finds, therefore, in the triple character of existence—individual, temporal, and in motion—the foundation of its irreducibility to reason. The problem is acutely stated, but far from being resolved. Unamuno is going to take it over at this point, and he will not be able to find a metaphysical solution for it either. He tries rather to avoid the problem by a detour whose fruitful consequences, perhaps unforeseen by Unamuno himself, will later become clear to us.

"Intelligence is a terrible thing," he says. "It tends toward death as memory tends toward stability. The living thing, that which is absolutely unstable, absolutely individual, is strictly speaking unintelligible. Logic attempts to reduce everything to identities and types, wants each thing to have only one identical content in any place, time, or relation we encounter it. And there is nothing which remains the same in two successive moments of its being." "Identity, which is death, is the aspiration of the intellect. The mind seeks death, for the living thing escapes it; the mind attempts to freeze the fugitive

* Sören Kierkegaard, *Concluding Unscientific Postscript to the Philosophical Tidbits*, tr. David F. Swenson and W. Lowrie (Princeton, N.J.: Princeton University Press, 1941), part 2, section 2, chapter III, 1. This work of Kierkegaard's is the one which had most influence on Unamuno, and he frequently quotes it under its Danish title: *Afsluttende Uvidenskabelig Efterskrift til de Philosophiske Smuler*.

current into blocks of ice, tries to immobilize it." "How, then, can reason give access to the revelation of life?" *

It would be difficult to find a briefer, more compact, or more accurate expression of the problem as it was felt to be at that time in European philosophy. We find in Unamuno's words all the elements which we have been examining: the stability of reason as opposed to the fugitive and ever-changing plasticity of life; the tendency to generalization which Bergson emphasized, and the inability of reason to reach the unique and irreplaceable individual; the abstraction of time, which does not include the temporal reality of living things. All is contained in Unamuno, who remained permanently rooted in this state of science and philosophy. Unamuno's work is essentially conditioned, in a way that might be called negative or in the nature of a limitation, by the state of science at the time he reached maturity, and he is affected by temporality in this most concrete form. It must be realized that the intellectual formation of a thinker—save in exceptional cases—becomes defined in broad outline at a time in his life which may vary between the ages of thirty and fifty. After that date the ideas he acquires become incorporated, to be sure, into his intellectual resources, but in a different sense; they are not living ideas which form his mind but learned things, objects of knowledge but no longer effective principles of which he makes use in order to understand reality. Unamuno was born in 1864; his *Vida de Don Quijote y Sancho* [Life of Don Quijote and Sancho] dates from 1905; the mentality of its author is not yet fully constituted. But in 1912 he publishes his *Del sentimiento trágico de la vida,* a capital work in one particular dimension; at that time Unamuno was forty-eight years old, and his thought was by then well defined; he never passed this stage in any substantial way. The philosophical works of Scheler or Heidegger or Ortega, in the measure in which he may have been acquainted with them—it is not easy to find allusions to them in his writings—must have been inoperative for him, must have remained outside his living thought. It is enormously difficult, in maturity or as one approaches old age, to rise above the general level of one's own thought; it is painful and hardly possible to be one's own suc-

* *Del sentimiento trágico de la vida,* chapter V.

cessor. This is the intimate tragedy of some philosophers, especially those perspicacious enough to divine the near future, who feel that their work, scarcely written, or even before they have finished formulating it, requires one more step essentially different from that on which they have spent the strained effort of a lifetime.

For Unamuno reason is, above all, discursive thought; and as a consequence of this, discourse itself, speech. Strictly speaking, the ineffable and the irrational are for him coincidental; and, as the Logos in this sense refers to the generic and the permanent, there is no use in applying it to individual vital reality, which is incapable of being expressed. Unamuno understands reason as the faculty of confining its objects in fixed and universal formulas. And when these objects, as is the case in human life, are by their essence individual and ever-changing, he believes that reason is incapable of attaining them. Unamuno does not even consider the possibility of arriving at another idea of reason, according to which its task would be to apprehend reality—not this or that form of it—exactly as it is, that is to say, not by imposing upon it a mold taken from some partial sphere of reality but adapting itself to reality's intimate texture. Today—but not at the time of Unamuno's effective formation—philosophy imposes upon itself the necessity of arriving at this idea and this use of reason. From the phenomenology of Husserl to the analytics of existence of Heidegger, and passing through Scheler's theory of the perception of one's fellow man, decisive steps have been taken in this direction. And perhaps the clearest and most explicit have been those of Ortega y Gasset, who postulates thematically, as opposed to the mathematical or Eleatic reason which has dominated philosophy from Greece to rationalism, a historical or vital reason. (The clearest and most precise expression of his thought in print is to be found in his book *Historia como sistema.*) * But we shall have to return to this point later.

For Unamuno, then, reason and life are in opposition, and the rational instrument is incapable of close contact with the living thing

* See also my *La escuela de Madrid* (Madrid: Revista de Occidente, 1959) in *Obras,* volume V, and especially *Introducción a la filosofía* in *Obras,* volume II. The latter appeared as *Reason and Life: the Introduction to Philosophy,* tr. Kenneth S. Reid and Edward Sarmiento (New Haven: Yale University Press, 1956).

without making it inflexible and killing it. Reason cannot draw close enough to the man of flesh and blood to satisfy his need to know whether he is to die completely or not. But Unamuno realizes that it is not possible either to choose one of these two alternatives, to cling only to it and abandon the other. "Reason and faith," he says, "are two enemies neither of whom can stand without the other. The irrational seeks to be rationalized, and reason can operate only on the irrational." And later, "Life cannot be sustained except by reason, and reason in its turn cannot be sustained except by faith, by life, even by faith in reason." Here Unamuno grasps very accurately an essential characteristic of life, which is its demand for rationality, whether fulfilled or not. Man needs to know what to hold to, he needs a manifest certainty about the questions which are truly important to him, those which are really necessary for his life. And this is what can most properly be called "reason." Therefore Unamuno's "sole question" is indeed a problem for all men, and is by no means made superfluous by faith. Faith in life everlasting is a conviction on which the existence of the Christian depends; but it does not exclude, rather it presents, the problem of asking rationally what life everlasting is and how it is possible, just as faith in God does not eliminate theology but exactly the contrary: religion is the moving force of theological speculation. And, on the other hand, Unamuno sees clearly that reason is not simply a mental game, but that it must be rooted in life itself and in a faith, that is, in a previous, immediate, and prerational condition of belief.

The problem, therefore, is defined again more sharply than ever; it is an aporia, as a Greek would have said. Now Unamuno, who desires to know, who cannot do without reason even at the moment in which he draws away from it—and from this arises his agony—turns to feeling, to the reality of his problem itself, to his own vital anguish, and declares that what he is going to say is only phantasmagoria or poetry, mythology at the very most. But maybe he declares it with a conjecture—and therefore that "perhaps" which we observed before—that he can enter by this method into new paths of knowledge, scarcely confessable in the light of the science current in his day. He neither wishes nor finds it possible to assert that what he produces is philosophy; but, at least for him, it has value as knowledge. He is not so daring as to try to establish a new kind of science worthy of the name, and perhaps does not even believe that it is possible to do so, but he does seek a kind of knowing which he presents from the outset as "irresponsible."

Because of his belief that reason is incapable of solving his intimate problem, Unamuno finds himself impelled to write novels; for this negative reason, and for another no less important which it will be of interest to examine.

## REALITY

As is well known, Unamuno puts on the same plane both Cervantes and Don Quijote, Hamlet and Shakespeare, his characters Augusto Pérez or Abel Sánchez and himself, Don Miguel. This has been observed and repeated a hundred times, but sufficient notice has not been taken of it. It might be said that this is an arbitrary occurrence which cannot be taken too seriously, that Unamuno himself did not take it literally. This is true, but by denying the ultimate seriousness and consistency of his attitude, we have not even begun to understand it. Why does it occur? There is obvious exaggeration; but it must be emphasized that exaggeration is always the overstatement of something which is not exaggerated; therefore, the exaggeration emphasizes at the same time that it hides a nucleus of meaning, of truth, upon which a proper light must be thrown. Exaggeration consists in emphasizing out of all proportion a *real* dimension of something, and by this means drawing our attention to it; but if we see only the lack of proportion and reject what is presented in this way, we will fail to observe the germ of truth, which is what really matters. Strictly speaking, the relation of men with objects is always exaggerated; whenever we speak, we emphasize one aspect of something which is never given alone but mixed with other things. When we use vitally any object whatever, we isolate one of its possibilities: when I eat an apple, I choose in an isolated and arbitrary way its qualities of tastiness and edibility, ignoring its geometrical characteristics, its general physical properties, its ability to reproduce itself, the fact that it is capable of being used as a projectile hurled from my hand. And this is true in everything; any vital act is an interpretation, and by that token an exaggeration.

What concept of reality had Unamuno which allowed him to confuse it arbitrarily and deliberately with fiction? He must have had some basis for making this farfetched identification; reality itself must have led him to it. We have seen that Unamuno's theme was man, for him the most important reality. But man not as an abstract being, a fixed essence, a rational animal, or anything of that kind, nor yet man as an object among other objects or a biological organism. It is the living man, he who is born and dies, who journeys from birth to death, taut between the two, in the process of forming his personality. He is a life, a history. Unamuno will also resort frequently to the metaphor of the dream; and naturally the important thing about the metaphor is not that it deals with dreaming as opposed to wakefulness—that is, as something unreal—but rather with the type of reality a dream represents. This reality is not a thing, but something which is being made, something temporal, which ceases to be even as it comes into being. This is why, when Unamuno makes use of the two great literary references to this metaphor, that of Calderón and that of Shakespeare, he is always careful to point out the difference in their meaning, and to make us see that the really important one is the second. Calderón says that "life is a dream," that we ourselves dream the world and life, that we are not a dream. Shakespeare, on the other hand, declares that "we are such stuff as dreams are made on," or that we ourselves are the substance of dreams. Unamuno is to find in this point—anticipating, perhaps, the gravest problem of the philosophy of our century—a profound difficulty not easily overcome. The dream, precisely because it is unreal in the light of things, because it does not appear mixed with things and dependent on their being, is the purest and most consummate example of that subtle mode of temporal reality, of novel or legend, of which our life consists.

It is in this mode of being—though in other ways they may differ —that men coincide with literary characters, with the realities of fiction: Don Quijote with Cervantes. When Unamuno says that his characters are as real as he is, it must be understood that their mode of being coincides with his, and resembles his more than that of, say, a stone or a tree. They are lives, they are stories, they have a legend, something which happens—and not merely *is*—in time, something that can be told, that can be the theme of a narration. They have, therefore, biography, though not in the usual sense; for the character of fictional literature is a person conscious of the legend that he is. Compare Shakespeare, after his death, with Hamlet or with a stone. Are not the first two linked by a common definition of the verb "to be" in contrast to the second? This is the conclusion which must be inferred from Unamuno's arbitrary identification; it is the revindication of the temporal and personal mode of being, consisting, for the moment, in a story, the special province of man in contrast to the other things of this world. Beside this essential difference, do not all others that can be found among the various historical modes of being seem pale and secondary? What happens to me in dreams is not so different from what happens to me "really" in the waking life, as is the reality of the life of the table I rest my elbows on or the wholly real paper on which I write. The reality of the fictional character resembles mine in that it is not finished, in that it keeps on forming and can be narrated, and this fact is precisely what constitutes its drama or its novel. To be Don Quijote does not mean to weigh so much, to measure a certain height, and to have a particular composition, but to think, feel, and act, within the framework of time, certain things, in a peculiar manner, and to be finished only at the end, in death. The being of the literary character, like that of man himself, is a result.

"The essence of an individual," says Unamuno, "and that of a people is their history, and history is what is called the philosophy of history: it is the reflection which each individual or each people casts on the events which occur to them, which occur among them. For events, once they have taken place, become facts, ideas made flesh." Note how Unamuno insists here upon the purely historical, and therefore human, factor—there is no history other than that of man—because a mere succession of facts, as is the case with the evolution of an animal or a plant, is not enough for him. First of all, events are essential to him, they are something that happens to someone; furthermore, knowledge of these events is a necessary condition if they are to be possessed by their subject. Without reflection on temporal happenings there is no history. They would not exist in the form of a web of events; each would disappear as soon as it came into being, and would not survive in the total complex. It is not in vain that two different meanings are linked in the term "history," which is essentially equivocal: historical reality and historical knowledge. It is useful to distinguish between these two meanings, but at the same time we must not lose sight of their basic implication: strictly speaking, there is no historical reality without some knowledge of it, as there is no temporal person without memory. "Life," writes Unamuno, "is continuous creation and continuous consumption, and is, therefore, unceasing death." * And this leads him to interpret memory as the basis of individual personality and tradition as the foundation of the collective personality of a people.† Later, when we try to understand the difference between the character of fiction, the living man, and God, we shall see the implications of this point.

It can be said that fictional characters are not real. But this implies a previous state of agreement as to what is understood by reality. It is evident that reality is in some sense a part of them; we can speak of Othello or Ulysses with a perfectly clear sense, and they have a certain existence or at least consistency of their own. Just as iron is hard, susceptible to rust, and denser than water, or the number 9 is uneven and indivisible by 5, so the Moor of Venice has a structure and an internal logic which define and individualize him perfectly. We are dealing with very different spheres of reality, but reality includes them all. Further, for Unamuno "everything which acts exists, and to exist is to act," § and with this he gives us an initial idea, though a very vague and insufficient one, of what he understands by reality. And it is clear that Don Quijote acts, and that he influenced Don Miguel de Unamuno forcefully and decisively.

* *Ensayos,* III, 2.

† *Del sentimiento trágico de la vida,* chapter I.

§ *Del sentimiento trágico de la vida,* chapter IX.

That is to say, one finds in fictional characters—in a rather spectral and dependent way, if you like—the same being as man's, that being which for Unamuno is the true reality and at the same time the theme of his anguished preoccupation. Therefore his meaning is perfectly clear when he says, "Fictional being? Real being? The reality of fiction, which is the fiction of reality." This, far from being, as is commonly thought, a "paradox," almost a play on words, is something perfectly clear and coherent, almost obvious. The character in a novel possesses, in fact, that mode of reality which consists in being fictitious—as opposed to the stone, which has a physical being, or desire, which belongs in the category of psychic being—and what his author imagines in him is precisely the full and true reality which is man and man's life.

On the other hand, Unamuno does not lose sight of the problem of the man who is dead. He who once lived and exists for us only in memory, in the survival of fame, also exists in a mode which is in a certain sense spectral, closer to that of imaginary characters. Again the problem of immortality is sharply posed: whether man, after death, exists in himself and has consciousness, or whether he only relives in us when we dream him anew. This is the problem. And this question, as can easily be seen, involves two other very important ones: first, that of the peculiar consistency of that life, of that dream, for we must ask ourselves in what sense and to what extent life and dream are independent; the other, the question of *who* it is who lives and dreams, whatever the nature of what he lives or dreams. These two questions are implicitly raised in Unamuno, and must at least be defined. In doing this we shall have to take up, if only in a tangential way, the gravest and most difficult problems of present-day metaphysics: the problem of life or existence and that of the person, which in their turn lead us inexorably to the problem of God.

## COMMENTARY AND NOVEL

In an essay published in 1911 Unamuno, referring incidentally to the question, wrote: "It is useless to belabor the point. Our gift is above all a literary gift, and everything here [in Spain], philosophy included, is therefore converted into literature." * Just before this he had stated that his *Vida de Don Quijote y Sancho,* a commentary, "above all else attempts to be an essay on Spanish philosophy." And later, in *Del sentimiento trágico de la vida,* he asked himself: "Is it not possible that fantasy and myth are revelations of an ineffable truth, an irrational truth, a truth that cannot be proved?" And, finally, in 1927, in *Cómo se hace una novela* [How a Novel is Made], he wrote, "System—which is consistency—destroys the essence of dream and with it the essence of life. And, in fact, the philosophers have not realized how large a portion of themselves, of the fantasy which they are, they have put into the effort of systematizing life and the world and existence. There is no more profound philosophy than the examination of how philosophy is produced. The history of philosophy is the perennial philosophy."

These four quotations, separated from each other by time and circumstance, taken together form the justification for all we have been saying. They are the stages through which Unamuno comes to have a sense of the reasons for his own work. In that work we see how he comes to discover the value of knowledge represented by his myths, his novels, his histories. System destroys the essence of the dream and with it the essence of life: this is what Unamuno believed, basing his belief on the idea he had of reason and of systematic thought, which today we would be unable to share. All the metaphysics of these latter years has bent its best efforts toward overcoming not only irrationalism but also the lack of systematization of all knowledge relating to life. In contrast to the opinion current at the end of the nineteenth century, of which Unamuno was a part, the philosophy of our century has discovered the systematic structure of our life, and demands that our knowledge of it adjust itself to this contexture of its object; this naturally obliges us to alter profoundly any possible idea we might have of reason and of system itself. The clearest and most understandable expression of this position, and at the same time the most mature, can be found in Ortega y Gasset's short book *Historia como sistema,* in which he sets forth the prin-

* *Ensayos,* VII, 207.

ciples of a metaphysic of vital reason, explicitly postulated therein.

Because of this belief of his, Unamuno sought modes of knowing which would be in harmony with that dream, which would permit dreaming it again. Therefore it was important for him to relive what had already been lived, to make it come into being again and not be lost in the past and in nothingness. This is the underlying reason for the reiteration or repetition so characteristic of his style. Each moment must be made present over and over; in this way each renews its life and comes into being again. This process takes the place of the actual presence or, better still, the action of all the elements in a given system, by sustaining each of them and causing each to come into being. Observe that there is a profound connection between this and the idea of that other great nonsystematic thinker, Nietzsche, who was also deeply troubled by the problem of life and its survival, and who resorts to the *ewige Wiederkunft,* the eternal return of all things, which is merely a simulacrum of eternity, for within it each thing repeats its temporal and fleeting existence indefinitely, without escaping into time or even evanescence.

This also explains the motive for Unamuno's commentaries. In his writings, especially those which are not novels, his essays no less than his poetry—and this is what is most revealing—he does little more than comment, comment incessantly on other writers' texts. Wherever he is not dealing with imaginary characters, he constantly depends on the persons of other writers. It would be ingenuous to believe that Unamuno's quotations are sources of authority: they are sources of personality. He quotes them, yes, to make use of them, not logically but vitally: to demonstrate that everything that has been said, has been said by a man, in relation to a particular human life or history; and, further, with the purpose of reliving that life. It is enough to note how he insists on saying that he is speaking of the man Kant, the man Luther, the man Pascal, and his eagerness to use the Christian name—not just the surname—and how he translates it into Spanish too, if they are foreigners: Manuel Kant, Guillermo James, Benito Spinoza. He needs them, he needs them personally, lives and all, not their mere doctrines, and that is why he calls them familiarly by their names. Unamuno always needs a history or a novel which he can bring to life again, and if it has already existed, if it is about one of the men we call historical, so much the better.

In *La agonía del cristianismo* [The Agony of Christianity] he writes, "I have relived with Pascal in his century and in his ambit, and I have relived with Kierkegaard in Copenhagen, and I have done the same with others. May this not be, perhaps, the supreme proof of the immortality of the soul? Do they not feel themselves in me as I feel myself in them?" As we see, it is a question of reliving rather than rethinking the ideas of others; this is why he insists on the identity of atmosphere. Unamuno is always aware that life essentially goes hand in hand with the historical circumstance, though it might be said that he considers the circumstance communicable. The possibility of imaginatively repeating the life of some dead fellow human leads him to believe that life has a certain consistence—subsistence, if you will—which in the last analysis would be equivalent to persistence or immortality. But of course the central problem still remains, that of the person, the problem of who it is who relives or survives, and this leads Unamuno to a dramatic confrontation with questions of supreme importance, as we shall see.

Of the two modes of survival of which Unamuno spoke, that of the immortality of the soul, which he most often understood in a historical way, sometimes as a simple survival of name and fame—a means of evading, in his moments of doubt and agnosticism, the great problem set forth above—was the one which led him to make commentaries. And his ardent desire for the resurrection of the flesh gave fatherhood an extremely deep significance for him. Both meant an analogy of the survival of the individual. In fatherhood he sought a creation, a living proof, a visible sign of the perpetuation of the flesh, just as in exegesis he sought a demonstration of spiritual immortality.

Above all Unamuno felt the necessity of creating spiritually, out of his own self and from his own consciousness, other lives and other histories to keep him company—we have already observed that he never did anything alone—and that these lives should at the same time be his. His, but different. By this means he sought the kind of company that can be provided only by what is not oneself; this is the great problem of coexistence, clearly visible in friendship and in love, and one of the keystones of human history. At the same time, he needed existences to which he would be superior, which would receive life and death at his hands; this meant that he placed himself, if only figuratively, above them, and was thereby delivered from his anguish. Underneath, what he wanted was to play the role of God in relation to his creatures. This is why that dialogue of Don Miguel with Augusto Pérez, the protagonist of *Niebla* [Mist], has such a deep dramatic meaning in spite of its deliberate conventionality. In it Augusto rebels against the decision that he is to die, and brings to the attention of his author—that is the correct word—the certainty that he too will die. It should not be forgotten that when Unamuno speaks, using the common metaphor, of an author's creation or of engendering spiritual children, he is not referring primarily to his works but to his characters. His spiritual children are not so much *Niebla, La agonía del cristianismo,* or *Abel Sánchez,* as Augusto Pérez, Angela Carballino, or Abel Sánchez—the man this time, not the book. Therefore, as we have seen, Unamuno writes novels and dramas that he may have human children of his spirit. And, when this is not so, he dramatizes his writings by means of commentary, and peoples his work with living and breathing creatures in the obscure hope that they will be with him in the hour of his death and that he will survive in them, just as he served them in life as a vital source of strength.

In addition to all this, the life of an imaginary character, which is spiritual creation, offers for this very reason a maximum transparency of thought, and permits its author to submerge himself in its furthest depths without encountering the fundamental opacity of the real. Later on we shall see the importance and fecundity of this fact. A fictional history, unmixed with reality in the sense of things, demonstrates the purest example of human drama and at the same time the greatest identity and similarity with the mind which tries to penetrate it. This is specially true, of course, if there is a question of penetrating that history imaginatively as it is being created. It means the projection of oneself outward, in transparent nakedness. This is what Unamuno attempts in his novels.

We have now seen how the deep roots of Unamuno's own problem, given the actual position in which he stands in relation to the philosophy of his time—which is not of course our own: let us not forget that he was born in 1864—impel him to write novels, those strange novels of his which are suffused with anguish and seem encircled by a halo of metaphysical problems. And we see as well that they are the most decisively and individually and profoundly characteristic productions of his entire work, the point in which it necessarily culminates. Just what are these novels? We must try to find out.

# III.

# *THE PERSONAL NOVEL*

## WORLD AND PERSON

Unamuno's novels differ from almost all others in many ways, but one difference is so apparent at first sight and bulks so large, that Don Miguel himself spoke of it many times in order to explain it. It is that they contain no descriptions of any kind, neither scenery nor depiction of customs, and hardly any indication of place and time. Unamuno says that they are written as intimate dramas, presented in their bare bones. "The fact is," he wrote in one prologue, "I believe that by presenting the spirit of flesh, of bone, of stone, of water, of clouds, of all visible things, I present true and intimate reality, leaving to the reader the task of clothing it with his imagination." In other places he adds other reasons, pointing out that the descriptive obstructs the interest the reader feels in the narrative and the human passions displayed in it, and thus isolated, the narrative is purer and more cohesive.

This characteristic, apparently one of simple literary technique, is revealing. It discloses the peculiar character of Unamuno's novel and shows how different it is from the usual one. In the majority of novels that exist in this world the author gives a view of the characters, locates them as accurately as possible, and makes them move and act in relation to each other. The setting, the variety of characters who are brought together to live in their pages, and the events that take place are the important elements. In the great novels especially, we are given the view of a country, of a period, or of a society. While reading

Dickens one is transported to the England of the last century with more life and precision than one can find in books on British history or politics. Balzac makes us see at once the ambit of the French bourgeoisie after the Empire. That is, the traditional novel gives us a *world,* and within it a number of characters who move and live and die.

In these novels, being is understood in the sense of things; those things—among them human beings—are there and must be displayed, described in their environment. Their mutual relations, their actions and reactions, the effects of these, the new events which take place, all this must be outlined by the author. It is the way in which we gain knowledge of those realities. But in fact they are all nothing but *things,* in the broadest sense of the word. A mountain, a river, a wharf on the Thames, a street in Paris, a human countenance, a popular festival, a state of passion, a homicide, or a wedding—the enormous differences matter little. Note that I include in this catalogue of things psychic realities, states of mind or consciousness, along with, say, landscape. They are things, facts which exist in the world or are produced in it, set forth along with their causes. A torrential rain may produce a flood, or a state of jealousy lead to a crime; but in either case the novelist's function is usually the same: to describe as exactly and minutely as possible the causes, the act which is taking place and its consequences. We move in a world of things, whether they be physical, social, or psychic; a world—exterior or interior—which must be described.

Instead of all this, Unamuno cleaves to the bare narrative. This is the decisive factor: the narrative. Not a description of things, nor of characteristics and customs, nor even of states of mind, but narration, drama. What truly happens to the character, what he is making of himself, what he *is*. And observe that the novelist cannot tell us what the character is from the very beginning, as if he were in on the secret, but only what the character is, or, better, what he comes to be, what he is gradually becoming: that is the novel. Let us not forget that the novel is something which is told; it is history, something which moves essentially within time. But the important point is not that it should be a particular time, that of the French Revolution for example, but temporality itself, the intimate time in which the character lives and within which the novel is formed. Unamuno is interested not in giving us a world—I repeat, in the sense of things—but persons. And only as much world as his characters need in order to exist, that is, the world of the characters, a temporalized world, included in the narrative. This is fundamental.

The total contrast which I have just sketched between Unamuno's novels and others is, of course, exaggerated. It had to be, in order to be understood. Similarly, it is a deliberate exaggeration to place opposite these novels all the others that have ever been written; we shall see that there is a whole series of grades and shades. But it is useful to define things by their tendencies, by carrying them to extremes; it is the way in which they show us their being, the being toward which they incline, the one they are heading for, their truest being. This is especially true of living realities, as Bergson realized very clearly many years ago. It is well to point out, then, that the novel as a genre accentuates the characteristic of temporality, of dramatic reality which creates itself as it goes along, in contrast to other types of literature. It will suffice to compare any novel which is one in the strict sense, Stendhal's *Le rouge et le noir* or Galdós' *Misericordia,* for example, with the *Iliad;* it is obvious that the latter concerns itself much more with things and the world of things. That is, the novel as such tends to be what it is in Unamuno, even though he carries it to an extreme. During periods of decadence and adulteration, as in so-called "realism"—although this term should not be applied to everything which is so designated in the histories of literature—the novel is held captive in the being of things and loses its narrative or historical quality, becoming mere description or presentation of customs or states of consciousness.

One point should be clarified here. Among Unamuno's novels there is one—only one—which departs from this description. It is *Paz en la guerra* [Peace in War], his first novel. In it there are descriptions, and landscapes, and minute details of the social environment, and fields, and mountains, and picturesque types, and episodes of battles or of the siege of Bilbao, and all of Biscay. Why this exception? Had Unamuno not yet found his way? Should this novel be excluded from the list of those which are characteristically his? Unamuno says that he later abandoned the procedure he had followed in it, and this would lead us to think that it was a first attempt at a novel in the other sense. But, as soon as we begin to look closely into the matter, we see that there is a more substantial and decisive reason, and that this apparent exception throws more light on what we have seen before. The protagonist of *Paz en la guerra* is not a man, nor an individual person at all, but the whole of Bilbao, the Bilbao of the second Carlist war. This is the novel of a collective protagonist: its subject is a collective and communal life, an existence which is not individualized. And naturally the main character, the very protagonist itself, is in this case a *world*.

Unamuno perceived this also, and it is why he said in the prologue to the second edition, twenty-six years after writing the novel, "This is not a novel; it is a people." And, more specifically still, in Chapter I of *Del sentimiento trágico de la vida,* he seizes this possibility of personifying the collective, and writes, "Neither a man nor a people —which is, in a certain sense, a man as well. . ." The protagonist of *Paz en la guerra* is in fact a people, and the apparent description of things is, if looked at carefully, the narrative of what happens to the collective protagonist, of what is taking place in many people, in fields and streets and houses, throughout the years. This is the meaning of that exception which raises so many serious problems: aside from many specifically literary ones, it is that of the meaning of collective life—an extremely ambiguous expression—and of the subject and personality of this type of existence.

## CASE AND CHARACTER

If we leave aside the environment or "world" of the novel and turn to its protagonists, we see that the author can take two very different positions in regard to them. In some cases the novelist invents a plot, a complex of events which affect various characters, and these react in a certain way to the situations created. What defines the characters is precisely the situation; strictly speaking, each one of them is a "role," a "case," with a value which is generic and therefore universal. There is *the* picaro, lad of many masters, defined by a situation of hunger and low trickery; or *the* jealous husband who must deal with the situation created by infidelity; or *the* dreamer who lives in an unreal world and collides with the world of reality; or *the* fallen woman, or *the* despotic father, or *the* ruined nobleman. In all this repertory we are dealing with a character in which the *man* is unimportant: what makes up his essence is a "case," and his way of reacting to it is a "role." This last point must not be forgotten, for it of course constitutes part of the situation.

These novelistic characters are not, properly speaking, personages. They have no personality; if we were to encounter them in the real world we would not recognize them, unless they should find themselves in the "case" in which the novel has presented them. Would we recognize Don Gutierre, the Calderonian husband in *El médico de su honra,* if we were to encounter him as a bachelor, or married to Doña Mencía, without the trying situation created by the prince? Would we recognize Segismundo in *La vida es sueño* if he had not been exiled and imprisoned by his father only to be brought back to the court later? Is there anything which individualizes these characters apart from the "case," the situation in which the author presents them to us? In what do they consist if not in that? The strong relief in which they appear in our imagination does not proceed from the characters themselves but from what happens to them.

In other novels or dramas, by contrast, the important element is the personages as such, apart from what happens to them. Sometimes almost nothing happens—the minimum which can serve as a pretext for setting them in front of us and letting them live; above all, the plot, the concrete happening which causes them to act, is unimportant. The character here is a person, a mode of being. This is why we would recognize him if we should meet him, even though he might be engaged in other activities. Would we have any trouble in identifying Don Quijote, even though he carried no lance, rode no horse, tilted at no windmills, and conversed with no dukes? Would we not recognize him at once even in a sports jacket, or a monk's habit, as soon as we saw him simply *living?* Hamlet would always be Hamlet, even though he were not a prince and did not live in Denmark; and Julien Sorel would be unmistakable even without the seminary and the Restoration, as Raskolnikoff would be, without the poverty and the old crone of a moneylender.

In literature "cases" are much more frequent than true "personages." There is only a discontinuous line of fictional beings, created in the image and semblance of man, who have a kind of being which is their own and unique, who have a truly human consistency; the great majority are only subjects of a drama, living supports for a situation, of a fortuitous change of fortune or an abstract pattern of life. There is an obvious analogy between this difference in fictional characters and the distinction, emphasized by the philosophers of our day, between what can be called "authentic life" and "inauthentic or trivial life." In the novels in which only a "case" or "situation" is dealt with, the narrative is reduced to the trivial life of the character as a person, even though the actions which make up the narration may be unusual, extraordinary, or glorious. On the other hand, the novel which creates true personages descends to levels of authenticity which can be found in the commonest and most obscure of lives, and captures the essential nucleus of personality. Compare, for example, Amadís of Gaul with Benina, the old servant in Galdós' *Misericordia*. In the first case we find the extraordinary adventures of a dazzling knight; in the second, the obscure and poverty-stricken life of a beggar serving-woman in the drab atmosphere of the Madrid of the 1880's, in which practically nothing happens. What is the difference between them? Amadís' deeds are virtually impersonal, interchangeable, and could be performed by any knight-errant, at least any of the same character—that is, with his particular way of reacting. They do not reveal the depths of his vital and intimate being, the redoubt we call the soul or the person, and which we know and love in the fellow humans who are the object of our particular interpersonal dealings. The humble yearnings of Benina, however, bring us into contact with her very self, and we coexist with the old servant throughout the pages of the book; by the time we are through, she is someone irreplaceable for us, someone we pity and love personally; we love her, Benina, not her misfortunes or her virtues.

And it is possible to pass from one mode to the other. In Spanish literature, so given to abstraction and outline, the very few "personages" who do exist proceed from an initial "case": they transform themselves under the novelist's hands; they become individualized and personalized, perhaps somewhat to his surprise, until finally an authentic creature of fiction exists where only a situation or generic type had been visualized. The prime example is Don Quijote. At the beginning, it is perfectly obvious, Cervantes intends to create a parody of the knight-errant; he is a deformed sketch of an already sketchy type. At the same time, Don Quijote is the fiction of a fictional being; he is therefore fictitious to the second degree. For in the novel, as a general rule, a man is invented, but in *Don Quijote* an attempt is made to invent the most abstract of novelistic characters, of the kind we call "cases." But little by little Don Quijote declares his independence from his author's plan, and turns into someone with an individual and very definite personality. When Don Quijote, in that passage Unamuno liked so much, exclaims, "I know who I am!" he is no longer an exemplification of knighthood but a soul, a unique, irreplaceable person who accompanies us for the whole length of the book and lives with us forever outside its pages.

Something similar happens with Celestina, though perhaps to a lesser degree. The literary type is old and well-known; furthermore, it presents an almost professional function, a trade. Therefore we are dealing with a "case" in its strictest and most concrete form. (Trotaconventos, in the Arcipreste de Hita, to find an example within Spanish literature itself, is exactly the same thing.) But Rojas' Celestina is full of personality; she begins to live before our very eyes, and as she carries out her important function she shows us an interior, a mode of being, an idea of the world and of life disclosed particularly in her dialogues with the servants Pármeno and Sempronio and with her protegées Elicia and Areusa. Above all, Celestina reveals an idea of her own self, a personal essence, a *chez soi* from which she derives her existence; and this is, after all, what we understand a person to be. Something of the sort occurs with Lazarillo de Tormes; it will suffice to compare him with Don Pablos, the pure "case." To be sure, the problem of passing from one type to another is given in a double and extremely clear sense in *Lazarillo de Tormes*. Its beginning is strictly generic, defined by a situation: he is the "blind-man's guide" who will come to be called by his name, even down to his personal diminutive.* Then, in his life with the blind man, with the priest of Maqueda and with the squire, while he battles with hunger and has it out vitally and personally with his masters—let us not forget the moving relationship of the hungry scamp of a boy with the dignified and equally starved squire—he acquires the quality of a personage and behaves as such; but later, after he passes into the service of the Mercedarian friar and the seller of Papal bulls, he loses it again. It vanishes and leaves us only with typical descriptions suitable to a "lad of many masters." Lazarillo, then, demonstrates the complete cycle, though in a minor key which never attains the strong personality of other fictional beings.

From the beginning, Unamuno creates only personages. Contrary to what might be believed, Unamuno's protagonists are not "situations." At first sight their nakedness makes us think of sketches; the novel or drama of Unamuno is often interpreted as a symbolic creation, in which the author sets in motion conventional figures who represent universal problems or desires: motherhood in Raquel of *Dos madres* [Two Mothers] or in Aunt Tula; education in Don Avito Carrascal; envy in Joaquín Monegro of *Abel Sánchez*. But the fact is that in Unamuno these situations are problems of personality, not "vital conflicts" or cases. The situation is the pretext for showing the drama of the personality; the important thing is not that this or that happens, but the sense of "who I am" of each of the protagonists. Strictly speaking, the desire for motherhood of Unamuno's women is not the desire to have a child but rather to be mothers; to the point that the child can be someone else's, as happens in the two cases mentioned, and neither real maternity nor the actual child matters,

* In Spain the person who leads a blind man has come to be called "un Lazarillo," after the hero of this famous picaresque novel. Translator's note.

only the maternal being of the woman, her personality as a mother. So it is in his other novels.

## BIOGRAPHIES

To clarify the question still further, it should be looked at from another point of view. Compare the novel with the biography. In the latter the important factor is, from the outset and unequivocally, the history of a person and consequently of the reality of that selfsame person. The narrative, then, is in the strictest sense unavoidably limited by the theme. However, in a goodly number of the *Lives* we read, the only thing we find is a chronicle of the events which occur in the subject's life. These are presented in temporal and external succession, as happenings that took place in the world and nothing more. We are left in ignorance about everything which concerns the subject himself, and at the end of the biography he is a stranger to us even though we know everything that happened to him. Strictly speaking, what we do not know is to *whom* all this happened; the subject of the biography appears to be only the link connecting all these occurrences; he is nothing more than a simple localization. At the bottom of this is a philosophical idea of man dominated by realism, by the interpretation of human reality as a thing among other things, as a mere support for actions, or else a point of view determined by positivist psychology, which in the last instance goes back to the concept of the soul as a bundle of psychic acts—a concept related to the sensualism of the eighteenth century. We can see, then, that the essential matter is not the exclusive attention to a figure or person but the manner of this attention, the way in which the living narration of his history is presented, his own history as it is being made, arising from the roots of his personality, in his life. Learned biographies often provide examples of an immense amount of attention devoted to a man; the smallest events of his life are examined, but at the end we really know nothing about him outside of a multitude of things which happen to have happened in his life.

But of that life, of what he did with these things, and what they did to him, I repeat, we know nothing. What we are told of a man understood as a thing is absolutely meaningless.

This is true insofar as it appertains to the person. But biography also serves to cast light on matters having to do with the world. Compare, for example, a French biography with a German one. In general terms—which, naturally, do not eliminate exceptions—it is obvious that the technique with which the life of the person is presented is profoundly dissimilar. The German biographer is apt to lead us from the very beginning into the inner life of the man whom we seek to know. His feelings, his concerns, his ideas, what he thinks about things: this is the atmosphere in which we move from the outset. The surrounding world is seen from his viewpoint, not directly with our own eyes; everything is translated into the man's interior view, and we feel a trifle cramped. The subject of the biography is at bottom a solitary man, and the world becomes his interior world within which the reader must live all the time he is reading. We move from the beginning in an ambit of psychic realities, within a consciousness which is the first thing we encounter; and only through that consciousness, as through a pane of glass, do we see his circumstance. But do not forget that this last factor, though quite important, is not the decisive one; the previous factor is: the pane of glass is not merely a clear and transparent medium which leads us to something other than itself, but is presented as colored, and itself becomes the principal object of our vision.

The French technique is very different. It shows us the subject living in the world, with other people, in contact with them, busy tending to his affairs, related to his society and the topics of his day. It is curious to note that French biographies—whether one is dealing with Rancé's, written by Chateaubriand, or those of Cousin or of Disraeli written in our own time by Maurois—usually devote a good deal more space, especially at the beginning, to other people and things than they do to the subject and his own affairs. He is revealed to us from the outside. We are not let in on the secret of his inner self; we are not told what he thinks and feels; in particular we are not told the meaning which each event has for his life—which one generally "knows" at once in the German biography—but instead we come to divine it little by little. The biographer does not introduce us suddenly into the inner life of the subject, but makes us enter his circumstance, presents him to us—him and others, though calling him particularly to our attention—and we begin to see him live. We come to know him well, and from his exterior we deduce his intimate reality bit by bit. We know him as we know any fellow human, from the point of view of ourselves and the world we coinhabit with him, not from inside himself. At the end of the book, in the great French biographies, we have a vast familiarity with the subject and with his world, and we know even how he thinks and feels; but we have come to know this by dint of watching him greet his friends, give speeches, make love, fight battles; in order to become acquainted with his inner self we have begun by watching his movements, the way he takes off his hat, enjoys a landscape, or talks to a woman.

Does this difference coincide with that fundamental difference in the novel of which we spoke earlier? Does this mean that the French biography gives us a world, a description of things, and the German one a person, a narrative of true history? It would be a grave error to believe this, though at first sight we might be persuaded to think so. The two distinct types cross each other without coinciding, and this is what defines them best. Man's life includes the world he lives in; the world, then, is essential in the biography as well as the novel. But this world must be the world of the man, not just a physical world, a world of things only. The world must be incorporated into the narrative. If it is independent and subsists all by itself, it is of no use to us and has no importance; it has to be the world in which and with which the subject is formed. In this way the French biography *may* give us the more living and temporal narration of a particular life. And, on the other hand, the German one cannot accomplish this by the mere tactic of its interior view as such. Quite apart from the false premise implied by this transfer to the subject's intimate self—a self which is not fictional and therefore is not oneself, but essentially alien, another's, with a real and opaque body and an interior which is by definition arcane—apart from this, I repeat, that interior world in which we are made to reside *may* be a world of things, of psychic or psychological things—the two are not synonymous—no less alien to the pure temporal being of the person as he forms himself than the most prolix and "objective" external description. The narrative can equally well dissolve into the physical circumstance or a series of happenings or a complex of states of consciousness. "Realism" can operate with all manner of *res,* with all sorts of things, notwithstanding their interior quality or their subtlety.

## PSYCHOLOGICAL NOVEL AND PERSONAL NOVEL

The nineteenth century gave us the psychological novel. And this was not by chance, for it was the period of psychologism. Just as it tried to convert philosophy into psychology—and I say "tried" because it is very hard to change philosophy into what it is not—psychologism also took unto itself novels, dramas, and even in some sense music and the plastic arts. Of course this must be understood *cum grano salis;* I mean that psychologism is at the base of the paintings and the music of some sixty years ago and explains them, makes them possible; it is their foundation.

Positivism, which held that reality was made up simply of facts, and furthermore that these facts were always those of experience, understood man as a biological entity or, on the other hand, as a collection of psychic phenomena; and that when men joined together to live in common—this must have seemed at that time rather secondary and derivative—a new type of facts came into being, the so-called social facts. Because of this, attention to man usually takes, in the latter half of the nineteenth century, the triple form of a biology—usually evolutionary—an experimental psychology and a naturalistic sociology, like Spencer's, for example. Naturally, at that time there were some who sensed that the reality of man is very different from this, that there are strata of human reality, the most important ones, the existence of which the science then in vogue did not even suspect—we need only cite the names of Kierkegaard, Maine de Biran, Gratry, Brentano, and Dilthey, among some few others. But this avant-garde thought was unable to influence sufficiently the great mass of culture which was not philosophical but concretely literary, and which adhered to the convictions of the science of the day. (It would be interesting, though, to pursue the contemporary influence of the incipient metaphysic of existence and the person in other fields.) Literature, then, approaches the human theme from the point of view of these scientific assumptions more consciously than ever before, and becomes totally impregnated with psychologism.

The psychological novel attempts to make a minute analysis of the psychic or spiritual life of its characters. States of mind are dwelt upon with positively loving delight. Love of any kind, unhappiness, doubt, fanaticism, ambition, world-weariness, understood principally —this must not be forgotten—as feelings. And observe that the psychological novel, once more following the tendency of the period, has a special predilection for the abnormal and tends to interpret human life pathologically. These states of mind are described, analyzed, divided into their component parts, and pursued in all their consequences. The reader is shown the reality of an unhappy soul, overcome by sensuality or dominated by maternal love, for example. The novel, that is to say the novel as such, the narration, consists in the exposition of the conflicts posed by these states of mind and the way in which one conflict leads to others. As a characteristic example among many which might be mentioned apart from Zola, one could read Alphonse Daudet's *L'Évangéliste*. That this approach is both desired and sought is shown by the fact that the author dedicates it as a case study to Charcot, the famous psychologist of the Salpêtrière. This also accounts for the pathological tone referred to earlier which is so common in the novels of the later nineteenth century, until we come to the so-called *roman expérimental,* which has very little of the novel about it.

In contrast to these, there arises early in our century, and closely related to the progress of philosophy, a new type of novel whose most extreme and most decisive example is found in Unamuno. It could be called the personal novel. At first sight, the fact that it also takes place in the interior self of a person, that there is little action in it in the sense of external events or happenings, might make it possible to confuse this novel with the previous type. But on close examination it will be seen that radically different things are being dealt with. What is important in the personal or "existential" novel—we shall see later the meaning of this dual name—are the characters, not their feelings. In the psychological novel the protagonists are simply supports for their respective states of mind, and it is the latter which are of interest, the true subjects of the narration. The personal novel is the expression of a life, and that life is of a person, of a personage or fictional creature who imitates the mode of being of a concrete man. Therefore the novel of Unamuno is not descriptive but purely narrative, temporal, and there are no conflicts of feelings in it but always a problem of personality.

If there are love, hate, sadness, and envy in these novels, they are never mere states of consciousness but modes of being. A passion is not a feeling, a mere psychic affection, for Unamuno; he understands and interprets it as a mode of being, as a concrete passionate being, that is, in an ontological way: it is not something that happens to one, what one feels at a given moment, but what one is. "I saw that that undying hatred was my soul," says Joaquín Monegro, the character in *Abel Sánchez,* when he has that agonizing encounter with himself, the self that consists wholly in hating. What has this to do with describing the stimuli of a hatred, and its psychic ingredients, and how it fills a soul, and how it and other feelings are in conflict within that soul? That would be the "history"—I use the word with extreme and deliberate impropriety—of the feelings of a character and of his conduct, but it is not what interests Unamuno. What interests him is the story of Joaquín Monegro, the man himself, not his psychic apparatus or his social relationships. It is clear that Unamuno does not always have a full consciousness of this; instead, he acquires it little by little, makes half-guesses, and then tries somewhat haphazardly to find justification for the character of his work. Unamuno's prologues are full of allusions to the strange style of his novels, which he feels to be something new and unusual, and from this arises his initial joke of calling *Niebla* a "nivola," even though he always insists later that it is a true and authentic novel.* The subtitle of *Abel Sánchez* is "A history of passion," and in the prologue to the second edition of this book, written in 1928, Unamuno notes the strangeness of this expression and says that perhaps "History of a passion" would have been better. But the interesting point is that, in spite of the fact that the latter title is the more obvious form of the expression, Unamuno chose the first and more arresting one because it illustrated his purpose better. It is a matter of writing not the history of a passion, but of a man—two men, if you will—and that history is of passion; passion is not its subject, but quite simply its essential characteristic.

Man is not exhausted when his physical or biological or even his psychic side have been investigated; rather man begins when one has probed deeper than this. Then the person is encountered, and the person is what gives meaning to biological and psychic life and makes them possible. The novel of Unamuno descends into this deep stratum of the soul or the personality, much deeper than all the feelings, which is why it can capture the secret of existence through its dramatic or narrative form. And so it is pure narrative, a narrative which barely needs to be enmeshed with the web of exterior events or even with details of action, because it takes place in living time, in the temporality of the existence which is being made in it. And this is the reason why Unamuno scarcely bothers with plot, or the framework of events, or the way in which the vital fortunes of his characters are resolved. At times these factors do not exist, or are specifically denied, as in *La novela de Don Sandalio, jugador de ajedrez* [The Novel of Don Sandalio, Chess Player]. Unamuno is interested not in any single event in the lives of his characters, but in their existence as such, in the life itself; and the sole problem of that existence is existence itself, the problem of their personality, and the only solution is death. With this we confront the great question again. But first we must find out just what strata of that reality

* In chapter 17 of *Niebla,* one of Unamuno's characters says that he is writing, not a "novela," but a "navilo . . . nebulo . . . nívola . . . nivola!" Thus, no one will have the right to say that it goes against the canons of its genre.

Unamuno shows in his novels: the concrete man, who lives and dies.

## EXISTENCE AND PERSON

I have used two different expressions to describe Unamuno's novels: "existential" and "personal." Are the two synonymous? Do they mean fundamentally the same thing? Or is Unamuno's novel only one of these two things, and the other term inappropriate? What do those two words so impregnated with meaning really stand for: existence—or life—and person?

First of all, we must not use too much precision; in this particular case it may be the only way to be exact. While talking of Unamuno we should take care not to unload onto this word existence all of Heidegger's metaphysical speculation, what he calls *existenziale Analytik des Daseins,* nor the ontological study of life made by Ortega y Gasset. Unamuno does not go into these rigorous investigations, and if we tried to raise his thought to their level we should have to alter it. We can make use of them only to understand conceptually from their viewpoint what in Unamuno is only *lived,* glimpsed and guessed.

We have seen that man cannot be reduced to the purely psychic; at every moment, man has experiences which determine the direction of his consciousness: now I think and perceive, later my psyche is filled with a feeling of pleasure, then some desire overcomes it, still later painful memories beat in upon it and my soul is flooded with sadness. But I do not exhaust myself in this, in the continuity of my psychic experiences. All these acts occur *in my life;* life or existence presents itself to me, for the moment, as a totality, defined by my relationship with things, with the world in which I am, and constituted by my actions in relation to these things, my vital dealings with the world. Within that life, as separate moments of it, psychic acts take place, but they are essentially different from it. On the other hand, that life has a shape, a structure, a meaning, which is shown in the vital plan it essentially supposes, in that which makes me choose at every instant what my life is to be in the next. All vital action, as Ortega has very clearly shown, has a why and a wherefore, and these elements are imbedded in the structure of life as such, in the scheme of life which every living man makes for himself. So-called "psychic life," then, is only an abstraction, one of the elements of authentic life, and cannot exhaust it nor, in consequence, be confused with it.

This life is temporal, historical; it takes place in time, in the instants of time and through its periods; therefore life is biography, not merely biology, and its expression is a narration. But, on the other hand, I am distinct from my life. This expression may of course be understood in the sense that I am not all of my life but only an ingredient in it, together with things. This is the sense in which Ortega says, "I am I and my circumstance." The moment of "I-ness" in man—the second "I" of Ortega's phrase—does not exhaust the human being, as idealism once held. But just now we are more interested in the first "I," the one which includes the circumstance, the one which is not a mere subject of living, center of a circumstance, and which is thereby one and at the same time *circumstantia.* The circumstance is in fact defined by being around—circum—an "I": that is what gives it its unitary and circumstantial, or vital, character; but we cannot simply define the I through the circumstance as its central point. The I is inseparable from the circumstance and has no meaning apart from it; on the other hand, the circumstance can exist only around an "I," and not just any I, a mere subject of acts and doings, but an "I myself," capable of self-analysis, an I which is not a some*thing, res,* but a some*body,* a person. We might say that I am defined by my circumstance, but my circumstance does not define me; that is, I exist only within it, and it decides my being, but does not exhaust it. My being—my future being, if you will—is not given when my circumstance and an abstract, single point of "I," a pure subject of it, are given. The circumstance is "my" circumstance; and this possessive does not indicate a simple localization but an effective possession. Because I am "I myself," because I have selfhood and am master of myself, I can possess something which is mine. "I-ness" does not exhaust the man, but neither does mere subjectivity—that is, the function of being subject of the "objective." I am not referring to immanence; the I is not a mere support or substratum of the circumstance, it is not merely *he who* lives with it but *the one who* lives, the one who makes his life together with the circumstance, giving that "who" its strictly personal sense. Man, besides being an "I" and the subject of his vital acts, the support of his world, is also a person.*

These slight and summary indications will suffice here, for this is not the place to introduce the metaphysical problem which they imply. I have wished only to clarify the primary meaning of the two expressions used to describe Unamuno's novels. And now we see—and will verify later on—that his novel is, for the moment, existential, not psychological, because it holds to the temporal narration of a life, not the description of its mechanisms. But it does not exhaust itself in this; the last redoubt of Unamuno's novel transcends even this vital narrative. How? When it comes to an end, in death. Unamuno is concerned with life insofar as it is a condition for understanding death; and death is, as we have seen, his true and anguished question. Through death, therefore, he transcends life and reaches the person who dies after having lived. I can take up a position relative to my life; I can be opposed to it; above all, I can lose it, for I am not my life. When the point of death is reached, life ends; but this is just the point where Unamuno begins to be really interested. He cares, first of all, about who has lived and is now dying, yearning to survive. This is the reason why his novel descends to the deepest stratum of man, and is, more than anything else, radically personal.

## THE IMAGINATIVE ANTICIPATION OF DEATH

We have seen how Unamuno approaches the novel, this "existential" or "personal" novel whose characteristics we have been describing, impelled by his idea of reason and of the temporal and dramatic reality of man. He uses the novel to create fictional beings, spiritual creatures with a history in which he can see himself reflected and in

* For a fuller treatment of the problem, see my *Introducción a la filosofía, Obras,* volume II.

transparency, outside himself, and thus can relive human history and understand its truth. He also makes use of the novel, and very importantly, to probe into the great experience, the one that can never be repeated and which for that very reason presents us with the problem of survival: namely, the experience of death.

Death, in fact, cannot be repeated; a person dies only once, and there is no room for repetition; this gives the fact—or the act—of death a meaning essentially different from that of all others, putting it on a level only with birth. But birth is not an act, nor is it even a fact which exists for the person who is born; therefore death remains as something absolutely unique, the one odd quantity. And observe that, even though immortality or resurrection is postulated, that is, that we keep on living and existing after death, the radical meaning of death is not diminished in the slightest degree. Survival, far from making death cease to exist, is precisely what gives death its full reality; only in everlasting life is a fully realized death made possible. For in this life—while life lasts—there is only the expectation or menace of death, which are two different things. If man ended along with his life, then, strictly speaking, he would only "stop living," he would not *die*. In order for death to be fully realized for the man who dies, it is necessary for him to survive past it; if not, death would be only something which takes place outside oneself, which happens to other men. The Greeks, especially the Epicureans, believed that, if man is not immortal, death does not exist while he lives; and when it does arrive, man no longer exists, he is not there to wait for it, he does not meet it; consequently death has no reality for him.

But everlasting life is that in which one can no longer die; and therefore death admits of no repetition at all. The only thing one can do with it is to anticipate it; to anticipate it, which is not the same as expecting it or counting on it or knowing that it must come. All these things are done from inside life; they consider death as something future, something as yet nonexistent, in fact, as something outside life, even though it is connected with life in the sense of a boundary, an after-fact. To anticipate it, on the other hand, is to see it and live it in itself; it is to make it arrive and have it already present in one's own life. To anticipate it, of course, imaginatively; since reliving it is impossible, it can be prelived. And this is what the novel can be used for.

Death occurs in almost all Unamuno's novels. This does not mean that it serves as the solution of one of those tragic *impasses* which life presents, nor is it the loss of a character. It is the real dénouement of the novel, the thing which gives full meaning to the history and consequently to the narration. This is particularly true in *San Manuel Bueno, mártir* [St. Emmanuel the Good, Martyr], Unamuno's best work in one genre, and perhaps his most personal and intimate book, in which the death of the character is the necessary culmination of the novel. For Unamuno each novel is an attempt to live death, to pass through it, to let it arrive, to enter its chilly ambit and stay there, in spite of everything, so as to see it from the other side, that is, consummated, in order to look anxiously behind oneself.

This is certainly an imaginative attempt. But Unamuno said of the imagination that "it is the most substantial faculty, the one which puts the substance of our spirit into the substance of things and of our fellow men." * Therefore we cannot doubt the importance of this anticipation or the burning desire to *know* which motivated it. Later we will see the broad implications of this. For Unamuno, it is imagination which allows him to penetrate the very substance of death, which can make him taste the truth of it as rational and systematic thought could never do. It can be said that the experience of another's death does exist. This is true, and it is what brings us up against death and makes us feel its mystery. But understand it? To understand it as death, not as a loss or an absence or a fact in the world, means placing oneself inside the viewpoint of the person who dies; death must be seen from his perspective. For he who remains alive, another's death is simply absence or loss, a deprivation. The positive reality of death exists only for the one who dies; if we see or glimpse it, it is also thanks to imagination. Solely by means of this faculty can we place ourselves in a certain sense in the mortal situation itself, or better still in the point of view, the very being, of the one who dies. We must solve the riddle of death imaginatively. In a certain sense we must coexist with the one who dies; but this, if looked at

* *Ensayos*, V, 73.

carefully and taken in its strictest sense, is impossible: it is a contradiction. It is possible only while he has not yet died; when death arrives, the witness' coexistence stops, and nothing remains but death's great silent presence. From this comes the absolute solitude of death, that each must die without companionship, and accounts for the most terrible despair when we watch a person die whom we love as our very selves. This is the true impotence: not the inability to save him, but the inability to be with the one who dies. It is the abyss.

And because of this imaginative anticipation, all of Unamuno's novels are a *meditatio mortis.*

## THE DEPTHS OF THE PERSON

We have already seen how the novel of Unamuno differs from the psychological novel in that it deals with modes of being rather than feelings. We must fix our attention on this for a moment because it will help us to discover one of the essential traits, perhaps the decisive trait, in what we have been calling the personal novel.

I said that it deals with modes of being. At the same time, we have seen very clearly that what characterizes the novel, and Unamuno's novel in particular, is the temporal narrative, the history, what goes on in the life of the man or fictional character. But is this not also the case with feelings? Are they not also something which happens to us men? Does not the feeling of sadness, or love, or envy, at some moment constitute the content, the very reality of our life? And yet we have presented both things as opposites, and have denied that feelings can be the stuff on which the personal novel can feed. Why is this so?

We must distinguish between two things which differ considerably. That which simply happens in my life and that which I am, what constitutes me, are not the same. In Spanish the very use of idiom makes this distinction, though not too rigidly; our language distinguishes sharply between the two verbs "to be," *ser* and *estar.**

* The use of *ser* denotes inherent characteristics, while *estar* denotes a state of being which does not imply permanence. Translator's note.

It says "I am good" *(soy bueno),* but, on the other hand, "I am sad" *(estoy triste).* However, we cannot take linguistic forms too literally, for we would be led into error thereby. And there is a profound reason for this: language is communal, belongs to no single person, and is formed on an almost impersonal basis, on a trivial and inauthentic mode of being. The subject of language is primarily society, people, anybody. Naturally the most authentic personalities influence language, and leave within it a precipitate of individual and private life, but the general forms of speech are topical, and respond to the collective daily state of man; this is why they sometimes hide the essential nature of certain human realities which acquire their true being only in the authentic modes of existence. Especially in those dimensions of man in which they appear equivocally, in both the trivial and the authentic life of the person. Take "love," for example. The usual phrase is "to be in love" *(estar enamorado),* and this might lead us to think we were dealing with something sentimental, accidental, and nonessential. And in reality this is true of what we usually call love; but, in regard to true and primary love, it is not the case at all, rather it is entirely opposite, as we shall see at once. But let us not forget that even in Plato there is a difference between the celestial Venus and the popular or demotic one: beside the 'Αφροδίτη οὐρανία there is an 'Αφροδίτη πάνδημος.

It is possible for me to feel a grief or a joy without their affecting my being; I do not think of them as radically mine. They can disappear, and my state of mind can change, but I keep on being the same. This is not true with other things, for example, authentic love or living faith. Nor does this mean that such qualities are totally fixed and inherent in me, that they cannot survive or disappear, but that their existence or nonexistence—not simply their presence or absence—alters me in what I *am.* To be in love does not mean to have certain sentiments connected with another person; it is an ontological determination. Many feelings are possible in love, but love is by no means a matter of feeling, but of being. The one loved is included as such in the very being of the one who loves: that is, in this concrete mode which love is. A man can fall in love without having done so before, or he can cease to be in love, or love another; but then he is another person. The loved one actually forms part of the life of the one who loves, as a moment of his ontological constitution, and without the loved one he cannot be understood. The person who loves is not exhausted in himself, but transcends himself and includes another person; this is an essential ontological possibility of man. Love—that which is truly love—has no reference to the qualities, to the actions, much less to the feelings of the loved one, but to his existence, and, more strictly still, to his person. (Existence and person, though very different, are inseparable, and therefore love includes them both at once, just as the novel, as we saw, inevitably has reference to the complex of the person who is being made in existence or life.) Therefore it is possible to discover love in oneself; that is, to find another person included in one's own being, to the degree to which that person is loved. This is why love is fulfilled, that is, one is *(estar)* or is not in a state of love, or better still, one is *(ser)* or is not—though the possibility also exists of not knowing it or being mistaken about it. And it is precisely this possibility which proves the ontological character of love and shows that it is in no case a sentiment. It is possible not to know it exists or to be mistaken about what it is—always within certain limits. But, on the other hand, would it make any sense to be mistaken about one's feeling of joy, of whether or not one was happy?

Love, I repeat, refers to existence and to the person who exists. This is why the problem can arise of whether simultaneous and plural states of being in love are possible, of whether a man can, for example, be in love with two women at once, and of the intimate and ontological conflict—not just the external one, of course—to which this would give rise. If love were a matter of feelings, it is obvious that this would be perfectly normal and possible, and that furthermore it would not constitute the slightest internal difficulty so far as the person in love was concerned. Also because of this it is possible that love can survive the loved one, and that it becomes part of the being of the one who loves, in the concrete mode of loss. In the last instance, only by following this path would we come to comprehend the ontological possibility and the real meaning of marriage as a sacrament, which has reference to persons and confers graces which are intended not for each one of the individuals, but for both together in their essential unity, and whose scope is not limited to their actual living together in this world but is extended, as a matter of course, into eternal life.

All of this is absolutely fundamental, and only the profound process of trivialization which afflicts modern man has made it possible for him to lose the meaning of it and to ignore it as the authentic sense of love, more often than not confused with realities which are very different. And do not forget that in authentic love, along with its essential features which my teacher Ortega has so perspicaciously discovered in *Estudios sobre el amor* [On Love]—especially the point of "self-surrender through enchantment"—there comes a decisive moment of necessity, a consequence of its quality as an ontological determination, which explains in its turn the strictly matrimonial meaning of fully realized love. He who truly loves feels united to the loved one by a necessary bond, independent of his will or his feelings, for it resides in much deeper strata than these. He realizes that he is not able to separate himself from the person he loves; and when I speak of this impossibility I do not mean simply that it would be distressing or painful, but actually impossible, because the very being of the lover necessarily involves and includes that of the loved one. Man is open to things, and things also make up his existence; he lives in reference to them, and the things themselves are an element of that reference. Among the ontological determinations of the man A we find that of the being who is in love; and not only this, but being in love with B. Therefore the woman B is necessarily included in the integral reality of the man A.

Much the same thing occurs with religion, with living faith, in which man is also in an ontologically determined situation with regard to God. Nor is it a question of any sort of feeling—for example, the famous feeling of dependence Schleiermacher speaks of—nor of opinion, but of a mode of being. Either man is rooted in God or he is uprooted from Him. This is what makes possible the existence of conversion, which is not a mere change of ideas, or even of beliefs, but a change in one's being; and thus the convert becomes another man. Almost from the beginning, Christian thought has had a more or less clear and explicit view of this. The atheist is defined, from the Psalms onward, as a *fool,** as one who, consequently, is deprived of

* *Dixit insipiens in corde suo; non est Deus.* Psalms, 14.

his reason; conversion consists in his coming to himself, in finding himself within his own mind, in his own senses; and, since he was outside himself before, out of his mind, when he comes back to himself he also becomes someone else, a different person from the one he was before.

This is why St. Paul speaks of the new man and the old man, not of new feelings or new opinions or even of the new conduct of that man, but of the man himself. *Christianus alter Christus.* In the last instance, this is what conversion is all about, and it can be understood only in that light, from the point of view of being. But to investigate this question with sufficient thoroughness would carry us too far afield, and I merely wished to show, with a couple of examples, the nature of those modes of being in man in which it seems the very depths of the person are being reached.*

This long detour was indispensable in order to understand the ultimate basis of Unamuno's novel. We saw that what interested him was the very life of his characters, and that this led him to the question of death, the sole dénouement of existence. Very well then, Unamuno is looking for what he sometimes calls the "soul," that which gives meaning to life itself, which makes man live and be who he is. "Your life ends, and you will remain," he often repeats. For what happens in one's life is not enough, although this may be of the deepest and most intimate nature that can occur to man, even though it is what he himself makes of himself; it is still necessary that what he does is done to himself, that a man be who he is and no other: the *personality.*

Unamuno tries to penetrate the depths of the person; the passions that grip him, which are the substance of his novels, are those in which personality is brought into full play. In *San Manuel Bueno,* his most intimate and moving story, it is the yearning to save the protagonist's own personality by rescuing others from despair, making the whole town live with faith in the other life without being able to

* For a more profound view of the problem, I refer the reader to the article of my teacher Zubiri: "En torno al problema de Dios" *(Revista de Occidente,* no. CXLIX), included in the book *Naturaleza, Historia, Dios* (Madrid: Revista de Occidente, 1944); and to my book *La filosofía del Padre Gratry. La restauración de la metafísica en el problema de Dios y de la persona* (Madrid: Revista de Occidente, 1959) (Obras, volume IV).

share that faith, wanting to believe in them and through them and thus to become eternal himself. In the church of Valverde de Lucena, Don Manuel, the tormented priest, recites the *Credo* aloud with all his flock, his children: "And when he came to 'I believe in the resurrection of the body and the life everlasting,' Don Manuel's voice was swallowed up, as in a lake, by the voice of the whole town, and he fell silent." He was silent, making the rest believe through him and dream that they were immortal, dreaming along with them. The dream is, in the last instance, charity, though Unamuno never even mentions the word. And in *La novela de Don Sandalio, jugador de ajedrez,* he presents the negative personality, deliberately made a vacuum: that is the mystery. In *Abel Sánchez* it is the hatred—or envy—of Joaquín Monegro, which includes the hated man in the very being of the hater, in the same manner, as we have seen, as with authentic love; for Joaquín, to be alone is to be with the other man, with Abel, while Abel "didn't even know how to hate, he was so full of himself." In the same novel, Joaquín says, "I wondered if when I died I would die with my hate, whether it would die with me or live on after me; I wondered if hate survives the hater, if it is something substantial and can be transmitted, if it is the soul, the very essence of the soul."

It could not be more clearly stated; we are not dealing with feelings—what role can feelings play at the depth in which we are moving?—but with personality and its temporal unfolding in the course of existence. Hate—or the incapacity for hate—affects the very essence of man and depends upon his intimate ontological structure. Abel cannot hate because he is so full of himself. Joaquín, on the other hand, is full of the other man in the dimension of envy, which is a very concrete mode of metaphysical relation. So it is in all of Unamuno's bare and stripped-down narratives.

Now we perceive the point which Unamuno reaches: the question of the ultimate reality of temporal, concrete man who lives and dies, the very depths of the person. And he reaches these depths by means of the novel, that novel which, in all strictness, deserves to be called *existential,* and, above all, *personal.* What significance has this for philosophy?

# IV.

## *THE NOVEL AS A METHOD OF KNOWLEDGE*

### UNAMUNO'S PURPOSE

One thing is abundantly clear after a careful reading of Unamuno's books, and I have tried to show the reasons for it since the beginning of this book. It is that when Don Miguel de Unamuno undertook a literary work he did not plan a task of an aesthetic or artistic nature in the strict sense, but everything he wrote tended to set forth and relive—and perhaps to solve, if it were possible—that "sole question" which he described almost at the beginning of his career. When Unamuno speaks of the literary value of his works he usually avoids the word "literary," or at least tries to clarify it by using another word, "poetic." And he gives this word its immediate and original meaning of creation: creation of fictional beings in his novels and dramas, or re-creation of historical personages and the fictional characters of others in his books of essays or poetry, which turn into commentaries, as we have seen and will confirm in more detail later on, especially in regard to his poetic work. For Unamuno it is always a question of moving among human lives, of being able to monologize in the form of dialogue, of seeking essential companionship. For, if talking is to make any sense, even though it be a soliloquy, someone must hear us; God, at least. And this is the path we must follow to introduce the extraordinarily complex question of Unamuno's religion, which will help us to enter still more deeply into the total meaning of his work and of his whole life.

Unamuno is determined to *know.* This point is decisive. The sole question is to know what will become of every man when he dies—not living in one way or another, or enjoying life, or creating beautiful things, or even simply surviving, but *knowing.* We must know in order to live, certainly, and we move in this quest or search impelled by the necessity of surviving and of knowing ourselves destined to survive. The motive force is therefore this necessity of surviving, of being immortal, but the question is one of knowing. Since for Unamuno the desire for immortality is both the basis and point of departure of philosophy, and its object the concrete man of flesh and blood who is born, lives in time, and dies yearning to be eternal, Unamuno's purpose becomes formally identified with that of philosophy as he understands it. Because he believes that reason is not vital but antivital and the enemy of life, and that it therefore bars the way to comprehension of life's reality, he must make a new attempt to penetrate the secret of life, and this attempt is the novel.

As early as 1902, in an essay entitled "El individualismo español" [Spanish Individualism],* Unamuno conjectured about the value as knowledge which a history or narrative has as a projection of ourselves outward, in contrast to introspection. It may be the first time he divines the meaning of narration, and also the meaning of some important philosophical truths which we shall examine with more care later on. "We contemplate ourselves directly a good deal," he writes, "and truly this is not the best way of getting to know ourselves, of responding to the collective and social 'know thyself.' Introspection is very deceptive, and if carried to an extreme leads to an actual vacuum of consciousness, like that of the yogi who does nothing but contemplate his navel. For a state of consciousness which consisted purely and simply in contemplating itself would not even be a state of consciousness, because it would lack content. This supposed reflection of the soul upon itself is nonsense. To think that one is thinking without thinking of anything concrete is nothing. We learn to know ourselves in the same way we learn to know others, by observing our actions; the only difference is that, as we are always with ourselves and scarcely anything we consciously do escapes our notice, we have more data for knowing ourselves than we have for

* *Ensayos,* IV, 65–66.

knowing others. But even so, we rarely know what we are capable of until we put ourselves to the test, and we often surprise ourselves by doing something we did not expect. It follows from this how useful it is for a people to know its history in order to know itself." Here Unamuno still is thinking more about collective knowledge—and history—than about the individual and the novel. But he has already remarked on the necessity of knowing ourselves in our actions and our temporal process of living, and of arriving by this means at our ultimate, mysterious, surprising nucleus. Though at first sight the expression might resemble it, this is very far from "behaviorism," for the "observation of actions" he speaks of takes place within oneself, as is revealed by the allusion to the important fact of "our being always with ourselves." Strictly speaking, he should have said that we learn to know others in the same way we learn to know ourselves. The knowledge of my fellow man is founded on self-knowledge, specifically that of my real life, in those actions which point to realities different from myself. This is the important thing.

Twenty-five years later Unamuno wrote with greater clarity in his brilliant but not fully realized book *Cómo se hace una novela,* the key to his whole work, "Reader, I want to tell you how a novel is made, how you yourself make and must make your own novel. The inner man, the intra-man, when he becomes a reader, an observer, if he is a living man at all, must make himself the reader, the observer of the character which he is forming at the same time he is reading, creating—the observer of his own work. The inner man, the intra-man—more divine than Nietzsche's trans-man or superman—when he becomes a reader becomes by that very action an author or an actor. When he reads a novel, he becomes a novelist; when he reads history, a historian. And every reader who is an inner man, a human being, is, reader, the author of what he reads and what he is reading. What you are reading here and now, reader, is what you are saying to yourself, and it is as much yours as mine. If this is not so, you are not even reading." A little later he adds this vehement and revealing sentence: "Is not retelling a life perhaps one way, and maybe the profoundest way, of living it?" *

Thus, in intimate coherence with the purpose of his whole life,

* Pages 140, 150.

he could say, summing it all up in one phrase in some pages written toward the end of that life: "Everything, and especially philosophy, is strictly speaking novel or legend."* This is when he declares that all his works, even that entitled *Del sentimiento trágico de la vida,* are novels, and consist in "pulsating dramatic narratives, intimate and deeply personal realities, without stage settings or realistic details from which the true, the eternal reality, the reality of the personality, is often left out." And then he includes among the works he calls novels Kant's *Critique of Pure Reason,* Hegel's *Logic,* and others of the same kind, as well as the histories of Thucydides and Tacitus, and "of course the Gospels of the story of Christ." All this shows with the maximum degree of clarity the unity of his work as a whole, and reveals his purpose in writing it.

I have employed this series of quotations, stretched out along the whole span of Unamuno's career, to show that there is a constant and recognized design in his work, even though masked by appearances, which periodically manifests itself and makes him turn again to his problem. He distracted and consoled himself with his novels and with the contemplation of his own anguish and agony; but, from time to time, the problem irrupts in his mind in its authentic form and causes him to meditate *in modo recto* upon the great question. And that is when his whole work—and with it his own self—becomes problematical, and he feels a desperate nostalgia for philosophy.

## WHAT THE NOVEL CAN AND CANNOT GIVE

Unamuno's novel puts us in contact with that true reality which is man. This is its principal role. Other modes of thought—for we are dealing with thought—have their point of departure in previous and abstract diagrams. For example, they consider human life from a biological point of view, based on the perhaps unconscious supposition of the fundamental unity of everything we call life, and therefore they cast human reality into modes of apprehension which are alien to it and which cannot contain it without deforming it. Or again,

* The prologue-epilogue to the second edition (1934) of *Amor y pedagogía.*

they move from the outset within the compass of what we could call "culture," leading us to an extremely deficient and nonessential view of man. Unamuno, on the other hand, tries to obtain the highest possible degree of nakedness and authenticity in the object to which he is trying to find access. He attempts to reach the very core of the human drama, and simply to recount it, letting it be just what it is. The purpose of the existential or personal novel is to make plain to us a person's history, letting his intimate movements develop before our eyes, in broad daylight, and thus uncovering his ultimate nucleus. The purpose is, simply, to show human existence in all its truth.

To achieve this Unamuno uses the method which best accommodates itself to life's temporality: the narrative. We are not dealing here with the static demonstration of a psychic structure, for example, nor with a "figure," nor even with the stages in which that figure develops, but we are present at the very constitution of a personality in time. Thus human life can be seen from inside its very self; it can be relived without being turned into a thing, without being considered as something ready-made which is outside of ourselves. The novel takes place in time; it has duration, and, even more, captures a vital time, a rhythm which may be hurried or leisured but which is the rhythm of a life, very different from the clock time that ticks away as we read; thus, the novel is the proper instrument for showing us something which also takes place temporally. Both novel and life consist essentially in temporality.

Compare this mode of presenting human life with some of the others which contemporary philosophy has essayed. If we leave aside the scientific "explication" of the static and mechanistic or, at most, the "evolutive" type of the psychology of the nineteenth century, we find the idea of *description,* which has meant such a great step forward. On the one hand, Dilthey's "descriptive and analytical psychology" *(beschreibende und zergliederdernde Psychologie),* although it is grounded in a radical historicism, leads nevertheless to a "typology," a repertory of possible forms. On the other, is Husserl's "description of essences," which attains the apprehension of ideal objects and of equally ideal a priori links between them; therefore, it always moves in the realm of the universal or specific, and at the same time in the intemporal, leaving out simultaneously the individual and the temporal. Essential intuition or *Wesenserschauung* leaves out what is peculiar to life, its quality of being mine and of taking place in time. Therefore existential philosophy (Heidegger) has had to take up later an essentially different position within phenomenology. "Description" cannot be understood in the sense of a botanical morphology; rather its very character depends on the nature of what is to be "described." This is why Heidegger affirms that the meaning of phenomenological description is interpretation, and the phenomenology of "existence" is hermeneutic in a basic sense. "Der methodische Sinn der phänomenologische Deskription ist *Auslegung.*" "Phänomenologie des Daseins ist *Hermeneutik* in der ursprünglichen Bedeutung des Wortes, wonach es das Geschäft der Auslegung beszeichnet."* And as "existence" is defined by *Sorge,* or *cura,* care, and the meaning of this *Sorge* is temporality, time is in the very center of existential analytics, that investigation of "existence" which is always, essentially, "mine" *(je meines).* This is the radical about-face which philosophy has been obliged to perform in recent years; but we should not forget that in the period in which Unamuno's thinking was formed, philosophical thought still resided in the forms indicated above, and even these represented a bold anticipation and were far from being the current state of affairs of European knowledge.

However great the merits of the novel for giving us the truth of human existence, they are still insufficient to satisfy all the demands of strict knowing. On the one hand it is a pure narrative, an imaginative construction of the temporal reality of a life which is making itself; but the narration, along with its temporal quality, possesses another which must be noted: its verbal or, if you will, logical quality, according to the Greek. The narration is a saying; and simply living is not the same as narrating or telling, though both may take place in time and to narrate may be one mode of living. To say always means to say something about things, to say what they are; to interpret them, therefore, from the point of view of certain *assump-*

* *Sein und Zeit.*

*tions;* further, saying requires words, therefore meanings or concepts. At the base of all saying there is conceptualization. In order to give the temporality of the narrative we have to express it with words, with names; and the mere naming of something already means giving an interpretation of it and understanding it in a mode of being, in a category. Consequently it has been said, and Unamuno knew this very well, that all language implies a more or less rudimentary (but especially an unconscious and a passive) metaphysic, which is carelessly used and which, without our even being aware of it, slides into an area of commonplaces that are alien to the comprehension of all which is the object of our saying.

Very well, the novel does not possess any mode of conceptualization of its own. It must resort to the very depths of language, and language consists in its turn of a more or less confused precipitate of the ideas of the philosophic past; one need only recall all the metaphysics, of an Eleatic kind, implicit in that most unimportant word "thing," which is constantly on our tongues and which seems not to compromise us when we pronounce it. That is, concepts are indispensable, and we need them; the novel does not possess them in and of itself, and all its discoveries necessarily go only halfway, without ever coming to the point of establishing a knowing in the strict sense of the word, in the sense of philosophy. When Unamuno says, "What follows has not come out of my reason but out of my life, even though I have to rationalize it in a certain sense in order to transmit it to you," he is aware of this essential necessity of reason. Simple intuition or contemplation of human reality is not enough; we all live our life, and its reality exists for our consciousness, and yet the majority of men do not have a true knowledge of it; life must be understood in categories which reveal the modes of the human being to us. What is required, then, is an ontology of human existence, which the novel cannot give at all; and it is only at this point that philosophy, properly speaking, begins.

In the second place, a delimitation of the object is necessary. It would be indispensable to achieve a presentation of the object of our study in such a way that the object would appear in its true being. And Unamuno's novel responds to partial interests which leave large areas of human reality in shadow in order to concentrate on others. There is an arbitrary breaking-up or limitation of the theme. This limitation would be acceptable and would carry no risk whatever if it were presented as such, with awareness of itself and knowledge of its dimensions and of the relation of the part illuminated by the novelist's attention to the whole. But this does not happen, and therefore the limitation involves a falsification, because the reality of each part also includes its concrete reference to the whole. Each part can achieve its truth only if it is understood as a part, in a way which immediately relates to the whole—better, the organism—of which it is a part. The very nature of reality demands a systematic interrelation of knowledge; its elements appear in an essential unity, a dynamic structure, and all have need of one another. For a strictly philosophical truth to exist, it must necessarily be given in a *system*. And this requirement clearly does not proceed from any a priori idea of what knowledge ought to be, but arises from the necessity of adapting itself to the very context of reality, especially the living reality of human existence, which is, in and of itself, essentially systematic—though this was not the opinion of Unamuno nor in general that of his time. All this is by definition impossible for the personal novel, which remains a deficient and secondary mode of knowledge, if we understand the terms in their strictest sense, although it is no less strictly effective.

The novel, then, in its function as a mode of knowing, is based on assumptions which go beyond itself and which constitute its deepest substratum. It is not, nor can it be, a primary and autonomous method of knowledge, for it requires a foundation; and this foundation may be, in turn, either a strict ontology or a repertory of unconnected convictions without evidence or final justification. In the first case, the novel can make use of a precise conceptual system, can move in a dimension of existence which is not unaware of other dimensions, and can thus maintain itself rooted in the systematic context of human life. Then it becomes a subordinate and dependent mode of knowledge, though strictly real nevertheless, whose implications we must investigate. In the second case its cognitive value is always dubious and it is liable to that form of error, common in abstract thought, which we call exaggeration.

The foregoing affects every authentic novel, although in very different degrees and forms. It would be exceedingly interesting and unexpectedly profitable to make a study of the novel from this point of view, which could lead to a comprehension of it vastly superior to that which the usual "literary" or "psychological" methods of investigation provide, and at the same time would disclose the assumptions on which novelists act. These assumptions mean nothing less than the radical modes of apprehending human reality current in each age. Not the philosophers' ideas, conscious on the one hand though on the other representative of a minority and ahead of their time, but the convictions on which the collective consciousness of a particular age are founded. Such a study could cast a light on the comprehension of the inner core of human history at its deepest levels, but we have no time here for even a sidelong glance, though our mind is tempted.

## THE SIGNIFICANCE OF THE NOVEL AS METHOD

What is the meaning of Unamuno's novel considered from the point of view of philosophy? The personal novel is a method which ontology can use as a preliminary step. We have seen how the temporal and living nature of the narrative brings us to the very reality of the human character's history or life. This is its most productive function. It represents an approach to the object, which is human existence and its personality, to what is to become the theme of philosophical inquiry. It can put us in contact with the very reality which we must describe and conceptualize metaphysically. And this is method in its full and original sense. Unamuno's novel gives a primary intuition of man which is both alive and effective; and this is necessarily the point of departure for all possible metaphysical knowledge: the encounter with the reality which is to be its theme. We have seen that this encounter takes place in what we call the existential or personal novel with a purity and a fidelity to the nature of life, which is temporal and alien to being in the sense of things, to such a degree that it is difficult to improve upon them. In this novel we are given our object in the fullest possible way.

Let us not forget that present-day philosophy, especially the analytic of "existence," uses the method of phenomenology, which first of all sets up a "how" of investigation defined by its need to go back to things themselves. As opposed to arbitrary constructions, chance discoveries, concepts which are only apparently justified, and apparent problems, philosophy must come to grips directly with phenomena; that is, with things themselves insofar as they appear, as they come to light, and thereby manifest themselves. Phenomenon means what shows itself as itself, what is manifest: *das Sich-an-ihm-selbst-zeigende, das Offenbare*. And beings, things, show themselves in different modes, according to the way of approach to them. Since it is conceivable that they show themselves as they are not, the mode of access must be adequate for them to show their true being—this is what truth consists of, the unveiling or showing of the being—not just an appearance of it.*

A necessary point of departure for a philosophical investigation is therefore the presentation of the object in its authentic form, so that it manifests itself *as it is in itself,* with no previous deformation. Only upon this contact with the phenomenon in its bare and pure and primary form can the Logos operate; and it is only in the Logos that strict knowing is possible. Unamuno's novel shows us, through its temporal narrative, the object which later is to be the theme of metaphysical investigation.

It could be argued that this object has no reality when achieved in the novel because it deals with fictional beings, purely imaginary persons. But, aside from the fact that the fictional being is very far from being *nothing,* that on the contrary he has a peculiar reality, we need only recall the fundamental principle of Husserl's phenomenology—with which all the foregoing has such a profound relationship—according to which fantasy or imaginative intuition are as effective as the intuition of real facts in achieving the apprehension

* Cf. Heidegger, *Sein und Zeit.*

of essences, and may even offer more advantages; for the apprehension of such ideal objects in no way implies the position of any individual existence nor the slightest affirmation concerning facts.* Therefore the novel, like one's own experience of human life from which it in fact derives, can help us come to know the essences of the modes of being which make up man. Its meaning supersedes that of mere anthropology, of course, in regard to its possibilities, and it is capable of leading us to an ontological consideration.

In other words, the novel is the first step toward an existential analytic or a metaphysical study of human life and the problems which affect the person's very being. It represents a preliminary stage in which a first contact can be made with the object of philosophical speculation, a contact in which the object shows itself in its full richness and plasticity, in its true temporal being, and therefore in a position to serve as base and support for phenomenological reflection. This suffices to indicate the methodological significance of Unamuno's novel.

* Das Eidos, das *reine Wesen,* kann sich intuitiv in Erfahrungsgegebenheiten, in solchen der Wahrnemung, Erinnerung usw., exemplifizieren, ebensogut aber *auch in blossen Phantasiegegebenheiten.* Demgemäss können wir, ein Wesen selbst und *originär* zu erfassen, von entsprechenden erfahrenden Anschauungen ausgehen, *ebensowohl aber auch von nicht-erfahrenden, nicht daseinerfassenden, vielmehr "bloss einbildenen" Anschauungen.* (Husserl, *Ideen zu einer reinen Phänomeno-logie und phänomenologischen Philosophie,* I, 12–13.)

# V.

# *UNAMUNO'S NARRATIVES*

## THE PROBLEM OF THE CIRCUMSTANCE

We have seen the scope of the novel in general—when it is a true novel—as a vehicle for the knowledge of man; and that, compared with all other novels, Unamuno's are of a particularly conspicuous type, novels in which an imaginative or figurative image of human reality is presented in its maximum purity and depth. But now we must find out in what sense Unamuno's narratives—his novels, dramas, short stories, and, stretching the point a little, even his poetry and his essays—carry out their intent, and also to what degree they fail. To do this we shall have to return in somewhat greater detail to the problem of the reality of man, of the fictional character, and of the circumstance or world in which both live. Perhaps by doing so the meaning of that troublesome verb "to live" will become a trifle clearer to us, and we shall find out to what extent it can be applied to each of these realities.

In the prologue to *Tres novelas ejemplares* [Three Exemplary Novels]—*Dos madres* [Two Mothers], *El marqués de Lumbría* [The Marquis of Lumbría], and *Nada menos que todo un hombre* [A Hundred Percent Man, No Less], as the reader will recall—Unamuno says: "I call these novels exemplary because I offer them as an example—neither more nor less—as an example of life and reality. Reality! Yes, reality! Their "agonists," their combatants, that is—we will call them characters if you like—are real, extremely real; they have the most intimate reality, a reality they give themselves, made out of their simple wanting to be or wanting not to be, and not the reality their readers may give them." He then contrasts this personal meaning of reality with the idea which is at the base of so-called realism. "The figures of the realists," he writes, "are usually mere puppets who move on strings and have a phonograph inside them that repeats the phrases their puppet master has picked up in streets and squares and cafés, and has written down in his notebook." In other words, they are not personages but pure cases or sketches or puppets who serve as mouthpieces for speeches that are not their own, that do not arise from their own intimate reality but which are picked up outside themselves and then artificially attributed to them. "And reality," adds Unamuno, "is not made up of the backdrop or the stage scenery or the costumes or landscape or furniture or the limits of the stage or. . ." Therefore things, *res,* that which seems to be most real, have nothing to do with human reality; Unamuno sees this with perfect clarity. Yet, in different places, both in this prologue and earlier, in chapter I of *Del sentimiento trágico de la vida,* he insists that the real man, *realis,* is a thing, *res.* But it must be noted that an ambiguous point is involved here: Unamuno gives the word *cosa,* thing, the meaning of its etymological antecedent *causa,* and therefore he understands it as "that which acts," that which is a creator, and gives a dynamic meaning to human reality.

What, then, is the reality of man? "What," Unamuno asks himself, "is the intimate reality, the real reality, the eternal reality, the poetic or creative reality of a man?" Note the adjectives he uses. And he adds, "Whether he is a man of flesh and bone or of that kind we call fictional makes no difference." "What is the most intimate, the most creative, the most real part of a man?" Now Unamuno has arrived at the point of grappling thematically with the question of man's being; and the first thing he does, as usual, is to seek company for his opinion, finding it this time in the American humorist Oliver Wendell Holmes,* who said that when two men, John and Thomas, are conversing, there are really six in the conversation, three Johns and three Thomases; the real John, known only to God; John's ideal John, the one he thinks he is; Thomas' ideal John, the one Thomas

* *The Autocrat of the Breakfast Table,* chapter III.

thinks he is; and, correspondingly, three Thomases to match. Unamuno accepts this but finds it intellectualistic, and believes that there are another John and another Thomas, apart from the ones known by God, who are still more profound and real; and this realer man is the one he would like to be. "This one, the one a man wants to be, is in him, in his bosom; he is the creator, and he is the truly real one. And we will be saved or damned by the man we wanted to be, not the one we may have been. God will reward or punish throughout eternity the man one wished to be." What does all this mean?

To begin with, in the passage quoted above Unamuno sets himself doubly against that doctrine of "eternal return," Nietzsche's *ewige Wiederkunft,* to which I alluded before. On the one hand, it is not really a matter of return or repetition, but rather of an eternal—or better, sempiternal—state of being, which does not begin the same cycle over and over again. Most important of all, in Nietzsche it is that which *was,* a being already existent and finished, which is to return, while what seems to Unamuno worthy of becoming eternal is not the self which each of us has been de facto, but the one *we wished to be*—and I may have to return later to the meaning of that wish—though perhaps the self one wished to be has not been realized, nor has it therefore really been, aside from that peculiar and very human mode of being which consists in having been wished. This point of view has an undeniable relationship with the position of German idealism, especially Kant's, according to which the immortality of the soul is postulated on the necessity for an *infinite progress* leading to a full reconciliation of the will with moral law, and from thence to happiness. This supposes an infinite survival of the existence and personality of the rational being itself, which, says Kant, is what we call the immortality of the soul: "eine ins Unendliche fortdaurenden *Existenz* und Persönlichkeit desselben vernünftigen Wesens." * I cite this passage because Unamuno was very familiar with the *Critique of Practical Reason,* and in it the problem of immortality is presented not in reference to man's completed being but precisely to that being which is by definition unattainable, the one which in

* Immanuel Kant, *Kritik der praktischen Vernunft,* part 1, book 2, chapter 2, section 4.

this world can only be desired and hoped for without the slightest possibility of its realization. According to Kant, the impossibility of my being in this life what I would like to be refers me to the other life, so that what postulates survival is pure unfulfilled will, and man becomes eternal in the name of the self he wants to be, but as himself, maintaining into infinity his existence and his personality (between which Kant makes a careful distinction).

A little later Unamuno alludes specifically to Kant, and this allusion clears up the meaning of his statements at the same time that it discloses a serious question which Kant glosses over. Unamuno says: "This man, whom we might call noumenal, in the Kantian sense, this man of will or idea—idea-will or strength—has to live in an apparential, rational, phenomenalistic world, the world of the so-called realists. And he must dream life, which is a dream. And from the conflicts of those real men with each other come tragedy and comedy and the novel and the 'nivola.' But reality means intimate reality." This paragraph is revealing; it shows us the philosophical assumptions on which Unamuno based his thought and, at the same time, their radical insufficiency. Unamuno contrasts true reality—that of man as will or idea, as "idea-strength" (an allusion to Fouillée)—with the phenomenalistic and apparential, which is precisely the reality of the world. But this world is a world of things, what he calls the world of the realists, and at the same time the rational world; on the other hand, life is a dream, yet he says that it is the authentic reality. This is what has generally been interpreted as a *paradox,* a word which greatly annoyed Don Miguel because he realized there was a lack of understanding behind it. On the other hand he accepted it with scarcely concealed complacency as a proof of its original and hard-to-grasp truth, hard to grasp even for himself, for as we have seen he lacked the intellectual means to comprehend his deepest intuitions. Unamuno is aware that the realest thing we encounter is our life, and that this life is something which takes place in time, that it is narrative or dream—dream, as we noted before, not as opposed to wakefulness, but to things. That is why Unamuno finds the root of man's being in what he wishes to be, in the sketch or plan of that dream, and in the strength which impels him to make it come about. These two dimensions of imagination and strength are certainly included in his definition of wishing, but the weight of his own philosophical tradition causes him to interpret this temporal man he has discovered as a *pure I,* in conflict with an empirical world of things, which press in on him and change him. And Unamuno refuses to recognize this world, considering it a simple phenomenalistic appearance, in contrast to the substantial reality of the dream which is life. And this world is rational, bound by that reason which Unamuno considers incapable of grasping the essence of life. This, and no other, is the inner cause of Unamuno's disdain for the world, for the environment of his characters, and why it is lacking in some of his novels.

All this supposes that man has a temporal, though substantial and permanent, reality apart from his world, and that this reality can be discovered and entered into at the point when we do away with the world which masks it; then, Unamuno believes, it will be possible to arrive at the man himself, at what he calls "the soul of the soul," which is precisely what I have called "the core of the person." Unamuno writes in this same prologue, "A true man can be discovered, can be created, in a moment, in a phrase, in a cry. So it is in Shakespeare. And when you have discovered and created him thus, you know him better perhaps than he knows himself." What Unamuno wanted in substance was to come to know the "real John," the John who exists only for God; he tried to place himself in God's point of view, though he scarcely confesses it even to himself. Is this arrogance? Maybe not; perhaps it was quite the opposite, an intimate and ultimate neediness; and at the same time a lack of confidence in faith—the substance of things hoped for, as St. Paul says—and in reason, whose deepest meaning he never came to know; in the last instance, despair. For what Unamuno wanted to know and had to know was whether he was to die altogether or not, and because of this he yearned to see, as God Himself sees, the substance of man, and in that substance his subsistence or persistence. Therefore, for him to discover and to imagine meant to "create," a word which he uses over and over and clings to tenaciously. But is this possible? Can man really know his fellow man, even the one who is closest of all, himself, exactly as he is, no more and no less? That *moment* Unamuno speaks of, which encompasses the integral reality of man, is it not very like eternity, that *tota simul et perfecta possessio* Boethius spoke of? In other words, is it possible for a man who is rooted in temporality to gain direct access to the *person* without passing through the *existence* in which the person *is* and in which he forms himself? It seems more than problematical. And human existence inexorably includes a world, a circumstance, which is in no wise an apparential world of dead things but the world in which man exists, the *circumstantia* which is around every real man who truly lives. Does not Unamuno forget what an essential element circumstance is?

He undoubtedly goes too far when he tries to suppress what he calls the backdrop and the stage scenery, for this involves an essential mutilation of the man himself, whose pure essence he is trying to maintain. Man lives in time and space, in a circumstance which includes landscape as well as the historical period in which he happens to live, the social environment as well as his physical and psychic characteristics. Man *is* not these things, and in this sense Unamuno has had a flash of genius in divining the truth in the face of the beliefs of his time; but neither is man *without them* or apart from them, and they condition his being. The dream of life is dreamed here and now, in relation to the cosmic and human surroundings, and nothing in life has meaning without that concrete frame of reference. Human reality is circumstantial, and consequently so is everything that can be said about it, and if the circumstance is omitted there is nothing left but abstraction. This is the serious deficiency which threatens Unamuno's narratives: the loss of the circumstance or world, and in consequence the loss of an essential dimension of the living person, for the meaning of his life is only partially illuminated for us, that is, he is created by his author only in part. Or, rather, Unamuno himself lends his characters his own circumstance, and that is why, if one's spiritual ears are sharp, one can notice a rather excessive echo of Don Miguel's voice in most of his fictional beings. Unamuno forgets—truly a strange lapse—that, when God created man, He first created a world for him to live in, and, because "it is not good for man to be alone," at once gave him the essential companionship of woman. Obviously, living, for man, means living *in* and living *with:* living together in the world is the concrete form in which human existence takes place.

It would be an exaggeration to say, however, that Unamuno does away entirely with circumstance in his novels; he does not do so for the simple reason that it is impossible; there is only a tendency toward it in him. He himself realizes that a world is necessary, but he sees that it cannot be the static world of things; and then he believes that it is an interior world—he really means a human or existential one —or has recourse to Kantian concepts which are inadequate to his vision of that world. "The reality in Don Quijote's life," he says in the same prologue I have been commenting upon, "was not the windmills but the giants. The windmills were phenomenalistic, apparential; the giants were noumenal, substantial. It is the dream which is life, reality, creation." Unamuno sees here that what is dreamed—the giants, "the world"—is an ingredient of the dream, which is not exhausted in the dreamer. A little later he adds: "Balzac was not a man who lived his life in the world or passed his time taking notes on what he saw or heard from others. He carried the world inside him." This is true: Balzac did carry it inside him, and so did Unamuno, though he was a trifle cramped by his ideas on reality and reason. Therefore Unamuno's narratives, especially the most successful and most intimate ones, present a real world, fleshless but authentic, which describes itself almost in spite of its author, and creates a circumstance in which human life beats and throbs and reveals the personal basis of the drama. We shall examine this by using some of his works as examples.

## THE DIMENSIONS OF THE PERSON

Reality is always individual, but human reality is so to a particularly high degree, because for man *to be* is to be *himself.* My life is essentially *mine,* and this characteristic is in no sense something added to its reality, but constitutes it. Therefore man, qua person, has a name of his own, and the common name that shows *what* he is does not suffice; he must have one that shows *who* he is. This extreme individuality of the human entity makes him exhibit to the maximum degree the traits which define a real individual; a certain infinitude and an essential opacity.

Any real entity whatsoever, as philosophy has traditionally held, contains an infinite number of notes; because of this, there can be no possible definition of the individual, but only description, and description can never be exhausted. But in man this happens in a much more radical sense, so much so that there is hardly any point of contact with the individuality of things. For things are, in fact, already what they are; they have a fixed being, a particular consistency, which in principle would be exhaustible. It is possible for me to think that I can know any single note of a thing, and that the impossibility of understanding it refers solely to its totality, not to any individual facet of it as such. The individual essence is, then, inaccessible de facto, but it can be conceived of as known in its totality without encountering any impossibility for this a priori. But with man the case is not the same. Man does not have a being which is already made but one which is in the making; furthermore, his being consists in the making.* Thus Heidegger can say, putting it in an extreme form, that his essence consists in his existence: *Das Wesen des Daseins liegt in seiner Existenz.* Man's being is affected by temporality, by the past's *no longer* and the future's *not yet;* and between the two we have, in an essentially fleeting form, the *now* of the present *in-stant.* The impossibility of grasping the totality of individual existence is here essential and by definition, not merely factual. Human reality is strictly inexhaustible and cannot be grasped from the point of view of time. A total knowledge of the human creature would be possible only from the point of view of eternity, understood as simultaneous and perfect possession of a life; but these attributes are, naturally, alien to the ones we encounter in earthly and temporal life, and therefore the simple expression "eternal life" poses a tremendous problem.

On the other hand, I have repeatedly used the adjective "opaque"

* Of course this temporal characteristic of man refers to his life, whose reality takes place in time, and cannot simply be transferred to what is called the soul or the basis of the person. It should not be forgotten that life is given to me, but it is not given ready-made. See the further distinction between life and person, that is, who it is who lives this temporal life. See also my *Reason and Life,* chapter XI.

to describe the real. This must be explained. Let us compare an ideal object—a triangle or an octahedron or the number 5 or the species "table"—with a real object—an actual stone or the individual table I am writing on. It can be seen at first glance that the former, being "unreal" or "ideal," are transparent; our thought can penetrate them and they show us their entire being; we do not encounter the slightest resistance in grasping the whole nature of the polyhedron or of the table considered as a species. It is precisely in the absence of that resistance that we see how "unreal" an object is, and precisely because their being offers me another type of resistance, I discover that these objects have a reality different from that of things, though no less true, that which we call "ideal." No matter how hard I try, I cannot force 5 to be divisible by 3, or make a regular octahedron have pentagonal angles. Their essence is fixed and resistant, but transparent because they do not have existence; we might perhaps say, inverting the terms of Heidegger's proposition, that the existence of ideal objects is exhausted in their essence. Real objects, on the other hand, are opaque; they have an "inside" which cannot be penetrated at will. The three dimensions of the octahedron can be traversed without any difficulty, for they do not contain an innerness. But the dimensions of a stone do; it is made up of an exterior and an interior, inaccessible as such, and I can reach only a few of the "points" of the stone, among an infinite number of possible ones. Naturally, I can break open the stone and exteriorize any of its inner points; but an infinite number of them will still be inaccessible. I cannot make contact with the whole of the stone's being, though in principle this is possible for any particular point in it. That is why I say that a real being is essentially opaque, and therefore arcane.

This characteristic of innerness becomes sharply accentuated if we progress from pure cosmic being to living things. In the plant, and still more in the animal, there is a constituent innerness; the living body has an "inside" which is not indifferent and haphazard; the possibility exists of exteriorizing the interior of a living body, but then it dies and is destroyed as such. I cannot bring out the entrails of an animal, for it will perish, except insofar as it is a simple physical body. And, if we take a further step, if we reach the reality of the soul, we find a radical innerness which admits of no direct exteriorization. My grief, my desire, my joy, and my love are essentially mine and only mine; they are not accessible to anyone; they consist in ultimate intimacy; and therefore they are susceptible of being revealed or made manifest because they are arcane. Accordingly, all knowledge of human reality is hermeneutics, interpretation, and is affected by the time and the place from which it is made. In other words: knowledge about human life can in no wise exhaust its object. Furthermore, a perspective and a horizon are essential to that knowledge; this, which is characteristic of all real knowledge, is eminently the case with man because his mode of being is, as we have seen, the most extreme form of the reality of the intramundane being. Consequently, the human creature can only be discovered and interpreted in a particular dimension.

This is what happens with Unamuno's narratives. Each of them approaches the theme of existence and the human person from different assumptions, and in a number of senses: this is what constitutes the peculiarity of each novel or stage performance—for our purpose they are the same—the *drama* in which it consists. The attempt to penetrate the secret of life and personality must make use of commentary, of interpretation, of imaginary existences, and show them from a concrete angle of perspective which will uncover one of their dimensions. Each novel, therefore, signifies a point of view and causes us to acquire one particular facet of the human being. However, we should not pay too much heed to the partiality of this knowledge; no doubt it is essentially fragmentary and "relative," as is natural in view of the intimate structure of its object, but it is also systematic—though Unamuno does not realize this sufficiently—and each dimension contains and implicates, in a certain sense, all the others in the unity of the being which is being understood. In this sense—but only in this sense—can we make use of the statement of Unamuno which I quoted before: "A real man is discovered, is created, in an instant, in a phrase, in a cry." As soon as we get into contact with the personality of a man, we have some acquaintance with it; this does not mean that we know it in its entirety—for that is impossible—but we are acquainted with the personality itself. We all distinguish between knowing a great many things about a person or knowing the person, even though we may be unaware of almost everything that pertains to him or affects him. The problem is not one of wholeness but of selfhood, which is the root of the personal being. Unamuno, who divined something of this, although he was unable to see it, explained the procedure for knowing and creating human fictional beings. "Reader, if you wish to create artistically persons, agonists—tragic, comic, or novelesque—do not pile up details, do not set yourself to observing the exterior facets of those you live among, but talk to them, stir them up if you can, love them above all, and wait until one day —it may never come—when they will reveal the naked soul of their soul in a cry, in an act, in a phrase, and then take that moment and shut it up inside you and let it develop, like a seed, into the true character, the one that is truly real." * The method of knowing man through the novel is here described: Unamuno's practice was even better than his theory. For by this means, starting from a phrase or a cry—a situation—Don Miguel captured the throbbing nakedness of a personality in order to divine its intimate secret. Now let us try to find this personal and existential redoubt in Unamuno's most profound narratives.

## EVERYDAY LIFE: *PAZ EN LA GUERRA*

Unamuno's first novel was *Paz en la guerra,* published in 1897. As we have already seen, its structure sets it apart from all the rest of its author's novels because it is one essentially defined by a world. The characters are presented as deeply immersed in that world; they are scarcely differentiated, and none stands out above the others; at most, it can be said, there are agonists, not protagonists. And that world is not seen from the point of view of an individual existence but from the multiple perspective of a whole town, which is, as I said before, the true subject of the narrative; and the town is a social world, a collective life, attached to a definite time and space, to a landscape, and to a period.

* Prologue to *Tres novelas ejemplares.*

Unamuno recognized this peculiarity of his first novel at several different times, and specifically in the prologue to the second edition in 1923; there he points out his change of procedure and appears to consider it as something purely technical, founded on mere convenience. "In this novel," he says, "landscapes are painted and time and place sketched in and colored. But afterwards I abandoned this procedure, creating novels outside a specific time and place, skeleton novels in the form of intimate dramas, and leaving the contemplation of landscape, skyscape, and seascape for other works of mine. Thus, in my novels *Amor y pedagogía, Niebla, Abel Sánchez, La tía Tula, Tres novelas ejemplares,* and other lesser ones, I have preferred not to distract the reader from the narrative of the unfolding of human actions and passions. And I have brought together my artistic studies of landscape and skyscape in special works, such as *Paisajes* [Landscapes], *Por tierras de Portugal y de España* [Travels Through Portugal and Spain], and *Andanzas y visiones españolas* [Spanish Wanderings and Visions]. I do not know whether or not this differentiation has been successful."

But is this the whole story? Is it not rather that Unamuno's intention changed between some of his novels and others? For the environment described in *Paz en la guerra* does not consist of "artistic studies of landscape and skyscape," but in the presentation of a stage where the collective life of Biscay takes place. The real personage of the novel is the people, the common man, and this personage is defined by its common life in a common world. But the deeper reason why Unamuno utilizes a plurality of characters living in common, within a world which at times seems to occupy the front of the stage, is that the dimension of existence into which he tries to penetrate is what we call everyday life. Being everyday, it is collective and visible in the world, not the opposite; and it is significant that Unamuno should begin with this kind of life, arriving later at other kinds which we will study further on.

What interests Unamuno is to make us penetrate the silent and permanent core of each day's process of living; we shall soon see what his final intention is. When he describes, he positively *inscribes* us into the circle of his characters' common life; this is the reason he seeks neither the picturesque touch, nor the "real" or plastic detail, as Pereda might have done, for example. On the contrary, he seeks what is most obscure and most commonly accepted: custom, the very substance of everyday life, what underlies personal opinions and mere events, the intrahistorical substratum of human existence. When he shows us Pedro Antonio Iturriondo, the chocolate-maker, the old soldier of the first Carlist war, he says, "In the monotony of his life, Pedro Antonio took pleasure in the newness of every minute, in the joy of doing the same things every day, in the very fullness of his limitations. He lost himself in the shadows, nobody noticed him; inside his own skin, like a fish in water, he enjoyed the intimate intensity of an obscure, silent life of toil, in the reality of his own self and not in the appearance of others. His existence flowed like the current of a peaceful river which makes no sound, and which is never noticed until it stops." In these short sentences we see summed up with tremendous accuracy a number of the notes of everyday life: monotony, renewed reiteration, shadow, inclusion in a medium—the fish in water—one's own reality, absence of reflection, and that happy discovery, "the fullness of one's limitations." It would be difficult to put more into fewer lines. Unamuno goes on to tell us of Pedro Antonio's relation with the cosmic—and urban—surroundings of the shop, the streets of Bilbao, the sunny or rainy days. "For many years his eyes had calmly gazed on that part of the city, leaving an imperceptible halo of thoughts of peace and toil in every one of its corners; in each of them dwelt a faraway echo of moments of life forgotten simply because they were all alike and all silent. And he loved the gray days when the rain fell slowly because they made him love the cozy intimacy of his shop all the more. The warm, sunny days seemed ostentatious and blatant to him." This is enough: it never occurs to Unamuno, not even in this novel, to describe the chocolate shop as a thing, with its external details, as a realistic writer might have done, showing us the shop "as it really was," we might say. What interests Unamuno is the existential relation of Pedro Antonio to his world. When he does give a detail of what a thing is like, it is never graphic or descriptive, but vital, related to its *use*. Thus, when he speaks of the old prayer book of Josefa Ignacia, the chocolate-maker's wife, he says only that it had "grimy margins and big print," and adds that it was in Basque and therefore was the only one understandable for her. Notice that he does not say, "It was the only one she could understand," but "the only one understandable for her," for it was not a question of her not knowing Spanish but that only her old Basque text spoke to her heart, and that only through it could she understand the written word intimately and personally.

Immediately after this Unamuno adds another layer to the human circumstance, the social confines of these lives: the meeting of friends in the chocolate shop. "Pedro Antonio looked forward to winter because, as soon as the long nights were joined to the gray days and the obstinate unending drizzle began to fall, the *tertulia* began in the shop. He would light the brazier, set the chairs around it, and wait for his friends as he nursed the fire. They would come in one by one, wrapped in gusts of damp and cold. Don Braulio, the returned immigrant, would arrive first, puffing. He was one of those men who, having been born to live, lives with all his heart and soul; he took long walks to test his "joints" and his "bellows," always spoke of America as "over there," and from one end of the year to the other never failed to make an observation on the lengthening or the shortening of the days, according to the season. Then came: rubbing his hands, an old comrade-in-arms of Pedro Antonio's, whom everyone called Gambelu; wiping his spectacles as he entered, for they were misted over, Don Eustaquio, an ex-Carlist officer and a pensioner under the terms of the treaty of Vergara, which supplied his only livelihood; solemn Don José María, who was not as regular as the others; and finally, Don Pascual the priest, Pedro Antonio's first cousin, who freshened up the atmosphere by gracefully swinging his cape off his shoulders. And Pedro Antonio enjoyed the puffing of Don Braulio, the hand-rubbing of Gambelu, the spectacle-wiping of Don Eustaquio, the unexpected appearance of Don José María, and the unmuffling of his cousin, at the same time as he watched the trickle of water from the enormous umbrellas the friends carried running along the floor, as he wielded the poker to stir up the coals." Here also, there is absolutely no "description" in the sense of things; we are not told what the members of the *tertulia* look like, nor the clothes they wear, nor what sort of character or psychic apparatus they have. Unamuno confines himself to telling us what they customarily *do* when they come in, and thus we see them creating an ambit within which their everyday existence moves. Compare this quoted passage of Unamuno's with the description of any similar meeting in a realistic writer; the difference between Unamuno and Pereda or a French naturalist is enormous and fundamental, but it is still a long way from Galdós—the least "realistic," in the authentic sense, of all Spanish novelists of the period, and therefore the best and the most penetrating—for Galdós does give a great deal of attention to the vision of "things," and of man as a particularly important species among them.

Throughout the novel Unamuno continues to disclose the forms of everyday life, always varied and always the same. There is scarcely any change or any happening; above the quiet and permanent intrahistorical depths the little tide of history, the comings and goings of the characters, the opinions, the words, even the events, are mere ripples; under all of this the deep strata of life lie unchanged. Immersed in custom, in tradition, in the repertory of social attitudes, lies the rockbottom of our existence, which is barely scratched by historical disturbances. And Unamuno emphasizes, perhaps unconsciously, the dimension of authenticity which goes along with these everyday modes of living; in their relations with their fellows, even in the extreme case when someone scarcely acts as a person, it is perfectly evident that there is a deep sense that, under all his acts, he keeps on being a person: and in this form the immediate personal situation of charity appears, quite apart from any "idea" or "theory." Unamuno tells of the visits made by Pedro Antonio's son Ignacio to a farmhouse near Bilbao; he writes, "In a corner, behind the cooking pot that hung from the ceiling in the center of the room, an old woman, Domingo's grandmother, blind and with her reason almost gone, sat in the shadow, counting the beads of her rosary for hours on end, praying for the blessed souls in Purgatory. Ignacio's heart ached when he saw how they had abandoned her, like an old piece of furniture that was in the way, and gave her the leftovers from their meals as they would to a beggar. What tears came to those dead eyes when a warm, young, slender hand, like an angel's, was placed on her skinny hands! What a good gentleman, God bless him!" This simple and moving passage shows us the unconscious and elemental introduction of the old woman into a world of persons united by charity; without realizing it, on the basis of old convictions, she feels linked to the souls of the blessed and closer to God; and Ignacio's hand, moved by a profound and scarcely confessed anguish, brings about this relationship and turns the old woman again into a person who feels intimately included in the order of personality and charity, in the hand of God.

Into this silent, intrahistorical life—whose theory we shall investigate later—the historical erupts in the form of war, into the activity of those who move on this traditional ground of everyday life. In this case it is the second Carlist war, which culminated in the siege of Bilbao in 1874. The events of the war, the ideas which set them in motion and go with them, in short, the abnormal, looms over the quiet web of everyday living and transforms it. On the one hand, everyday life becomes stronger, rises higher, and becomes more personalized; instead of feeling themselves submerged in collectivity as if they were almost vegetably implanted in a body, men feel as though they are participants in a historical destiny, subjects of that lofty event which is developing before their very eyes, therefore, personages. Each acquires the consciousness of being included in a society, and this, which at first sight seems to intensify the social feeling, weakens it in the last analysis, for social feeling as such is unconscious. With a sure touch, Unamuno evokes notes of this transformation of everyday life. "Good humor," he says, speaking of the besieged citizens of Bilbao, "which is usually spread through the tiny network of imperceptible daily acts; good humor, which in normal times each man kept for himself, bubbled forth out of everyone, as an act of social duty, and resulted in a collective gaiety." And then he adds, "Since the intensity of everyday life had grown greater, the smallest daily episodes came into strong relief, and were the subject of interminable comment. Nothing was trivial any more." This last phrase is revealing: nothing was trivial any more; that is, the very substance of everyday life, that which makes up every day and every hour, every crossroad or every street corner or little square, had disappeared, had vanished into thin air. Everything, instead of being lived silently and then forgotten in the personal collective, became individualized and talked about, inserted in a new world, the world of history.

But, on the other hand, this ebb and flow of the historical tide leaves the deepest layers of existence unchanged, just as at the bottom of the sea. In the midst of the military excitement, the bloody episodes of the campaign and the siege, everyday life slips by imperturbably: the anguished concern of Doña Micaela, slowly dying in the besieged city; Ignacio's primitive life in the Carlist camp, with the villagers and the Biscayan mountains; Rafaela's love, that everyday love which Unamuno defines as "care" and the care of those one cares for: "Loving him was only a way of tending him, of caring for his cares, of living with him, of adjusting to his habits, of cheerfully suffering his weaknesses and his misfortunes, putting up with his moods—ah, the moods of men! For Enrique she showed a mild and deeply felt affection, woven of the thousand little incidents of ordinary life, cosubstantial with life itself, an affection which quickly turned into a habit and as such became unconscious." And in the midst of this everyday life death appears, everyday too in a certain sense; we shall have to take up that point elsewhere. At the end, once the fleeting change is over, and even before it is over, everyday life gains the upper hand again and reestablishes its deep, silent power over man. When Unamuno speaks of Pedro Antonio Iturriondo, living alone, silent and melancholy, after the deaths of his wife and son, he writes these extremely meaningful words: "He lives in the depths of the true reality of life, free of all transcendental intentionality, above time, feeling in his consciousness, as calm as a cloudless sky, the slow invasion of the sweet dream of supreme rest, the great calm of eternal things and the infinite which sleeps within its narrow confines. He lives in true peacefulness of life, lulling himself, unheeding, in everyday occupations: day by day, yet resting in the calm of one detached from transitory things; in eternity; he lives day by day in eternity. He hopes that this elemental life will be prolonged on the other side of death, so that he can take joy of a nightless day, of light perpetual, of infinite brightness, of sure repose, in steadfast peace, sure and undisturbed peace, peace within and without, peace that lasts forever. This hope is the reality which makes his life peaceful in the midst of his cares, and eternal within its brief, perishable course. Now he is free, truly free, not with the false freedom sought in acts but with the true freedom, the freedom of the whole being; in pure simplicity he has become free."

In this everyday life, man lives in his reality, not in appearance; and this is why, as he follows the course of time and its cares, he is brought close to eternity and his soul is at peace, a deep peace which is, as Unamuno says, *freedom of being,* not of acts. Man retreats from what happens to him and what he does, to what he is; then he finds himself, and only thus does he find peace in war. The external and public "acts" make up only the surface, the skin of the soul, and they slide off the soul without affecting it, leaving it whole and quiet, master of itself and therefore free. As a contrast to this situation defined by Unamuno, we might consider the times in which we have been called upon to live, in which the world seems to have completely thrown out everyday and private life, and feeds exclusively, in a strictly inauthentic manner, on "public life," historical gossip and impersonal acts. This is why our time seems depersonalized, devoid of substance, deficient in intimacy, concerned only with the moment and with "events," with what happens and not with what remains. The so-called crisis of our time is, in one of its essential dimensions, the crisis of everyday life.

## THE TRANSITION TO INDIVIDUAL LIFE: *AMOR Y PEDAGOGÍA*

After *Paz en la guerra* (1897), Unamuno writes *Amor y pedagogía* [Love and Pedagogy] (1902). In the prologue to the second edition (1934), the author points out that this novel differs from its predecessor in that it dispenses with the so-called "realism" of description in order to hew to unadorned narration; and he also notes that in this novel "is present in embryo—and more than in embryo—the greater part, and the best part, of what I have shown later in my other novels." To what degree and in what sense are these two assertions true? To begin with, Unamuno dispenses with an exterior world and with any reference to a community, a people. The most that can be said is that far in the background the city is divined. However, it does not exist in itself but only as a simple echo of the actions of the characters; for example, the effect of Apolodoro's novel, the uncomfortable social situation which he fears so much, and a few other similar details. On the other hand, the protagonists are presented as clearly individualized: Don Avito Carrascal, Marina, Apolodoro, Don Fulgencio Entrambosmares, Clarita, and even the secondary characters. But are they, strictly speaking, personages? When Unamuno introduces Carrascal he says: "He appears on the scene of our tale as a young man enthusiastic about all progress and in love with sociology . . . Carrascal lives on a private income, and has secretly carried out a Herculean task, that of submitting all his instincts to the power of reason and making everything about himself purely scientific. He moves by mechanics, digests by chemistry, and has his suits cut out by projective geometry. . . But his forte is sociological pedagogy." That is, Unamuno gives us from the start the key of his character's personality, and turns him *ipso facto* into a role, a case. Don Avito Carrascal, a profoundly stupid man, with the folly of positivist "science" deeply rooted inside him, empties his life of human content step by step for the sake of his plans, although he constantly runs afoul of the real world, and on such occasions he mutters under his breath, "You fell, you fell into temptation, and you'll fall again!"

He decides "deductively" to marry Leoncia, the "solid dolicocephalic blonde" whom he has chosen with the aid of physiology and sociology to be the mother of the genius he intends to produce through really satisfactory teaching. And, when he is about to present her with his "amorous" declaration—a scientific treatise setting forth all the biological and sociological justifications—he is attracted by the eyes of Marina, Leoncia's friend, a blooming brachiocephalic brunette, and in the end presents the treatise to her and marries her "inductively." Later, when the future genius is born, the father names him Apolodoro, though his mother will secretly call him Luisito; and

Carrascal receives him in a manner worthy of his plans: "The father seizes the baby and carries him to the scales to weigh him; then to a special bath which he has ready, and—in he goes!—covers him completely with water so that he can see in the measuring tube how many liters of volume he has displaced. Using the weight and volume, the father will be able to deduce his density, the density of genius he has at birth. And he measures him and takes the facial angle and the angle of the skull and all the other angles, triangles, and circles imaginable. He will open his casebook with these details. The house is suitably equipped to receive the child: high ceilings, as the fashion is today; light, ventilation, antisepsis. Everywhere there are barometers, thermometers, pluviometers, aerometers, dynamometers, maps, diagrams, a telescope, a microscope, a spectroscope, so that no matter where the baby looks he will be drenched in science; the whole house is a rational microcosm. It even has its altar, its trace of religious practice, for there is a brick with the word "Science" on it, and above it a little wheel mounted on an axis; this is the only bit of the symbolic, the religious as Don Avito puts it, to which he is willing to give houseroom."

The story goes on in this way, ending with a melancholy finale of paternal disillusionment and the lamentable suicide of Apolodoro, the "genius"; and this is *Amor y pedagogía,* the grotesque tragicomedy, nearly always treated as a caricature, of these lives which are individual but not yet personal. Unamuno is slowly advancing toward his true theme, man himself, the man of flesh and bone; from the social community, from impersonal everyday life, he has progressed to a particular life extrinsically defined by one purpose, one passion, one mania, if you like. Don Avito as a character is sketched on the first page of the novel, individualized but not personalized, set in motion according to an external principle previously introduced into the narrative; there is not that fundamental situation, that *cry,* from which the soul of the character can be shown stripped of all pretence, which Unamuno later demanded in his novels. At most, the novel merely tends this way; its final pages begin to penetrate into the world of the personal, the deeply intimate. Little by little an elemental being is superimposed upon—or better still, begins to surge up within—the fictional character of Carrascal; this being, starting to be cured of his pedagogy, begins to have a certain intimate and direct reality. In this sense *Amor y pedagogía* anticipates the later novels and contains the germ of what is most substantial in them.

It is, in fact, the transition from communal life to individual life; but it makes this transition by following the thread of something which, though not collective, is not intimate and authentic either. Rather it is impersonal and abstract, subordination to a theoretical plan. It is a necessary stage, but let us not be deceived; in no sense is it a progress toward the real understanding of life. *Paz en la guerra* places us in close contact with an essential, though not fundamental, dimension of life; *Amor y pedagogía,* on the other hand, brings us into an individualized but strictly speaking inauthentic vital atmosphere. After showing us everyday life, Unamuno presents an inauthentic life, hollow inside, with its inevitable futility, its failure. And from this failure, from that turning in on oneself brought on by the vanishing of a dream, Unamuno approaches step by step the authentic dimensions of personal life. It is not by chance that the contrite remnants of Carrascal's personality appear in other novels; he is reduced to a poor, minimal, vanquished shred of human reality.

## FICTION AND REALITY: *NIEBLA*

Unamuno's novel fully matures in *Niebla,* published in 1914, two years after *Del sentimiento trágico de la vida,* which marks the climax of his intellectual formation. But it is an interesting point that, while none of his volumes of essays comes to surpass the *Sentimiento,* Unamuno's novel continues to advance and to reach still greater depths. Thus we see that the genre most truly alive in Unamuno is the novel, much more so than the writings with scientific pretensions.

*Niebla* is the first attempt to enter fully into the creation of fictional beings. Unamuno, who by now is in possession of his principal ideas on the fictional being and has made a very important trial of them by rethinking—or, better, redreaming—an imaginary life in his

*Vida de Don Quijote y Sancho* (1905), now feels fully capable of moving within the compass of this mode of being. This is the reason why, in *Niebla,* he uses a great many main characters, and these are surrounded in turn by other more marginal ones, some brought into the picture more or less haphazardly. They represent a varied fauna, and Unamuno establishes himself among them with evident complacency, a complacency which is not only literary and psychological but is ruled by the consciousness that he is their creator, the sense of his ontological domination over these lives. It might be thought that this multitude of characters is not new, for we find them in *Paz en la guerra,* but the reality is very different. We have seen how, in *Paz en la guerra,* the characters are individualizations of a collective, social, or still better a communal world; the primary thing is Bilbao, and the characters, rather than being this or that individual, are Bilbaínos, and are defined by belonging to this common world. In *Niebla* the process is reversed; the other characters rise out of one—Augusto Pérez—and their lives become intertwined with his. There is a horizon bounding the protagonist, but it is not collective, always individual; and the relationships which arise are always interindividual, multiple, between man and man, and define an atmosphere which is dense and at the same time imprecise, best characterized in the title of the book: *Niebla,* mist. Furthermore, Unamuno's desire to create characters leads him to include in his narration other minor ones, briefly sketched dramas which he puts into the mouths of his creatures, rather in the manner of the novels Cervantes inserts into the *Quijote.* There are no fewer than six of these in the slender compass of *Niebla.* Some of them, like the case of Don Eloíno Rodríguez de Alburquerque y Alvarez de Castro, who marries his landlady Doña Sinfo so that she can take care of him, on condition that he die promptly and leave her the minute pension due the widow of a civil servant (chapter XVII), or that of the strange and painful loves of Don Antonio (chapter XXI), are really autonomous tales by means of which Unamuno creates tiny, intimate worlds or worlds of grotesque triviality, interpolated into the misty atmosphere of Augusto's life.

This mist is given form, life, and drama by two components, time and personality, whose final confluence comes in death. The temporal preoccupation is constant: "Is life a game, or is it not? And why can we not play the hand over again? That's logic! Perhaps the card is already in Eugenia's hands. *Alea jacta est!* What's done is done! And tomorrow? Tomorrow belongs to God! And yesterday, whose is that? Ah, yesterday, treasure of the strong! Blessed yesterday, substance of each day's mist!" (chapter III). Later, in chapter VII, Unamuno writes: "Where has Eugenia sprung from? Is she a creation of mine or am I a creation of hers? Or are the two of us mutual creations, she of me and I of her? Isn't it, perhaps, that everything is a creation of each single thing, and each thing a creation of everything? And what is creation? What are you, Orfeo?," Augusto asks his dog. "What am I? Every hour comes to me pushed along by the hours that preceded it; I have not yet experienced the future. And now, when I begin to see dimly what the future is going to be, it seems that it is going to turn into the past. These days that pass. . . this day, this eternal day that passes . . . slipping away in a mist of boredom. Today exactly like yesterday, tomorrow exactly like today."

"This is the revelation of eternity, Orfeo, terrible eternity. When a man is all alone and when he closes his eyes to the future, to all his daydreams, the horrible abyss of eternity yawns before him. Eternity is not the same as the future. When we die, death turns us about in our orbit and we begin to go backward, toward the past, toward that which was. And so we go on endlessly, unraveling the skein of our destiny, undoing the infinite which has formed us in the course of an eternity, traveling toward nothingness, but never reaching it because it never existed."

"And now Eugenia's two eyes shine in the heavens of my solitude. They sparkle with the radiance of my mother's tears. They make me believe that I exist, what a delicious delusion! *Amo, ergo sum!* This love, Orfeo, is like a healing rain in which the fog of existence alternately dissolves and becomes solid. Thanks to love, I feel that my soul is solid, I can touch it. My soul, thanks be to love, begins to pain me in its uttermost depths. And what is the soul after all but love, but pain incarnate?"

"Look, Orfeo, at the silken threads, look at the warp, see how the woof comes and goes with the shuttle, watch the play of the bobbins;

but tell me, where is the beam overhead on which the fabric of our existence must be rolled up: where?"

In this long quotation we find the very heart of Unamuno's preoccupation. When he creates fictional beings he creates first of all fictitious histories, temporal events, material for narration, a reality of time from tomorrow to yesterday. And, if at first he has concentrated on the moment of creation, on the entity of his creatures, now their fictitious character troubles him, and he looks back to yesterday, that "substance of each day's mist." He looks back at memory, the basis of the personality, which gives solidity to the protagonist of the narration. He confronts the problem of the reality of existence, which dissolves into a tangled skein of insubstantial events which in their turn come to an end in the vanished mist, in nothingness. And in this monologue, this conversation Augusto Pérez has with his dumb pet, there are two clearly distinguishable steps which will bring Unamuno to the very heart of the problem. First, love, grief, resistance—the rough touch of things, as he says in a paragraph I have not quoted—which make him feel that his soul is solid, which give him an illusion of existence. Then, because that is not enough, comes the vital question: What is the center of those days, those tasks, those griefs? Where is the fabric of existence rolled up? In other words, *who* is the man who exists—whatever *to exist* may mean. Who am I? And this is the problem of personality.

All this culminates in the famous chapter XXXI of the novel, so often quoted and commented upon, in which Augusto Pérez goes to visit his creator, Unamuno, and a conventional but truly dramatic conversation takes place between them. At the end of chapter XXV, in an aside in which Unamuno speaks of his characters, he writes these revealing words: "When one looks for reasons to justify oneself, strictly speaking one is only justifying God. And I am the God of these poor *nivolesque* devils." In other words, as I mentioned before, Unamuno attempts to play in respect to other lives and other persons the role of God in respect to men. He does this, on the one hand, because of his desire to see the reality of the man himself; on the other, figuratively to conquer death by disposing as he wishes of another human soul. This is the reason why, in the conversation of

Augusto Pérez with his creator, which Unamuno fills with realistic details—his study, his books, his portrait, the work table of his house in Salamanca—a problem of personality, and especially of mortality, is being dealt with. Unamuno says to Augusto, "No, you exist only as a fictional creature; poor Augusto, you are no more than a product of my fancy—mine, and the fancy of the readers who will peruse the story I have written of your fictional adventures and tribulations." And Augusto answers this statement by comparing the reality of the author with that of the fictitious character. I have spoken of this elsewhere; now I should like to call attention to the point around which the "discussion" revolves.

"When a man, asleep and motionless in bed, dreams something," Augusto asks, "which exists more truly, he as a dreaming consciousness or his dream?" And, when Unamuno argues, "And if the dreamer is dreaming that he exists?," Augusto answers him again, "In that case, my dear Don Miguel, I'll ask you in my turn: in what manner does he exist, as a dreamer who is dreaming, or as he is dreamed by himself?" That is, the important thing is the dream as reality, what is dreamed, the temporal event which is dreamed or told, the narrative. In this sense the fictional being coincides with the real man, and that is what allows the former to justify his own existence.

But when Unamuno announces to Augusto that he has decided to let him die, Augusto is terrified, and immediately reveals the hollowness of that existence he has just affirmed to his creator. "Now that you want to kill me," he says, "I want to live, live, live. . ." He understands that his life depends on the author's, that he needs him in order to exist, that he is not his own master. "I want to be I, I, I. . ." In other words, what is revealed to him is the insubstantiality of his fictitious existence, which depends on another's existence and cannot live on its own. When he sees that Unamuno is not going to change his decision to let him die, Augusto makes use of his own despair to challenge the real existence of the author himself, and to deny him also ultimate self-sufficiency. " 'So you won't do it, eh?,' he said to me, 'so you won't? You don't want me to be myself, to come out of the mist, to live, live, live. You don't want to let me see myself, hear myself, touch myself, feel myself, hurt myself, be myself? So you don't want to? So I have to die as a mere creature of fiction? All right then, my dear creator Don Miguel, you will die too, you too, and you'll go back to the nothing from which you came. . . God will stop dreaming you! You will die, yes, you will, even though you don't want to; you will die and everyone who reads my story will die, all of them, every one, all of them without exception! Creatures of fiction like me; the same as I! They'll all die, all, all, all.' " And Unamuno adds, "This supreme effort of passion for life, of yearning for immortality, left poor Augusto quite exhausted."

The ontological sketch drawn here is absolutely clear: the fictional being qua *fictum,* inasmuch as he is a dream or narrative, is real. He is a temporal life or existence of the same mode of being as the human one, but, inasmuch as he is the result of a *fingere,* an author's dream, he has no substance and appears as a being without foundation, who cannot stand by himself in existence and falls into the void, into nothingness. On the other hand, if we move into the sphere of the reality of the real man we find an analogous situation: seen from God's point of view, man also lacks substantiality and depends on his Creator; a radical and essential mortality also affects man. That is why Augusto says, "God will stop dreaming you." Human reality also appears as a dream of divinity, as fiction of a superior order capable of producing fictions of a secondary order, which are those called fictional beings. There is, then, a clear ontological hierarchy: God, man, the fictional character; they are three degrees of the personal being, of the kind of being that can say "I" and have selfhood and a sense of intimacy, that possesses itself. Fiction and reality are permanently linked in a relation of subordination: the reality of the character is fictitious seen from man's point of view, as is man's when seen from God's.

It would be difficult not to divine in this an echo of Spinoza's metaphysics, which so much troubled Unamuno, as is seen throughout his work and very explicitly in the *Sentimiento trágico de la vida.* Spinoza, who accepts the Cartesian idea of substance as that which needs nothing else in order to exist, as that which is independent, carries Descartes' thought to an extreme. When Descartes says that substance needs no other thing, he means any other created thing, leaving out the necessity of God. Spinoza abolishes this restriction and so must deny substantiality to individual things—and most especially man—in order to reserve the characteristic of substantiality to Divinity alone, *Deus sive substantia.** Spinoza believes that the essence of things lies in a desire or endeavor to persevere in their being indefinitely, in an appetite for eternity which in men is conscious and is called *cupiditas,* desire.† *Cupiditas est ipsa hominis essentia,* Spinoza says; that is, the passion for life, the yearning for immortality of which Unamuno speaks.

We see, then, that the lack of ultimate self-sufficiency of the fictional being and even of the real man leads Unamuno to God; this is perfectly reasonable and clear. But, when he gets so far, instead of finding the point of support which sustains all created reality in existence, Unamuno takes a step backward and proclaims the equally fictitious character of human reality. The reference to God, instead of serving as a foundation, reveals to him the insubstantiality of man. How is this possible? And, above all, what does it mean in the last instance? For now we must leave these questions unanswered. We shall have to look at the several further steps Unamuno takes on the road to knowledge of the personal self, and, still more important, we shall have to try to translate these findings into ontological language, the only language in which they can be fully effective and as such achieve their reality. Suffice it to say that at this point we encounter a capital moment in Unamuno's thought, in large part the key to the basically frustrated metaphysic we find in him, and at the same time the key to his ambiguous religious position. Later we shall have to tie up this dangling thread, which at the moment we must leave hanging loose.

## THE DEPTHS OF THE SOUL: *ABEL SÁNCHEZ*

The first novel in which Unamuno came to full maturity as a narrator was *Abel Sánchez,* "a history of passion," published in 1917, three years after *Niebla.* In this narrative he tries for the first time to de-

* *Ethics,* part I.
† *Ethics,* part III, propositions vi-ix.

scend to the profoundest depths of the person, to what he called "the depths of the soul," to capture the secret of existence and even of personality. Of individual and naked existence, of course; none of Unamuno's stories—except *Nada menos que todo un hombre,* which has such a profound affinity with this one—carries so far the bareness, the lack of reference to a world or a setting. Not even a social world, for the relations among the few characters are strictly interindividual, man to man—or woman—and all are seen from the viewpoint of the tormented soul of Joaquín Monegro, whose confession constitutes the nucleus of the story.

Starting from a situation—hate or envy—Unamuno attempts to penetrate the innermost recesses of the character and possess himself of his intimate substance. Hatred is, in a certain sense, the principal character. When Unamuno reedited the book, he wondered if it would have been better to subtitle it "History of a passion"; but that would not be accurate, for the hatred is not per se, as passion, the theme of the story; rather the theme is the dimension in which it is revealed, in which it consists, in Joaquín's soul. The terrifying decriptions in this novel are not psychological but existential. At the end of chapter III the initial atmosphere, charged with tension, thickens, and hatred appears under its own name, that is, made patent or real. "I began to hate Abel with all my soul and at the same time I resolved to hide that hatred, to fertilize it, to nurse it, to foster it in the darkest places of the depths of my soul. Hatred? I was not yet willing to give it its true name, I didn't want to admit that I was born, predestined, with the bulk and the seed of it inside me. That night I was born to the hell of my life." And then, in chapter V, when he speaks of the wedding of his adored cousin Helena to Abel, his intimate friend whom he simultaneously loves and hates, the two emotions closely intertwined, he describes his passion and is described in it. "In the days that followed that on which he told me they were getting married," Joaquín wrote in his Confession, "I felt as if my whole soul were freezing. And the ice pressed in on my heart. It was like flames made of ice. I could hardly breathe. Hate for Helena, and especially for Abel, because it was hate, cold hate whose roots choked my spirit, that had turned me to stone. It wasn't a weed, it was like a sheet of ice that had pierced my soul; rather, my whole soul was frozen by that hatred. And the ice was so transparent that I could see everything through it with perfect clarity." And later, "As the fatal moment came closer, I counted the seconds. 'Soon,' I said, 'everything will be over for me!' I think my heart stopped. I heard the two 'I do's,' his and hers, clearly and distinctly. She looked at me as she said it. And I felt colder than ever, without a qualm, without a tremor, as if I had heard nothing that affected me. And that very fact filled me with a diabolical terror of myself. I felt worse than a monster; I felt as if I did not exist, as if I were nothing but a piece of ice, as if I would be one forever. I even touched my skin, pinched myself, and took my pulse. I said to myself, 'But am I alive? Is this really I?' "

Note the way in which Unamuno aproaches the specific theme of the lover who witnesses his beloved's wedding and is present at the consummation of his despair. One might expect that Joaquín would think of his memories, of his past hopes, of Helena, of the now-closed horizon of his future life and of the imaginary boundary which once had meant hope to him, of what might have been. One might perhaps have expected him to show the bitterness or the grief or the animosity that filled his soul. But there is nothing of this. Joaquín keenly describes his own reality; it is this that concerns him, not so much his hatred, his passion of hating, but the fact that he sees himself as turned into hate, petrified, frozen in hate. It is something that concerns his own self, and he feels terror and anguish at himself, not at what has just happened outside him. For, in the last analysis, what crushes and shocks him is not the external event of another's wedding, nor even the loss of his hopes, but the transformation which is produced in him by the event. Strictly speaking, what Joaquín is witnessing is his own perdition, the horrifying alienation of himself, of his own personality. Joaquín will no longer be himself, Joaquín; he will be *the man who hates Abel,* and, consequently, the man who needs Abel in order to exist, the man who is not himself nor master of himself, the man who has lost his own selfhood. On the other hand, he writes this conclusive word about his friend Abel, "He didn't even know how to hate, he was so full of himself."

Therefore, when in the following chapter Unamuno tells of Abel's illness, and how Joaquín takes care of him, and how he dreams that his friend might die and that Helena might realize that she had always loved him, he adds: "'But he won't die!,' he said to himself. 'I won't let him die, I mustn't, my honor is involved, and anyway . . . I need to have him live!' And when he said, 'I need to have him live!,' his whole soul trembled, as the leaves of an oak tree tremble when a hurricane shakes it." From then on Joaquín Monegro lives on his hate, consists of it, and needs it; he needs it and its object in order to be—to be who he is, of course. So he recognizes clearly that any cure for his hatred will have to be, strictly speaking, a conversion, a becoming someone else, and at the same time a liberation, when he would stop being alienated and return to himself.

This situation dominates Joaquín and determines his whole life. When he marries Antonia, the daughter of the woman whom as a doctor he has treated until her death, his relationship with her is affected by the hate that fills his soul. "Antonia felt that between her and her Joaquín," Unamuno writes in chapter IX, "there was a sort of invisible wall, a glassy, transparent wall of ice. That man could not belong to his wife because he did not belong to himself. He was not his own master, for he was at once alienated and possessed. In the most intimate transports of conjugal relations, a sinister invisible shadow fell between them. Her husband's kisses seemed to her to be stolen kisses, when they were not kisses of rage." Then, in chapter XII, after he has read Lord Byron's *Cain,* which makes such a tremendous impression on him, Joaquín thinks of a possible cure or solution through love. "But did I truly come to love my Antonia? Ah, if I had been capable of loving her, I would have been saved. For me she was only another instrument of vengeance. I wanted her as the mother of a son or a daughter who would avenge me. Though I did think, wretch that I am, that being a father would cure me of all that. But did I not perhaps marry to create other hateful beings like myself, to transmit my hate, to immortalize it?"

Joaquín always fluctuates between two extremes: the desire to be cured, to free himself from his hate, and his profound attachment to it, the deep-seated bond which ties him to the passion that devours him. And this reveals that he feels his hatred to be his own reality, like an ontological moment which makes up his essence. Unamuno sees clearly that it is not a question of a feeling, but of a determination of the being; Joaquín *is* hateful, and because of that urge to persevere in one's being which Spinoza talked about, he clings to his being as a hater. He would only wish to escape from it in the name of another possible being of his, a deeper one perhaps, the one he would be if he had an authentic love, for his wife or for a child, that is, another ontological determination of the opposite sign.

Joaquín feels ever more deeply the metaphysical reality of his hatred and its undying character, written inexorably on his soul. "Until I read and reread Byron's *Cain,*" he says, "I, who had seen so many men suffer and die, hadn't thought about death, hadn't discovered it. And then I wondered if when I died I would die with my hate, whether it would die with me or survive me; I wondered if hatred survives the haters, if it is something substantial and can be transmitted, whether it is the soul, the very essence of the soul." And, a little further on: "I saw that that immortal hatred was my soul. I felt as if that hatred must have existed before my birth and would survive my death. And I shuddered with terror at the thought of living forever in order to hate forever. That would indeed be Hell. And I had laughed so at belief in it! It was Hell!" The theological allusion was inevitable; Unamuno, who thinks of this hatred as something existing in and of itself, as a constituent element of the reality of the hater, is obliged to pose the problem of its survival. And, since life passes but *I* remain, one must also consider that hate or love do not die but survive and endure. Since Unamuno's view is of love and hate as ontological moments of man, not as mere psychic affections, he reaches a point of view from which the anthropology latent in all Christian eschatology becomes comprehensible. Man's reality delivers him to death, and death to survival; and in that reality itself he finds immediately postulated eternal love or unending hate, Heaven or Hell. The attempt to penetrate the last redoubt of human personality leads Unamuno to the horizon of Last Things.

This situation of hatred—or envy: "All hatred is envy," Unamuno says—for Abel continues to mold Joaquín's life. He envies all his friend's success: his marriage, his son, his fame as a painter, his easy charm, his ultimate indifference to himself, Joaquín. He feels the necessity of delivering himself from his anguish; but two opposing ways lie before him, in a new choice which tears him to pieces: to cure his envy with envy, or with love—with charity, it might be said. "This idea that they didn't even think about me, that they didn't hate me, tortured me even more than the other. If he had hated me with a hatred like the one I had for him, that would have been something, and might even have been my salvation" (chapter XIII). And later (chapter XXI) he analyzes this inclusion of the hater and this yearning—parallel to that of love—to achieve a hatred that would be returned, to feel himself to exist in the other, for in the last instance that is what we are dealing with; it is a mode of returning, in a certain sense, to oneself, of escaping from that situation which Unamuno accurately describes as being at one and the same time "alienated and possessed."

"In solitude he never managed to be alone, for the other was always there. The other! He even caught himself talking with him, supplying the other's words for him. And the other, in these solitary dialogues, these dialogued monologues, would say unimportant or pleasant things, and never showed him any rancor. 'My God, why doesn't he hate me!,' Joaquín would say to himself. 'Why doesn't he hate me?'

"And one day he caught himself on the point of asking God, in a shameful, diabolical prayer, to infiltrate Abel's soul with hatred for himself, Joaquín. And again, 'Oh, if only he would envy me . . . if he envied me!' And at this idea, which crossed the shadows of his embittered spirit like a livid flash of lightning, he felt a melting joy, a joy that made him tremble to the shivering marrow of his soul. To be envied! To be envied!"

Finally, Joaquín discovers the ultimate root of his hatefulness in the lack of love for himself, in the radical inversion of his person which makes him hate and envy himself. " 'But isn't it,' he said, 'that I hate, I envy myself?' He went to the door, locked it, looked all around, and when he saw he was alone he fell on his knees, murmuring with scalding tears in his voice, 'Lord, Lord! You told me: love thy neighbor as thyself! And I don't love my neighbor, I can't love him, because I don't love myself. I don't know how, I can't love myself. What have You done to me, Lord?' " And, in the final pages of the book, when he is about to die, surrounded by his wife, Antonia, his daughter, his son-in-law, Abel, the son of his now-dead friend and enemy, and Abelín, the grandson of the two of them, he asks himself again: " 'Why have I been so envious, so evil? What did I do to be like this? What milk did I suck? Was it a poisonous draught of hate? Has my blood been poison too? Why was I born in a land of hate? In a land where the precept seemed to be: Hate thy neighbor as thyself. Because I have lived hating myself; for here below we all live hating ourselves.' And he says to his wife, 'I never loved you. If I had loved you I would have been cured. I didn't love you. And now it hurts me that I didn't. If only we could begin all over again. . .' "

He cannot begin over, he cannot because death is already upon him; he even feels that if he were to live longer he still could not stop hating in this life. But Joaquín dies with his hate overcome, at least possessed and recognized to its very root. So far Unamuno goes. But one could keep on asking, pursue more deeply still this murky exploration of the depths of the soul, perhaps to emerge and *riveder le stelle.* In the first place, where does the man who hates himself hate from, or better still, from whom? Who is the deeper *I* that turns against his other, separated I? What ontological problem is posed by this strange possibility of love or hate for oneself? And, in the second place, what is the root of that hatred of oneself and of others? All hate is envy, says Unamuno; but then what is the sense of hatred toward oneself? It would not be difficult to find in it a root of pride, of hatred for limitation, for finitude, for the unaccepted necessity of dying; at bottom it might be said to be a satanic envy of God, an *odium Dei,* the absolute inversion of charity. From this inversion of charity in its primary meaning as *amor Dei* inevitably flows the destruction of charity as love for one's neighbor. And sometimes the concrete origin of the hatred for God and of the most profound despair is hate for His image, for man. So the circle closes. As St. John says, if a man say, I love God, and hateth his brother, he is a liar; for he that loveth not his brother whom he hath seen, how can he love God whom he hath not seen? *Si quis dixerit quoniam diligo Deum, et fratrem suum oderit, mendax est. Qui enim non diligit fratrem suum quem videt, Deum quem non videt quomodo potest diligere?* * We see, therefore, how far this attempt to penetrate the secret of the human soul can carry us.

## THE VACUUM OF PERSONALITY: *DON SANDALIO, JUGADOR DE AJEDREZ*

*La novela de Don Sandalio, jugador de ajedrez,* which Unamuno published in 1933 just after his *San Manuel Bueno, mártir,* represents in a certain sense the inverse of *Abel Sánchez,* and consequently is its complement as well. *Abel Sánchez* is an intimate study, a descent into the depths of a character's soul, a story narrated from within with scarcely any references to an exterior world, a pure display of intimate temporal occurrences which lays bare the last redoubt of a personality. In his *Don Sandalio,* on the contrary, Unamuno attempts to suppress inwardness totally, to ignore it, to try not to know or even guess anything about it. The author of the letters which compose the narrative, assailed by a hatred of stupidity which makes him flee the society of men, winds up in a provincial club and meets there a silent chess player with whom he occasionally plays a game, without knowing anything about him. There is no plot. The author of the letters occasionally hears vague accounts from others about the real existence of Don Sandalio—his son has died, he is later put in jail, dies there, and his son-in-law visits the man he used to play those silent games with and tries to talk to him about his father-in-law. But the partner does not want to find out anything; he does not want to know what happened to Don Sandalio outside the club; he is interested only in the man who played without talking, watching the movement of the pieces, the man who is dead as far as he is concerned. The writer of the letters, then, moves against a background of the vacuum or negation of a personality, and consequently of mystery obstinately maintained.

* I *Joannis* 4:20.

"Don Sandalio," Unamuno notes in the prologue, "is a personage seen from outside, whose interior life escapes us; perhaps he has none." After an allusion to the behaviorists, who believe that consciousness is an impenetrable mystery, he adds: "But is it possible that my Don Sandalio has no inner life, that he has no consciousness or interior knowledge of himself, that he never indulges in monodialogue? But what is a game of chess but a monodialogue, a dialogue the player maintains with his partner and opponent in the game? And furthermore, do not all the pieces on the board, the black and the white, carry on a dialogue and even a controversy among themselves? It is clear, then, that my Don Sandalio does have an inner life, and monodialogue, and consciousness."

When Unamuno presents his character he outlines his shape against a void and surrounds him with silence, and this is precisely what he is made up of. "There is one poor man," he writes in Letter IV, "who is the person who so far has interested me most. They call him—not often, for almost nobody speaks to him and he speaks to nobody—they call him, or he is called, Don Sandalio, and his occupation seems to be that of a chess player. I haven't been able to find out anything about his life, nor do I particularly care to. I'd rather imagine it. He comes to the club only to play chess, and he plays almost without saying a word, with a sick avidity. Outside of chess, the world seems not to exist for him." And later: "I haven't dared to approach his table myself, even though the man interests me. He seems so isolated among all the others, so sunk in himself! Or rather in the game, which seems to be a sacred function, a sort of religious rite for him. 'And when he isn't playing, what does he do?' I've asked myself. 'What profession does he live by? Has he a family? Does he love someone? Does he have griefs and disillusionments? Does he bear some tragedy in his soul?'" He asks himself these questions; but, when he has lived with the closed-up personality of his chess partner, when he has transmigrated to him imaginatively, when he has recreated him with his own spiritual substance and filled the void of another's personality and made it his own, he ends by rejecting the real data that come into his consciousness because he clings jealously to his own Don Sandalio.

Little by little, as he takes over his personality, the author of the letters begins to feel the necessity of living in Don Sandalio, of existing for him, though in a nebulous and hermetic manner. He begins to ask himself: "What must he think of me? What must I seem like to him?" And immediately after this the decisive question: "Who am I for him, I wonder?" Don Sandalio turns out to be a problem of his own personality, and he needs to see his personality in the other man, to know at least that he exists in the other, to encounter his own reality in the very secret of the impenetrable fellow creature, more real because impenetrable, for we have already seen that an essential opaqueness is a quality of reality.

Finally, the death of Don Sandalio, which is the culmination of the mystery, makes the meaning of that vacuum of personality even more patent. In Letter XVIII the author writes: "And now, Felipe, comes the most extraordinary, the most shocking thing! It is that Don Sandalio . . . has died in jail. I am not even sure how I found out about it. Maybe I heard it in the club, where they were talking about his death. And I fled out of the club and went up on the mountain, trying to escape from the comments. . . What has happened to me? Why did such a black dismay come over me, and why did I begin to cry—yes, it's true, Felipe—why did I cry over the death of my Don Sandalio? I felt as if there were a tremendous void within me. . . That man had died to me. Now I won't hear him not talking as he played, I won't hear his silence any more." This is the decisive point. *I felt as if there were a tremendous void within me. That man had died to me.* That strange capacity man has for including other people in his life is what makes this hollowness, this void, possible. Don Sandalio, insofar as he was a withdrawn and silent personality, forms part of his fellow player; and that is why he can die to him, and his death is a partial death of the other. The author of the letters later writes (Letter XXII): "The profoundest problem of our novel, of yours, Felipe, and of mine, of Don Sandalio's, is a problem of personality, of being or not being, rather than eating or not eating, loving or being loved."

In this novel Unamuno carries to its extreme his total separation from the realistic or the psychological; there are no things in it, no world, no psychic life; all that is rigorously denied, excluded. And this is the interesting point. If we take away exterior things, psychic reality, life itself, what is left? Only *personality*. By presenting it in a vacuum, Unamuno shows its irreducible reality. Where does Don Sandalio live, what does he do, what does he think, what does he possess? Unamuno does not know, does not want to know; it does not matter in the least. After this violent suppression of every other reality, one solitary and irreplaceable thing is left, a *thou* which is also an *I,* that of Don Sandalio: a *who,* a person. When Don Sandalio dies, his partner, his *thou,* avidly guards the secret, the vacuum of his personality, for he does not want to see it disappear by exchanging it for another, for that of the man he has not come to know, for one that is not *his*. When the son-in-law tells him that he believes he must have been fond of Don Sandalio, the friend quickly replies, "Yes, but I was fond of my Don Sandalio, understand? Mine, who played chess with me silently, not yours, not your father-in-law. Silent chess players may interest me, but fathers-in-law don't interest me at all" (Letter XX).

Unamuno achieves in this novel an extreme point of his theory of the fictional being; strictly speaking, his friend's Don Sandalio is an imagined character, a fictional being, but *cum fundamento in re*. His partner invents him, and by doing so fills the vacuum of his hidden personality. That is why he is afraid he will see him vanish like a dream when he comes into contact with another personage, with the Don Sandalio of the son-in-law or of any others, or even of Don Sandalio himself. It is no coincidence that here we encounter again that insubstantiality of Unamuno's characters—consider this well—the lack of foundation of that dream which each of us is for him. The real problem, the one to which Unamuno refers only obliquely and sometimes tries to avoid, is that Don Sandalio *himself* must be the one he makes himself, the one others see, the one God holds in His hand.

## LIVING TOGETHER: *LA TÍA TULA*

In his novel *La tía Tula,* written in 1920, Unamuno maintained his plan of a novel without a setting, without scenery or realisms. At first glance it is a narrative of the same type as the two I have just discussed, or like the three he called *Novelas ejemplares.* However, if we probe into the matter a little, we can find appreciable differences. In the first place, the narrative itself has more consistency than the others; it is not a mere pretext to show off the characters and bare their souls. Or, rather, they are bared by reason of the drama as it happens to them, as it develops, and form themselves within it as it proceeds. In the second place, there is a plurality of characters, in a very different sense from that which we find in *Niebla,* on the one hand, and *Abel Sánchez,* on the other. In the first of these novels it was a question of creating a multitude of fictional beings, of watching this living world of secondary creatures proliferate, and of weaving a web of relationships between them which formed an ambiance, a misty atmosphere in which they lived. In the second they are characters who play a necessary role, each in respect to others, and thus define the very structure of the drama: the man who envies, the man who is envied, the origin of the envy, the children who prolong the story. In *La tía Tula,* on the other hand, the plurality is the basis of a higher unity within which the life of each one of the characters takes place; they are together, all exist for the others and each for the family group. There are not merely several characters, then, nor even relationships between them—these exist already by themselves—but a living together, a common life, so that what each of them *is* comes to pass only within their unity. And Gertrudis, Tía Tula, is precisely the foundation of that unity, a foundation, as we shall see, of a strictly personal kind.

Gertrudis appears from the start as a strongly emphasized personality, but she is shown, not in isolation but in union—first to her sister Rosa, then to Rosa's entire family, which is to become even more truly her own.

"It was Rosa and not her sister Gertrudis," Unamuno begins the story, "who always went out with her, who attracted those anxious glances Ramiro used to send in their direction. Or at least that was what both Rosa and Ramiro thought when they first felt attracted to each other.

"The two sisters, always together, but for all that not always united in feeling, formed an apparently indissoluble pair and were always thought of as a single unit. At first it was Rosa's splendid and somewhat provocative beauty, her blooming flesh that seemed to open to heaven and light and wind, which drew people's eyes to the pair; but then it was Gertrudis' magnetic eyes which both attracted and kept at a distance the eyes that rested on hers.

"When you looked at them carefully and at close range, it was Gertrudis who aroused desire. While her sister Rosa opened splendidly to all the winds and all the light the flower of her living flesh, Gertrudis was like a closed and sealed coffer which hinted at a treasure of love and secret delights.

"But Ramiro, who wore his soul in his eyes, thought he saw only Rosa, and Rosa was the one to whom he was attracted from the beginning."

This defines the general situation of the novel. Ramiro, approaching Rosa, sees Gertrudis at close range and is attracted to her, as she is silently attracted to him. But Gertrudis, noticing Ramiro's hesitation, without letting him speak or explain himself, urges him with all the weight of her quiet gravity, her "great black mourning eyes," to marry Rosa quickly. "If you love her," she tells him, "marry her, and if you don't love her there's no room for you in this house." And Unamuno adds, "Her heart seemed to stop as these words came out of her cold lips. An icy silence followed them; meanwhile the blood, repressed before and now set free, rose to the sister's cheek. And then, in the pregnant silence, the racing, trembling beat of her heart could be heard."

Gertrudis, Tula, continues to accompany her sister, though from afar, and as the latter begins to have children—eventually three—she enters more and more into the life of the house and dedicates herself with total devotion to the care and love of the children: she is turning into Tía Tula. Ramiro, though he always remembers the enthralling impression of Gertrudis, becomes deeply attached to his wife, and when she dies he feels that he recognizes all the deep bonds which tied him to Rosa, all the powerful reality of their life together. It is then that he has an inkling of the meaning of everyday life, but within the strictly individual picture, not the collective one as in *Paz en la guerra,* where each man's daily existence emerged from the common depths of the life of Bilbao. Ramiro feels that his own life has been interwoven little by little with that of his wife, that the two of them have made one single life between them in the continuity of many days that were all alike; and that when Rosa, a member of this single life, died, the apparently paradoxical truth was that he had also died in part, but that Rosa lived again in the mutilated life of her husband.

"Now, only now that he was a widower, Ramiro realized how much he had loved his wife Rosa without even suspecting it. The greatest of his consolations was to shut himself in that bedroom where they had lived and loved so much, and to live over his married life.

"First their engagement, an engagement which, though it was not very long, was slow and quiet, in which it seemed that Rosa was stealing his soul away, almost as though he did not have one, making him believe that he would not know her until she was his once and for all; that quiet and reserved engagement, under the gaze of Gertrudis, who was all soul. . .

"Then came the wedding and the intoxication of the first months, the honeymoon; Rosa opened her spirit to him by degrees, but it was a spirit so simple, so transparent, that Ramiro realized she had not concealed or withheld anything from him. His wife lived with her heart in her hand and held out that hand in an offering gesture, with the innermost part of her spirit laid open to the air of the world, totally given over to the concern of the moment, like the roses of the field and the larks in the heavens. And at the same time Rosa's spirit was a reflection of her sister's, like running water in the sun, while the other's was like the closed spring from which it rose . . .

"She was like daily bread, like homemade everyday bread. . . Her glance, which bestowed peace, her smile, the impression of life she gave were the expression of a quiet, peaceful, and domestic spirit. . . There was something plantlike in that hidden but powerful strength with which she continually, moment after moment, sucked in the essence of the depths of everyday life, and in the sweet naturalness with which she opened her perfumed petals."

And that common life is the life that survives in the form of deprivation, better still, of mutilation, for Ramiro; not only does it survive in him, but also in that reality which is the home, into which Unamuno brings us with great skill, and which will be jealously preserved and maintained by Tula. "But did Rosa actually die? Did she really die? How could she have died while he, Ramiro, still lived? No, during the now-solitary nights, while he slept alone in that bed of death and life and love, he could feel beside him the rhythm of her breathing, her gentle warmth, though it brought him an agonizing sense of emptiness. And he would stretch out his hand and run it over the other half of the bed, pressing it sometimes." "No, Rosa, his Rosa, had not died; it was not possible that she had died; his wife was there, as alive as ever and radiating life all around her; his wife could not die" (chapter VII).

This form of everyday life—which is constantly maintained even after Rosa dies—is sharply cut in two by her death. Death puts life to the question, especially daily life, for death is the unaccustomed factor, the one which does not admit of repetition, and when death is not a mere ceasing to exist, it places us in the authenticity of life, which possesses itself in its ending and at the same time becomes problematical. "During the choking spells her eyes looked into the eyes of her Ramiro from the edge of eternity. And that look seemed to be a supreme and despairing question, as if, on the point of departing never more to return to earth, she were asking him what the hidden meaning of life was. Those looks of quiet sorrow, of sorrowful quietness, seemed to say, 'You, you who are my life; you, who with me have brought new human souls into the world; you, who have had three lives from me; you, my man, tell me: what is this?' It was an abysmal afternoon." Once again Unamuno looks for the secret of life in the creation of new lives; the man who is able to produce them is able, in a certain sense, to divine life's mystery; and this, which Unamuno applies directly to spiritual creatures, to fictitious personages, here refers to fatherhood and motherhood. Then he adds this profound metaphoric description—it cannot be described except metaphorically—of Rosa's death, which clearly tries to reproduce the radical anguish of that unique and irrevocable moment. "At last the supreme moment came upon her, the moment of transition, and it seemed as though, on the threshold of the eternal shades, suspended over the abyss, she clung to him, to her man, who trembled as he felt drawn in too. The poor creature tried to tear open her throat with her nails; she looked at him terrified, her eyes begging him for air; then, with her eyes seeming to plumb the depths of his soul, she let go of his hand and fell back on the bed where she had conceived and borne her three children" (chapter VII).

Unamuno speaks of the abyss, of the eternal shades, of a fall, but he takes good care to call death a transition. It is indeed a question of falling into an abyss, into the depths of oneself, into an unknown death; of falling, of something happening, not that nothing happens. Unamuno shows death as a reality, as something that one accomplishes, or at least that is accomplished in oneself. Man dies; he does not simply cease to exist.

This death divides the novel, as it does the life of its characters, into two parts; now, in the home of Ramiro the widower, it is Tula who is everything. She is the spiritual mother of the children, whom she feels to be her own, more than her own since they are not children of the flesh, and Gertrudis has a constant obsession with purity. With the passage of time Ramiro feels more strongly than ever the attraction for Tula which has always been alive in him, though concealed by Rosa's authentic everyday love. Her brother-in-law's love, in the last instance returned by her, galls Gertrudis; she rejects it because she is reluctant to succeed her own sister, in spite of her deathbed request, for fear that children of her own would affect the love she feels for those who are only children of the spirit, and because of that exacerbated need for absolute purity which dominates her in spite of herself. "If I married Ramiro. . . then I would really be a stepmother," Gertrudis says, "and even more so if he gave me children of my own flesh and blood. . ." Unamuno adds: "And the thought of children of her flesh made the very marrow of Gertrudis' soul shake with sacred terror, for she was all motherhood, but spiritual motherhood." At bottom this is again a problem of personality. Tula is in anguish, less for what she may do than for what she will *be* (we often forget that some of our actions turn us into other persons, and that is why we feel seized with terror when we contemplate them). She is in love with Ramiro, but she wants to be Tía

Tula, always virginal, the spiritual mother of Rosa's and Ramiro's children and even of Rosa and Ramiro, the foundation of their home, keystone of a common existence which she has created and to which she has dedicated herself. What is to become of those things? I repeat, it is not a question of a trivial conflict between opposing appetites, or between desires and duties or supposed duties, but of a problem of personality which affects the very being. This is why Unamuno says, "And certainly, in Gertrudis' closed-up soul a great storm was brewing. Her head battled with her heart, and both head and heart battled in her with something even more deeply buried, more private, more intimate, with something that was like the marrowbones of her spirit." This something is no other than what Unamuno called the depths of the soul and which I prefer to call the basis of the person, the "who" that each one of us is.

When Ramiro insists, Gertrudis, softened in her loving uncertainty through pity for him, gives him the space of a year to decide at the end of that time whether they should marry. But during that period Ramiro, overcome by the temptations of the flesh, falls into sin with the maid of the house, Manuela, "a nineteen-year-old girl from the orphanage, sickly and pale, with a feverish gleam in her eyes, of gentle, submissive manners, of few words, almost always sad." When Gertrudis finds out about it she feels great pity for her brother-in-law, and at the same time suspects that her own virtue may have caused him to sin, that she may have been inhuman. But, simply and imperiously she makes Ramiro marry the girl so that his new child can have a father and mother, and Tula can be spiritual mother of them all. When the orphan is about to have her second child, which will be a girl, Ramiro falls ill and dies. Shortly before, in a moving dialogue between brother- and sister-in-law, Tula bares her soul to him and Ramiro dies holding her hand. Gertrudis, "broken by a long exhaustion, the fatigue of years, pressed her mouth for one moment to Ramiro's cold mouth and relived their lives, which had been one life." Gertrudis renounces nothing; those who have departed survive in her, she tries to make them go on living in the house. This is the decisive point: she embodies all their sense of coexistence, which she nurtures with memories. When Manuela dies giving birth to her daughter, Tula is left alone with the five children, all of whom she thinks of as equally her children; and year after year she makes them live in intimate communion with the three dead parents, and even with the ancestors one step removed from them whom they have never known: Tía Tula's dead. She devotes herself particularly to Manolita, the youngest, the one who would not have been born had she not obliged Ramiro to marry the orphan girl, the one who never had a mother, the one she will form in her image and who will be Tula's successor in the family.

During this time, in which Gertrudis relives all her memories, in the serene seriousness of her maternal life, the meaning of the unity she has formed and defends at all costs becomes clear to her, as does her mistake in regard to Ramiro. " 'Do I love him or not?' she had asked herself sometimes when he was alive. 'Isn't that pride? Isn't it like the sad, lonely passion of the ermine, who won't jump into the mire to save his fellow for fear of getting dirty? I don't know . . . I don't know. . .' " And when she is about to die, after she has left her nieces and nephews, who are all really her children, grown up and united in the house of which she has been the soul, she tells them as a final piece of advice: "Think well, very, very well about what you are going to do, think very well . . . so that you'll never have to repent of doing something, and still less for not having done it. . . And if you see that the one you love has fallen into a pool of mire, a cesspool even, a sewer, jump in to save him . . . don't let him drown there . . . or drown together . . . in the sewer. . . No, we don't have wings, or if we do they're only chicken's wings . . . we are not angels . . . we will be in the other life . . . where there is no mire and no blood! Filth there is in Purgatory, flaming mire that burns and cleanses. . . This is the last thing I can tell you: don't be afraid of filth. . . Pray for me, and may the Virgin forgive me.' "

At last, after Gertrudis has died, her meaning as founder of the family's coexistence is made most clearly apparent. In the prologue Unamuno alludes explicitly to St. Theresa, and says that he did not notice the deep and hidden similarities to the saint until after he had written the novel. Tula is the founder of a domestic community which survives her; her life, her strong personality, is not destined to feed on itself but to realize itself in the common life of the house. Perhaps it is for this reason that Gertrudis' ultimate loneliness is so stressed, that loneliness from which she draws the intimacy necessary for the common life of the others.

"Did Tía Tula die?" Unamuno asks at the beginning of chapter XXIV. "No, instead she began to live in the family, with a new sort of life that was more inward and more life-giving than ever, with the eternal life of immortal family spirit. Tía Tula was the foundation and the rooftree of that home." And Manolita, the youngest girl, is the continuator of Tula's spirit. "She kept the other's archive and her treasure; she had the key of the secret hiding places of her who in flesh and blood was no more; she kept, with the doll she had had as a child, Tula's childhood doll, and some letters and the prayer book and Don Primitivo's breviary. She was the one in the family who knew the sayings and doings of the forebears still within memory: of Don Primitivo, who was no blood relation of hers; of the elder Ramiro's mother; of Rosa; of her own mother Manuela—no sayings or doings here, only silence and passions. She was the domestic history; the spiritual eternity of the family was continued in her."

This is the story of Tía Tula; Unamuno is gradually closing his cycle of the exploration of human life. From collective everyday life, which he fathomed in *Paz en la guerra,* he goes on to abstract individuality founded on ideas *(Amor y pedagogía).* Then, abandoning these historical or ideological pretexts, he affirms the reality of fiction as such, and creates characters which acquire more and more personality; but he carries this so far that he strips them of their flesh, leaves them naked, and—an obvious error—isolates them: *Abel Sánchez* or *Nada menos que todo un hombre* are the extreme examples of this. At last he feels the insufficiency of the isolated man, his fundamental lack of reality, and he returns to the concept of common life. But this common life in *La tía Tula* is very different from that of his first novel; in the latter a communal life was being dealt with, personal only to a slight degree; in *La tía Tula* everyday life is trivial in the other characters, but it is strictly authentic, dramatic, intimate, and solitary in Gertrudis. She is the person in her world; in a tiny family world of interindividual relations, but nevertheless a world. Unamuno has taken a step forward in comprehending human life as it is. A further step will be necessary: the family circle must be broken; the person must be placed in a world which is also social, and open to transcendence. This is what his last and most important novel, *San Manuel Bueno, mártir,* will give us.

## PERSONAL LIFE: *SAN MANUEL BUENO, MÁRTIR*

Unamuno's most deeply felt and profound novel is *San Manuel Bueno, mártir,* published in 1931, and again in 1933 with three other stories. At the same time it is the most characteristic, the one in which Unamuno achieves the greatest fidelity to himself and to his attempt to penetrate the reality of life and human personality. It is a story suffused with deep emotion, even with a sort of rough tenderness seldom found in Unamuno's pages, as if it crept in in spite of him, but which at times dominates the whole narration, as happens in *La tía Tula* and again in this novel.

Unamuno states (page 27 of the 1933 edition) that the problem to which he gives expression in this novel of his, as in the others, is "the terrifying problem of personality, of whether one is what he is and will keep on being what he is." But the new element in this book is that he decides to confront directly in the novel that problem of personality in the dimension in which it most seriously troubled him: that of personal immortality, of finding out whether we must die altogether or not. Don Manuel, the parish priest of Valverde de Lucena, that "matriarchal man," full of charity and goodness, is tormented by the anguished need of survival, by wanting to believe in everlasting life without being able to do so. Death and the necessity of surviving imbue the whole novel, and this places it squarely and from the outset in the authentic atmosphere of living, though in the most everyday of senses, in a tiny hamlet near the lake of San Martín de Castañeda in Sanabria. Thus, Unamuno can say of this novel: "I am convinced that I have put into it all my tragic sense of everyday life." We shall soon see the scope of these two linked expressions: tragic sense and everyday life.

The structure of this novel presents some interesting features. In the first place, after stressing the often commented on bareness of his narratives, Unamuno nevertheless states: "There is a setting in *San Manuel Bueno, mártir* which derives from that marvelous and suggestive lake of San Martín de Castañeda in Sanabria, below the ruins of a Bernardine convent, and where the legend still exists of a city, Valverde de Lucena, which lies in the depths of the lake's waters" (page 9). And later (page 11): "The scene of the activities of my Don Manuel Bueno and of Angelina and Lázaro Carballino postulates a greater development of public life, poor and humble though it be, than the life of these terribly poor and humble villages warrants. Which does not mean, of course, that I believe that there might not have been, or still are in these places, very intimate and intense individual lives and tragedies of conscience."

We see, therefore, that Unamuno considers the existence of a *world* with certain conditions, with a particular spiritual and even physical circumstance, as decisive for the reality of the lives with which he is concerned here. For the first and only time in all his work, Unamuno overcomes the abstraction of the *I* and places it fully in a world; and as was to be expected, not in a world of things but in the world of the person. The person in his world, stressing the *his,* might be the formula of this novel's structure.

But there is more. The central character in the novel is Don Manuel, a priest; and this priesthood is in no way accidental, for the novel takes its meaning from the fact, the sacerdotal function of the protagonist in relation to his people, a collective and anonymous character, or, if you will, a thousand unknown names. For Don Manuel is a Christian priest, and for the Christian as such there are no masses or multitudes but only fellow men, irreplaceable persons, each one with his name, which, though it be unknown, is known at least to God. And the narrative is placed, not in the mouth of Don Manuel nor directly in its author's, but on the lips of a young girl, Angela Carballino, who grows older during the course of the novel. By this means the protagonist is seen from outside himself, like a fellow man also, but from inside the novel, inside the world of fiction in which he lives. There is a circle of persons qua persons—Don Miguel, Angela, and her brother Lázaro—with a strictly interindividual relation, and there is the daily life of the whole town which surrounds them like the far-off murmur of the sea, and for which the three live. From this care for the childlike soul of the silent town, which ensnares the three vigilant and tortured personalities, arises that tragic sense of daily life alluded to before.

Don Manuel is described by Angela, at first externally and physically; soon after, in his aspect as spiritual leader of the town he serves; only later will she penetrate the secret of his soul. And the description is never realistic, but vital; it tries to bring to light the human reality that lies under the physical body and the actions. "Our saint must have been about thirty-seven at that time [in Angela's childhood]. He was tall, slim, and straight, carried his head as our mountain peak carries its crest, and all the blue depth of our lake was in his eyes. He attracted everyone's attention, and with it their hearts, and when he looked at us he seemed to look into our hearts, seeing through the flesh as if it were glass. We all loved him, especially the children. What things he used to tell us! They were things, not words. The town began to sense an odor of sanctity in him; we felt full of its aroma, drunk with it" (page 40). A little later she adds (pages 44–45): "And how he loved his people! His whole life went into mending unhappy marriages, reconciling rebellious sons with their fathers or fathers with their sons, and helping everyone to die well." That was his life, Unamuno says, not his duty or his occupation, but his very life. Further on Don Manuel says: "I ought not to live alone; I ought not to die alone. I should live for my people, die for my people. How am I to save my soul if I do not save my people's?" (page 60). What is the meaning of this?

Don Manuel lives oppressed by the idea of death, not precisely by the fear of death but by the idea that, if one has no hope of the other life, this life is intolerable. "I have watched poor, ignorant, illiterate villagers die well," he says, "people who have scarcely ever left the village, and I have learned from their lips, or been able to guess, the true cause of their mortal illness, and I could see, there at the head of their deathbed, all the blackness of that abyss which is the weariness of life. A thousand times worse than hunger!" (page 86). At the front of the book he puts St. Paul's words to the Corinthians: "If in this life only we have hope in Christ, we are of all men most miserable." Don Manuel has a secret anguish, which he zealously hides from his people, and to ease the burden he must confess it to Angela and Lázaro: his anguish about life everlasting, faith in which eludes him. Without that faith life is intolerable, mortal, and he takes care to keep faith alive in his people so that they will always believe themselves immortal and so be able to live. When Angela goes to confession, she raises the question. "Daring greatly and all trembling, I said to him: 'But do you believe, Father?'

"He hesitated a moment, then recovering, told me: 'I believe!'

" 'But in what, Father, in what? Do you believe in the other life? Do you believe that when we die we don't die entirely? Do you believe that we'll see each other again, and love each other in the other world that is to come? Do you believe in the other life?'

"The poor saint was weeping. 'Look, my daughter, let's not talk about that!' " (pages 82–83).

This is the root of Don Manuel's sense of community with his people: a root of charity, for he takes care with more zeal than anyone else that his people shall not lose their faith in the other life and with it their satisfaction in living; at the same time, and for charity too—charity, if properly understood, in fact begins in oneself, though it does not end there—he tries to save himself in this union with his people, to save his faith in the faith of all of them together. The whole town, congregated in the church, was reciting the Credo with a single voice. "And when they came to 'I believe in the resurrection of the body and life everlasting,' Don Manuel's voice was swallowed up, as if in a lake, by the voice of the whole town, and it was because he was silent. And I heard the bells of the town they say lies submerged at the bottom of the lake . . . , and they were the bells of the sunken town in the spiritual lake of our people; I heard the voice of our dead, who were resurrected through us in the communion of the saints. Later, when I came to know our saint's secret, I understood that it was as if a caravan were marching in the desert with its leader dead as they came near the end of their journey; and as if his people lifted him on their shoulders to bring his lifeless body into the promised land" (pages 50–51).

Don Manuel, in anguish, tries to make the rest, his brothers, believe for him when he cannot, to have those whom he has strengthened in their faith help him. He seeks to save his personality through that of his people, to believe with all of them since he can no longer believe alone. And, when he is about to die, when he feels that his hour has come, after an intimate conversation with Lázaro—who follows him in his anguish and in his care for the people—and with Angela, who still believes with a living faith, he has himself carried to the church to pray with all his people and to bless them. "And when they came to 'the resurrection of the body and life everlasting,' the whole town realized that their saint had given up his soul to God. And no one had to shut his eyes, for he died with them closed" (page 101).

After the deaths of Don Manuel and then Lázaro, Angela stays in the town, keeping the memory of both alive—Angela, the girl who comes to be a mature woman, completely identified with the town, the recipient of the priest's charity and of her dead brother's. At the end, as a summing up of this life of intimate tragedy, Angela writes: "And now, as I write this Memoir, this intimate confession of my experience of another's sanctity, I believe that Don Manuel Bueno, my Saint Manuel, and my brother Lázaro died believing they did not believe in what we are most interested in knowing, but believing it without belief, believing it in an active and resigned sense of desolation." "And I believed, and believe still, that our Lord God, for I know not what sacred and inscrutable designs, made them believe themselves unbelievers. And that perhaps at the end of their passing, the blindfold fell from their eyes" (pages 110–111).

In this novel Unamuno does not content himself with the bare personality, but makes it really live. The human person exists only in living; but life can be lost among things, in the world, and then it is trivial, inauthentic, impersonal, and not human. On the other hand, when life turns back to itself, when it concentrates on itself, when it lives from its own depths, its own roots, then it is a *personal life,* the making of a person as such, in his world, in the vital circumstance in which it was fated to take place and have temporal being.

And this can happen without unusual events, within the normal calm of every day. The concern for eternity, for life everlasting, what Unamuno has called the tragic sense of life, turns us back toward ourselves, into our ordinary daily life, and makes it be a personal life, immunizes it against triviality. Unamuno leaves room for belief that doubt, and the anguish of trying to conquer unbelief, are not necessary. Living faith in everlasting life, no matter how firm it may be, the unquiet expectation of eternal life—for all expectation is unquiet, the more so perhaps the more it is hoped for: *inquietum est cor nostrum donec requiescat in te,* says St. Augustine, whose hope was so firm and lively—is enough to maintain man deeply rooted in essentials, spared from triviality and emptiness, master of his personality.

Therefore, every man who daily prays with the Credo: *exspecto resurrectionem mortuorum et vitam venturi saeculi,* honestly, that is, actually looking for them, not merely saying that he does, that man, whatever the external shape of his existence, maintains himself in his personality. Men are persons to God, and for the Christian, who knows this, everyday life is always personal too.

We have followed the internal evolution of Unamuno's narratives through their most important stages, from *Paz en la guerra* to *San Manuel Bueno, mártir.* In this long exploration we have seen how Unamuno stations himself from the beginning in the field he is to cultivate all his life, that of human reality, and how at the same time his work will be a constant progress—or rather, regress—toward himself. From everyday communal life, from the human world as such, he keeps descending into the depths, the abysses even, of individual existence and the isolated personality. As we saw some time ago, Unamuno tried at the beginning of this exploration, in an error caused by a certain arrogance, to capture the person directly, paying no attention to his circumstance or the existence in which he was formed. This is the negative side of his lack of setting and plot; the positive side, it will be recalled, is the unerring replacement of the realistic world of things by the temporal world of human life. But, after carrying this tendency to its extreme, Unamuno begins to feel that it is deficient, and begins to let in reality as it is, the person in his world, the world with which he makes his life—a reality that cannot be seen as absolute transparency, even though a creature of fiction is being dealt with, for fiction must imitate the same mode of being as reality, and a living man is by his very nature mysterious and arcane. Tula or Don Manuel partially disclose their secret, which is not fully known even by them; the last redoubt of personality is veiled even to that personality itself, for only God has perfect possession of Himself.

Unamuno, then, impelled by his profound sense of narrative and of human reality, in fact corrects his own theory. His novel gains in narrative truth and at the same time in its value as knowledge. Little by little Unamuno renounces the point of view of God to hold to the vision that one man can achieve of another, even though that man be himself. And every justified and authentic renunciation increases and buttresses that knowledge. After attempting the comprehension of the person "from nowhere," taking neither time nor place into account, Unamuno proceeds simply to make his characters live before the eyes of the soul. By following the process of living, which is also our own, he makes us penetrate imaginatively the substance of reality itself, and we divine and possess it by the mysterious route of fellow-feeling and spiritual affinity. The doctrine of knowledge as love, of which Unamuno spoke so often, has its best application in his later narratives.

And when these narratives end, always with death, the enigma of personality, instead of being resolved as something completed and therefore exhausted, ended, gives rise to the thorniest question of all. When the person dies, he does not dissolve and show us his inner self, but instead closes in upon himself, reassumes his reality, recapitulates it in that last act, and leaves us an unanswerable question, precisely the most living question imaginable. "Your silence is the pledge of all eternity," Unamuno writes, addressing the star Aldebaran. The same could be said before the silence of a dead fellow human, not dumbness but silence, for it conceals the last nucleus of the mystery only guessed at in real or imaginary coexistence. That hermetic secret, that silence of something which might be spoken, emphasizes the latent reality of the person hidden in death, and thus postulates his everlasting life. This is the ultimate meaning of Unamuno's novel.

# VI.

# *THE POETRY*

## THE VALUE OF THE VERSE

Running parallel to Unamuno's prose work is an abundant though rather late production of poetry, from the volume entitled *Poesías* (1907) to the last writings of his *Cancionero* [Songbook], published and known only in part. The volumes in between are: *Rosario de sonetos líricos* [A Rosary of Lyric Sonnets] (1912); *El Cristo de Velázquez* (1920); *Rimas de dentro* [Rhymes from Within] (1923); *Teresa* (1924); *De Fuerteventura a París* (1925); and *Romancero del destierro* [Ballads of Exile] (1927). To these can be added the poems included in *Andanzas y visiones españolas* (1922), in the *Cuaderno de la Magdalena* [Notebook from La Magdalena] (1934), and in periodicals. A fairly complete idea of Unamuno's poetry can be obtained by reading an extensive *Antología poética* (Ediciones Escorial, 1942), which contains, with very few important omissions, the most substantial part of his poetic work.*

And we might ask ourselves why Unamuno, at the age of forty-three, after a long period of literary activity, begins to publish poetry, and does not stop doing so until his death. Why, when he is sunk in his central preoccupation, when he has become accustomed to writing in a harsh and fiery prose which affects to ignore and disdain all artifice, does he turn to the supreme artifice of verse—a verse with little music in it but full of profound resonances—and pour so much

* An ample selection of it can be found in my edition of Unamuno's *Obras selectas* (Madrid, 1946). The *Cancionero* was published in 1953.

of himself into it? What does verse add to the customary power of language? What does Unamuno mean when he says he needs rhythm in his expression? What does he expect of his verses?

They were always very important for him; he always wrote them—and published them—with profound seriousness. In the Introduction to his poetry, when bidding farewell to his verses to give them to the world, he says:

> "You are the summing up of all my works,
> you are my acts of faith, my only true ones;
> the roots of all my deeds float loose and freely
> on that fleeting current which is Time,
> while my songs' roots are fixed securely
> in the rocky bosom of the eternal."

Unamuno attempts, then, to give some substantial part of himself in his verses, something more personal and heartfelt than his acts themselves. He demands density of his poetry, demands that the feeling be thought and the thought felt. All of this, which has generally been understood in a trivial way, has made many people believe that Unamuno's poetry was poetry "of ideas," this expression being taken to mean that it consisted in expressing in verse what he could have and perhaps should have said in prose. But this represents a total incomprehension of Unamuno's poetry. At the beginning of his first book, in his *Credo poético,* he says,

> "Not he who embodies a soul in flesh
> nor gives form to the idea, the poet is;
> but he who finds the soul behind the flesh,
> behind the form encounters the idea."

That is, his procedure is the inverse; his point of departure is a poetic reality to which verse—flesh and form—is essential. And in that reality, as he thinks it, as he brings it into being poetically, the poet must find the soul, the idea it carries—the idea in itself—the poetic experience from which it has arisen. Unamuno's poetry is by no means an addition, but springs from its own and irreplaceable source.

We have seen throughout this book that Unamuno believes reason does not avail for the understanding of life, that life's findings cannot have logical or conceptual expression, for this kills living reality; hence his novels, in which he shows human life descriptively and imaginatively, in its temporal element, in its intimate internal mobility. Very well, poetry is the culmination of that irrationalist tendency, that flight from concepts. In poetry expression is stripped bare, is made allusive, draws away from direct reference to things the better to capture their meaning. In the narrative, Unamuno reveals and describes figuratively the reality he perceives, which he lives in a very immediate way. In his poetry he goes still further: at the highest moments, when he grasps a truth he considers ineffable and even indescribable in narrative—but which, after all, retains a logical structure since it is a Logos, a saying—he has recourse to the poem, to pure metaphor, which barely brushes reality, which does not confront an experience in order to reveal it but attempts to provoke it allusively, by means of a sort of contagion. The poem tries to carry the one who reads it or hears it—the latter, more properly, for poetry is a thing of the ear—into the very situation in which the poet was when he wrote it. Thus, Unamuno can say of his verses that they "are fixed securely/in the rocky bosom of the eternal." At the same time, since they carry the very situation of the poet, they preserve it, keep it alive, able to relive in every reader, and this is a mode of survival. Let us examine this through some examples.

Knowledge of death is always sought by Unamuno in all imaginable ways; he attempts to prelive it from the point of view of *afterwards,* and even from the point of view of divine, immortal eternity. This is why he concentrates on the death of Christ, to find imaginatively the fulcrum of Divinity, and from it to look at human death *(El Cristo de Velázquez,* second part, verse II):

> "You were alone with your Father—
> alone, face to face with Him—
> and your looks mingled—the blues
> of His heaven with your eyes—
> and when infinity, His heart, lamented,
> the shoreless, depthless sea of Spirit trembled.

And God, feeling Himself man,
tasted of death, divine aloneness.
Your Father wished to feel what dying is;
one moment saw himself alone, without Creation,
when you, your head bent, offered up
your human breath to God's last sigh.
And to your last moan there only answered,
far-off and faint, the pitying sea."

The expectation of death, the reality of death whose uncertain inevitability threatens—*mors certa, hora incerta*—reveals itself, makes itself felt and lived in an immediate and heartfelt way in a poem from his *Romancero del destierro* called "Vendrá de noche" [She Will Come by Night]; by night she did come to him, to Unamuno suddenly and softly, when he died in 1936.

"She will come by night, when all is sleeping;
she will come by night, when the ailing soul
is muffled in life;
she will come by night, with her quiet footstep;
she will come by night, and lay her finger
upon the wound.
She will come by night, and her fleeting spark
will fan the fatal lament to flame;
she will come by night
bringing her rosary; she will loose the pearls
of that black sun which blinds us as we look
in a vast torrent!
She will come by night, night who is our mother,
on a night when memory cries, barking afar
like a lost omen;
she will come by night; and the far-off barking
will drown her footsteps, and in the West
will leave a rent. . .
Will she come on a night that is quiet and vast?
Will she come on a night maternal and chaste,
when the moon is full?

She will come, arriving with eternal coming,
she will come on a night of the very last winter. . . ,
        a quiet night . . .
She will come as she went, as she has always gone—
the fatal howl sounds faint and far away—
        she will keep her hour;
it will be by night, though it be the dawn;
she will come at her hour, when the air is weeping,
        weeping and musing. . .
She will come by night, on a night of brightness,
a moonlit night that shelters us from sorrow,
        a naked night;
she will come. . . , to come is to become. . . , the past
which passes and remains and stays awhile
        and never changes. . .
She will come by night, when time is waiting,
when the daylight lingers among the shadows
        and waits for dawn.
She will come by night, on a night of pureness,
a night when the blood is purged from the heat
        of noonday sun.
A night must be when she comes and enters,
when the worn-out heart will give itself to her,
        a night of calm.
She must come by night. . . she, he, or it?
By night she must stamp her dusky seal,
        night without care.
And night will come, the night that gives us life,
in which the soul forgets all night at last,
        and bring the cure;
the night will come, the night that covers all,
and reflects the heavens in the shining mire
        that purges it.
She will come by night, yes, she will come by night,
and her dark seal will fasten like a brooch
        and clasp the soul;

she will come by night without the slightest sound,
the barking will die away, far off and faint,
and calm will come. . .
and night will come. . ."

What is Unamuno *saying?* Strictly speaking, it is not a question of saying anything; he never even names death, nor speaks of it, nor takes up a position in regard to its being. He simply creates the atmosphere of its coming, of its arrival at a moment unknown to us; he makes its imminence felt, he makes us await it. The elements which could be discovered in this poem—night, silence, the faraway barking—are neither descriptive nor conceptual: they are only vital, and their purpose is to provoke, more than a state of mind, a temper, one which corresponds to the expectation of death. This is accomplished principally by the rhythm, by the reiteration of the verse line and the capital phrase—"she will come by night"—like an insistent litany which gradually submerges us in the expectant situation. The attempt to be on the other side, to see death consummated—that is, the central purpose of Unamuno's novel—becomes poetically lived in these lines:

"she will come. . . , to come is to become. . . , the past
which passes and remains and stays awhile
and never changes. . ."

and the immediate imminence, the imaginative anticipation, the feeling of "here it is," appears with insuperable force in a single line:

"A night must be when she comes and enters."

Finally, in the concluding lines, Unamuno captures the reality of consummated death, at once despairing and hopeful, extinguishment and dense silence, which persists in its silent being. Unamuno artfully avoids nothingness by means of an allusion to calm—calmness supposes a state of being, that is, a continuing to be—by means of the reiteration of a rhyme which he does not conclude, and even by the use of the line of dots, the living pause, which negates the ending:

"she will come by night without the slightest sound,

the barking will die away, far off and faint,
and calm will come. . .
and night will come. . ."

The whole circle of Unamuno's preoccupations, the whole repertory of his themes, almost what we might call his *Weltanschauung,* appear poetically condensed in his poem "Aldebarán" in *Rimas de dentro.*" The tonalities of the Universe, God, the relations between the two, infinity, consciousness, personality, love, death, and disquiet of mind are all transfigured in the poem. Its most characteristic note is that Unamuno manages to give faithful expression to his inner world, to what I have called his *Weltanschauung,* by means of the constant use of questions. It is the poetic expression of the problematical. Unamuno substitutes for enunciative speech—Aristotle's λόγος ῆοφχντικὸς, which affirms or denies—the pure question, which creates by its reiteration the atmosphere of unsatisfied disquiet, of agonized belief. Let us look at part of this poem:

"Ruby burning on the brow of God,
Aldebaran,
brilliant mystery,
pearl of light set in blood,
how many of God's days
have you watched the earth,
that speck of dust,
spin in the voids of space?
Did you see the sun burst forth, new born?
. . . . . . . . . . . . . . . .

Are you one of God's sleepless eyes,
always waking,
an eye scanning the darkness,
counting the worlds
in His flock?
Has He, perhaps, lost one?
Has another one been born?

And far beyond all visible spheres
what is there on the other side of space?
And farther yet than infinity,
say, Aldebaran, what lies there?
Where do the worlds end?
Do all pass by alone, in silence,
never once together?
Do all look across the heavens
toward one another, moving, moving,
each one in its path alone?
Say, would you not draw near to Sirius
and kiss him on the brow?
Some day, will not God
bring all His heavenly stars together
into one fold?
Will He not make of them a rose of light
to lie upon His breast?
What impossible loves
are hidden in the void?
What messages of ageless yearning
pass among the comets?
Are you all brothers?
Does Sirius' grief grieve you?
Tell me, Aldebaran.
Are you all moving toward a single end?
Can you hear the sun?
Can you hear me?
Do you know I breathe and suffer here
upon this earth, this speck of dust,
ruby burning on the brow of God,
Aldebaran?
If your soul shines in your light
what does its light illumine: love?
Is your life a secret?
Or do you mean nothing, shining there

on the brow of that shadowy God?
Are you an ornament and nothing more
that He has hung there for His own delight?

. . . . . . . . . . . . . . . . . .

The first man saw those shining hieroglyphs
that God's hand drew upon the sky,
and forever undecipherable
they wheel about this poor earth of ours.
Their changelessness, which compensates
the fateful shifting of the centuries,
is our link of quietude, a chain
of lofty permanence;
symbol of everlasting desire,
of thirst for truth unslaked forever,
those unchanging figures mean to us,
Aldebaran.
The long, long dreams of many centuries
were dreamed of you, heavenly hieroglyphs,
you who enclose the universe's riddle,
cloudy and stellar,
like hidden cords
that link us to the man of caverns.
He saw you, in his night of pain and hunger,
he saw you, an unwinking ruby,
Aldebaran,
and maddened, perhaps, with bloodshot eyes
he saw you as he died,
bloody eye of heaven,
eye of God,
Aldebaran!
And when you come to die?
When your light at last
melts into darkness?
When, cold and dark,
space for your shroud,

you roll away forever into nothingness?
This night-roof of our earth
embroidered with enigmas,
this starry cloth
of our poor tent,
is it the same that one day saw this dust
which now our footsteps tread upon
when living, burning eyes it forged
in human brows?
That selfsame dust the wind
now flails and whirls
was once the living breasts
of breathing human beings!
And that dust of stars
that spherical sandy shore
on which the sea of shadows beats,
was it not a proud body too,
was it not a soul's abode,
Aldebaran?
Is it not one still, burning Aldebaran?
Mysterious star, are you not still
a drop of living blood
in the veins of God?
Is not His body murky space?
And when you come to die
what will that body do with you?
Where will God, fighting for health,
toss you away, a lifeless star,
Aldebaran?
On what tremendous rubbish-heap of worlds?

. . . . . . . . . . . . . .

Shed your blood-red light
upon my tomb, Aldebaran,
and if one day we return to earth
let me find you, motionless and mute,

the word of eternal mystery witheld!
If the Supreme Truth should bind us
we would all return to nothing!
Your silence is the pledge of all eternity,
Aldebaran!

We see that Unamuno's poetry has a value which is not only literary and aesthetic but its own and irreplaceable. It is the intent to transmit through spiritual contagion the profoundest and most ineffable part of his knowing or his yearning to know. Think of the function of the poems in the mystic work of St. John of the Cross, which sum up in a very concentrated form the spiritual content of his books in prose; and the verse is essential in this condensation, for without it that transference of the reader to a situation which cannot be expressed or is impossible to express in human terms cannot be achieved.

And there is yet more. Poetry represents the crystallization and fixation of form; in poetry, spirit is confined into permanent and material forms, which are transmitted and survive without alteration. It is rather like what occurs with the liturgy; and Unamuno is very conscious of the value of prayers, which he thinks of in a certain sense as verse. Thus, the personality of the author is preserved in the integral memory of the poem, destined to be repeated without change, to become present again and again in its rigorously identical form. The survival of name and fame which worried Unamuno so much has a higher form, which is the survival of the author's spirit in his readers; and this is achieved in the strictest and most faithful sense in poetry, a medal struck once and for all, which renews its living vibration each time its rhythm is reproduced. In one of his last songs Unamuno explicitly stated this lifelong yearning of his:

"I exile myself to memory,
I go to live on remembrance.
If I am lost to you, seek me
in the desert waste of history.
For life to me is sickness
and my sick man's life is dying.

I go, then, go to the wasteland
where even death will forget me.
I take you with me, my brothers,
to people my desert for me.
And when you think me most lifeless
I will stir in your hands as you hold me.
And here I leave with you my soul—
a book, a man—a true world.
When all of you trembles as you read
it is I, reader, who tremble in you."

## THE POETIC NARRATIVE

We have already seen how Unamuno always required spiritual creatures about him, how he needed outside companionship; and when he was not writing novels or drama, when he was not creating fictional beings, he made commentaries. Hence his books of essays, filled with quotations—sources of personality, as I said above—in which he supports every word on the statement of a living man to give it reality. In his poems he tends to do the same. Those which consist of pure lyric effusion are rare; and these are precisely the ones in which he is most present, in which he pours out his whole soul, and in which his own personality is enough for him. In the other cases he seeks supports to cling to, his own or those of others. Hence the abundance of dates, the desire to fix a concrete moment of his life with all precision: "On the train from Bilbao to Salamanca, near Orduña, 20-IX-10," is the note to one of his sonnets. And this is constant. In his *Rosario de sonetos líricos* there is hardly one which does not sum up some concrete instant, similarly noted, or enlarge upon a quotation from another author.

The same occurs in his books *Romancero del destierro* and *De Fuerteventura a París;* in the latter a commentary in prose follows the verse, which is in itself a commentary, and what is always sought is to create a spiritual circumstance. This is expressed in a more complete and deliberate way in his poem *El Cristo de Velázquez,* a commentary on a painting—and what is expressed in it—which follows the Scripture step by step, with the Biblical verses indicated in the margin in order to rethink and refeel poetically, alongside the poet's verse, the word of God. In his book *Cómo se hace una novela* Unamuno picked up Cassou's statement that all his work is only a commentary. He said: "But the fact is that to make commentaries is to make history. Just as to write telling how a novel is made is to make it. Is the life of each one of us any more than a novel? Is there a more novelesque novel than an autobiography?" *

This brings him to the poetic narrative, which of course cannot be a novel in verse, nor even a stage play, for in these cases the verse becomes trivial and loses its poetry in the continuity of the whole work, by the very nature of its presentation. For this reason Shakespeare and later the Romantics properly mixed prose and verse in their tragedies and dramas. Unamuno, who is strictly lyrical, cannot make up his mind to write what is usually called a "sustained poem," which is liable to lapse into prose when the tension of the verse is made too commonplace. He writes a collection of verses, joined by a unity of spirit, by a situation from which they all arise; and this discontinuous history of a soul, in short lyrical bursts, makes up an authentic poetic narrative: *Teresa,* the story of Rafael, a young provincial who has lost his sweetheart, Teresa, through death from tuberculosis; and he recalls her, relives her, as he waits for his own impending death. The subject is ordinary, elementary, essentially commonplace, and from this deliberate lack of originality arises the immediate originalness of Rafael and Teresa's simple and intimate passion of love. It is also a poem of everyday life, made authentic and turned in on itself and on transcendence by death and the imminent hope of the other life.

In the first group of verses the atmosphere and general sense of the drama are established; it is like a mathematical statement of the narrative, its minimal expression, which later will be extended in bursts of expansion, in the heartbeats of Rafael's life and even Teresa's, for she lives in his memory and in his love, which yearns to be realized. In these verses is given the keynote of the whole story, which is

* Page 47.

*shared death,* in the only way in which it is possible, the death of the two persons essentially united by love. That death, which at the beginning is merely suggested, acquires a clearer shape, a greater density in the course of the narrative, until it discloses to Rafael its imminent presence, and with it that of Teresa, now on the point of returning to him.

"I was near your window
not knowing how I came;
I spoke into your ear
telling of our love;
and you, all in confusion,
wrapped in your modesty,
listened while time was passing
and looked all about you.
The days were very long,
the nights were very short,
painful were my reproaches,
and you—you were not with me!
The bed slipped out from under
my heart, suddenly cold;
I felt emptiness beneath me,
clung to the bars at its head.
I saw myself as finished,
like a man who is dying,
I begged of you, yearning,
one drop of your faith.
And I lay down to death,
the death I dream of, Teresa.
Is it a bed or a grave?
Teresa, I no longer know.
The sad smile that fled
from your pallid lips
blew away in the breeze
the day that you died.
And then? Then I saw
you were dying too,

and one destiny joined,
fatally, our two deaths.
I know that your poor heart,
turned into holy dust,
awaits me there, Teresa;
the eternal hour will come.
Oh, what a dismal nightmare!
To be born. . . to live. . . and then
the fires of Purgatory
and death before our time."

Other verses follow, among them memories of their broken life together, meditation on Rafael's own interrupted love, whose meaning becomes ever more clear to him, and the invisible presence of death. Rafael lives in a state of tension, scarcely touching the present, suspended between memories of the past summed up in a death, Teresa's, and the anticipation of the future reunion of the two which will take place with Rafael's death. And life becomes a brief, unstable road, full of haste. Stanza 7—another interrogative poem—relives the astonishment in the face of one's own destiny which makes the whole of reality questionable. Once more Unamuno makes use of that artifice of language which is the question in order to provoke in the reader the suspension which has reference to the future, which demands and at the same time denies repose, the impatient and despairing waiting.

"And why those lilies the frosts have withered?
Why those roses the sun has burned?
Why must the young birds die as fledglings
    and never learn to fly?
And why the lives by heaven squandered
before new links of life are forged?
Why did your poor heart stop, Teresa,
    choking your maiden blood?
And why did our two bloods never mingle
in love's most holy sacrament?
Why could we never bloom and flower,
    Teresa of my soul?

Why and for what were we born, Teresa?
Why and for what were we two at all?
Why and for what does all mean nothing?
Why did God make us live?"

And at the end of the book the theme of common death, of *shared death* which love can accomplish by means of the union of two lives, appears in its full and true light. The death of one of the two lovers includes the other, it is a partial death for him; hence the unstable situation of the lover who is alive, with a foot in each world, tensed to take the step anticipated in his attitude. In Stanza 75 Rafael says:

"Man cannot see God's face and live;
together you and I have seen God's face;
now you are dead
and I, in the desert,
can only walk behind your saintly steps.
But I died too;
I died, and dream now of our mother Death;
I died in you,
that is the greatest love.
I saw God in your eyes and with them,
our mingled eyes saw God together;
our sight was common,
and then our two lives died together
in one embrace.
Since you and I saw living God together
by God's grace death has given me life."

After this the dénouement of the narrative arrives quickly; for it is, strictly speaking, a story whose solution, whose unraveling, comes with death. The yearning for death becomes stronger and stronger in Rafael; it fills him with a jubilant joy of arrival:

". . .Oh, when the day comes that I embrace you. . . !
Eternity will be too short!

. . . . . . . . . . . . . . . . .

I give you birth each day when I awake,
what a sweet death dreaming is!

I'm drowning in a sea of wishing;
oh, terrible wish to die!"

And in Stanza 93, when death is now very close, when Rafael feels it is certain, gratitude to God for imminent death, already within his grasp, surges forth:

"I thank Thee, Lord, now that at last I'm dying,
my God, I give all thanks to Thee;
no more a slave of Time that kills us,
for love has set me free.
Now all the heavens blush with roses,
now sings eternity;
now, now I feel that every creature
basks in reality.

. . . . . . . . . . . . . . . . . . . .

I know now why I've lived, what I was born for;
I know the why of everything!

. . . . . . . . . . . . . . . . . . . .

I thank Thee, Lord, now that at last I'm dying,
my God, I give all thanks to Thee;
for only now I praise our love most truly
and thank Thee for our love."

At last, in the final stanzas (94, 95) there is a series of metaphors whose intent is to capture the emotion or impression of approaching death; once more Unamuno tries to touch the irrevocable moment with his imagination, to feel its awesome nearness:

"I hear the murmur of Death approaching,
the velvet step of a naked foot. . .
I feel her winged arm brush the air. . ."

And then:

"She clasps me with her wings like a great bat,
to press me to the earth—a black, closed sea. . ."

Unamuno's poetic narrative, therefore, the only one he wrote in maturity, restates the central themes of his novels. Is it, then, just one more novel? By no means. If *Teresa* were to be told in prose it would be annulled, would vanish under our hands. To demonstrate this, Unamuno chooses an ordinary and extremely commonplace theme, a minimum number of personages, as far as possible from being characters, from literary myths. Not Romeo and Juliet, not Othello and Desdemona, but Rafael and Teresa, two poor country youngsters who die of consumption in the middle of their engagement. It is an attempt to capture lyrically the theme of death from the point of view of love's reality. And precisely this commonplace, though strictly authentic and therefore personalized, love raises the characters to the necessity of sharing death, turns them face to face with eternity. The poetry introduces us into this tiny world, brings us into the moving situation of the tale, binds us to it and places us in the tension of its inevitable outcome. The rhyme constantly repeats, repeats its moments, as in the monotonous life of the provinces or in the engagement—a waiting—and in the second waiting, that of waiting for death. And then the verse gradually sinks deep into the spirit and makes us relive, in the only direct and efficacious way, the profound story which is the flower of everyday life.

# VII.

# *RELIGION IN THE WORK OF UNAMUNO*

## THE POINT OF DEPARTURE

Unamuno's whole work is bathed in a religious atmosphere; in him, any theme whatever ends by showing its religious roots or culminates in an ultimate reference to God. And fundamentally he was not interested in anything unless he could reduce it in some way to the terms of his permanent preoccupation. From this arose his intimate literary and intellectual preferences, his dislike for the merely literary in an artistic sense or for the scientific and the erudite, and his manifest hostility toward the attitude which tends to turn man's attention to exclusive concern with his temporal and fleeting life, rather than occupying itself with the other life; concretely, in his implacable aversion to sociology and pedagogy, and still more to sociological and pedagogical perversions of religion.

Unamuno's readings, especially those which are most alive in him, those which appear most frequently and authentically in his writings, are predominantly philosophical and religious. Unamuno, a man of immensely wide reading, though with a spirit that was not at all erudite, showed his preferences very clearly, and they are revealing: Scripture above all, principally the New Testament, and within the New Testament St. Paul, who is rarely absent from Unamuno's thought. After that come a number of spirits essentially moved by religion in one form or another: St. Augustine, Pascal, Spinoza, Rousseau, Sénancour, Leopardi, Kirkegaard, Butler, St. Theresa, St. John of the Cross, and St. Ignatius. Then, the thinkers, like Kant or James, who have grappled most directly with the theme of religion, and the theologians and ascetics; the latter interest him more, and among the theologians he has an indubitable preference for the Protestants or for those who are close to agnosticism: Schleiermacher, Harnack, Ritschl, and Luther himself. On the other hand, the most rigorous philosophers and the Catholic theologians appear less frequently in his pages, and the mention he makes of them is not always cordial; he was not by any means enchanted with the figures of Aristotle, St. Thomas, Duns Scotus, Descartes, Suárez, Hegel, or Leibnitz. And, lastly, Unamuno enjoyed the poets in whom a profound and even religious sense of existence is displayed: the Greek tragedians, Leopardi, Antero de Quental, and especially the English Shakespeare, Tennyson, Wordsworth, Thomson, Byron, Browning; and, of course, Dante.

What is the nature of this evident religious preoccupation of Unamuno's? His point of departure is man himself and his yearning for survival, for immortality. In Unamuno, not God but man himself is the immediate basis of religious feeling; it is he who leads us to postulate God. He speaks of "the truly religious temper, which tells us through the voice of Paul of Tarsus, 'But, if there be no resurrection of the dead, then is Christ not risen; and if Christ be not risen, then is our preaching vain and your faith is also vain.' " * And he adds: "If religion is not founded on the intimate feeling of our own substantiality and the perpetuation of that substance, then it is not religion, no. Faith in God begins with faith in our own substantial existence." †

In chapter IV of *Del sentimiento trágico de la vida* he reiterates this point of view, and says that the specifically Christian is the discovery of immortality and belief in the resurrection of Christ: "He who does not believe in the resurrection of Christ in the flesh may be a Christophile, but he is not specifically a Christian." And this is why he says, in the essay I have just mentioned: "Faith in the resurrection, that is, in the immortality of Christ, which is the nucleus as it was the seed of Christianity, has been for Christians, whether they knew it or not, the support of faith in their own immortality,

* I Corinthians 15:13–14.

† "¡Plenitud de plenitudes y todo plenitud!" [Plenitude of plenitudes and all is plenitude!] *Ensayos,* V, 85–86.

fount of the intimate life of the spirit. And so Athanasius could say that Christ had deified men (θεοποιεῖν), that He had made them gods." These are ideas which Unamuno glosses at length in his poem *El Cristo de Velázquez* and in all his writings.

This point of departure, accurate though a trifle unilateral, since it pays heed exclusively to the immortalizing relation of God to man, to the guarantee of survival, without taking account of the actual relation of man to Divinity, seems to place Unamuno solidly within Christianity, and even in positive meditation about it. For he affirms his decision to seek the truth, to wrestle with the mystery, to strive untiringly toward knowing. In his essay "Mi religión" (1907), Unamuno writes: "My religion is to seek truth in life and life in truth, even in the knowledge that I am not to find them while I live; my religion is to wrestle unceasingly and untiringly with mystery; my religion is to wrestle with God from the break of day till the coming of night [*sic*] as they say Jacob wrestled with Him. I cannot reconcile myself to that idea of the Unknowable—the Incognoscible, as the pedants say—nor with that other idea of 'further than this thou shalt not pass.' I reject the eternal *ignorabimus.* And in any case I wish to clamber to the inaccessible." Unamuno postulates here a ceaseless effort to penetrate the mystery, to know God, realizing that he will not achieve it while he lives. There also appear to echo in this passage the *fides quaerens intellectum* of St. Augustine and the *Deum nemo vidit umquam* of Scripture. It could be expected, then, that Unamuno would direct his activity toward the achievement of an effective knowledge of God; faith, he frequently says, cannot rest but seeks the support of reason. It seems that the result of this attitude of Unamuno's would be a theological task, or a philosophical one if you will, concerned with the great theme of Divinity. Is this actually the case?

## APPEARANCE OF AGNOSTICISM

As a continuation of the paragraph just quoted, Unamuno writes the following sentences, which at once clarify and diminish the integrity of the preceding words. "[Christ] placed the unattainable as the goal and boundary of our efforts. And he did this, the theologians say, through grace. And I want to fight my battle without concern for victory. Are there not armies and even peoples who go forth to certain defeat? Do we not praise those who die fighting rather than surrender? Well, that is my religion." We observe several things of interest in this revealing passage: in the first place, Unamuno, after saying that God gives His grace to help men reach a goal unattainable in itself, drops the idea; in the second place, he does not say that he doubts the victory, but that he wishes to fight without concern for victory; in the third place, he alludes to praise of those who die fighting. What does this mean?

The first part might seem to be pure rationalism, the desire to attain truth through one's own reason alone; this, as Gratry has said, already involves a certain lack of interest in the truth, for the man who truly yearns after truth and needs it will seek it by every means, without eliminating any possible approach. Unamuno says elsewhere that into the search go his peace of conscience and consolation for having been born, all his interior life and the mainspring of his actions; if this is so, how can he renounce anything? This ultimate lack of interest is revealed in his phrase about not concerning himself with victory; the man who fights from necessity, not for sport or exhibition, fights for victory and, naturally, is concerned with it. And, lastly, what does praise matter? Can it not be that Unamuno is seeking the joy of combat, of his own agony, with a desire for praise, for appearing interesting and gallant, at least in his own eyes? May there not be an excessive complacency in that agony, which of course strips it of ultimate basis and seriousness? And, most especially, one must ask why Unamuno holds from the outset the belief that defeat is certain, that it is impossible to know, all of which eliminates *a radice* his own longing.

We find the reply to this question in the same essay, a bit farther on, and can follow its vital development in Unamuno's most concretely intellectual books, which are those of religious concern: *Del sentimiento trágico de la vida* and *La agonía del cristianismo*. On the one hand, Unamuno is not inclined—and this from the outset, which is a grave matter—to accept any orthodoxy, and particularly the Catholic orthodoxy, in fact the only one possible for him; the cause of this is a frivolous desire for uniqueness, for differentness. And I call his heterodoxy frivolous because Unamuno, who expressed so many philological opinions on heresy or choice *(hairesis)* and upon the possibility that the *other* opinion (heterodoxy) might be the *right* opinion (orthodoxy), sought above all to choose the *other,* isolated, solitary opinion rather than the right or true one; Unamuno is deliberately heterodox, a priori, without transcendental reasons, and this must be called, regretfully and severely, frivolity. "They want to try to pigeonhole me and put me in one of those square boxes spirits are crammed into, saying of me, he is a Lutheran, a Calvinist, a Catholic, an atheist, a rationalist, a mystic, or any other of those labels whose real meaning they are unaware of, but which excuse them from thinking any more about it. And I refuse to be pigeonholed, because I, Miguel de Unamuno, like any other man who aspires to full consciousness, am a species in myself." Note that Unamuno wants to avoid being pigeonholed; he does not say, "I can't" be orthodox, but "I won't"; he wants to be, as St. Thomas says of the angels, a unique species, exhausted in himself.

On the other hand, Unamuno does not believe—I repeat once more —in reason's capacity to achieve the truth about God. In the same essay there is a passage which clearly formulates his position in regard to this:

"I sincerely confess that the supposed rational proofs—the ontological, the cosmological, the ethical, etc., etc.—of the existence of God *do not prove anything to me;* that all the reasons which attempt to prove a God exists seem to me to be reasons based on sophistry and begging of the question. In this regard I stand with Kant. . .

"Nobody has succeeded in convincing me rationally of the existence of God, or of His nonexistence either; the reasonings of the atheists seem to me to be of a superficiality and futility even greater than those of their contradictors. And if I believe in God, or at least believe that I believe in Him, it is first of all because I *want* God to exist, and next because He is revealed to me, *by way of the heart,* in the Gospels and through Christ and history. *It is an affair of the heart. . .*

"I do not know, that is certain; perhaps I can never know; but I 'want' to know. I want to, and that suffices.

"And I shall spend my life wrestling with the mystery even without any hope of penetrating it, for that struggle is *my sustenance and my consolation*. Yes, my consolation. I have got used to extracting hope from my very despair." *

Unamuno rejects the traditional proofs of the existence of God; not only does he believe them insufficient, but he states that they prove *nothing*, which seems sufficiently precipitate and excessive; but, above all, he rejects them without trying to find substitutes for them, without attempting to complete them or to find others which might be workable, and almost without serious examination. The reflections he makes upon them in chapter VIII of *Del sentimiento trágico de la vida* are intellectually slovenly and represent no substantive effort to clarify the problem rationally. Rather, Unamuno takes as his point of departure the assumption that reason is impotent, and that consequently any attempt to achieve the truth by this means is idle. For him the only way of approach to God is cordial, a thing of the heart, in the double sense of wanting and feeling. Unamuno will always dwell lovingly on this struggle, which later he will come to call agony, on this sentimental zeal for God motivated by his yearning for immortality, but will never be capable of really bringing his faculties to bear on an attempt really to know. This is why he can accept without any difficulty the doctrine of Schleiermacher which places the essence of religion in the feeling of dependence: "Schleiermacher's doctrine, which places the origin, or rather the essence of the religious sentiment in the immediate and simple feeling of dependence, seems to be the most profound and accurate explanation." † This also explains his receptivity—partial at least—to the Modernist movement, which was at its apogee when Unamuno completed his intellectual formation. (See, for example, his essay of 1908, "Verdad y vida" [Truth and Life].)

We observe, then, a strict parallelism between the fate of both philosophy and religion at Unamuno's hands. He moves in an ambit of metaphysical and religious preoccupation; the problem of man

* The italics in the passage above are mine.
† *Del sentimiento trágico de la vida,* chapter VIII.

and the problem of God—and that of their relation—engross all his interest and all his mental activity. But in both cases, instead of launching himself upon the course of knowledge, even though he might return with empty hands at the end of the voyage, he gives up the task, the adventure, because he believes from the outset that reason cannot bring him to a safe harbor. At the same time, his desire to be different will not allow him to remain in an orthodox, received position which he shares with his fellows. And then, having turned his back on the most authentic aspect of the problem and yet unable to withdraw from it, he launches forth into marginal paths, seeking substitutes for reason in the enjoyment of his own initial anguish, which all too often inevitably deprives that anguish of ultimate authenticity. Unamuno's novels, as well as his poetry, and his "agonic" and capricious essays, all his literary genres, spring from this, wherein problems are disguised and sometimes falsified, though occasionally they appear in all their true drama. This is apparent more than anywhere else in certain deeply felt passages in his narratives which we have noted above.

Back in the eleventh century, St. Anselm, the true founder of Scholasticism, one of the men who has most deeply and profoundly plumbed with his reason the problem of God, clearly defined the intellectual position suitable for a religious man: "Christianus," he wrote in his epistle XLI, "per fidem debet ad intellectum proficere, non per intellectum ad fidem accedere; aut si intelligere non valet, a fide recedere. Sed cum ad intellectum valet pertingere, delectatur: cum vero nequit, cum capere non potest, veneratur." ("The Christian should advance by means of faith toward intelligence, not reach faith by means of intelligence or, if he cannot understand, retreat from faith. For when he can arrive by intelligence, he rejoices; but when he cannot, when he cannot understand, then he worships.") Unamuno, at least in his intellectual and written work, lacked faith; not only religious faith *sensu stricto,* faith in the total truth of the Christian religion, but also faith in the capacity of human reason to arrive at the point of understanding; he lacked too the splendid humility which worships a truth not understood, yet which he will not and cannot renounce. This is the reason for the agonized agnosticism which dominates a large part of Unamuno's work, although here and there he tears himself away from it long enough to show a more authentic and profound reality.

## THE RELIGIOUS CONTENT

Now we can ask ourselves what is, in the last instance, the religious content of Unamuno's work. But the question is not quite univocal; therefore we must draw some distinctions. In the first place, we are dealing with the presence of religion in Unamuno, passing over for the moment any problem of confession; in the second place, it will be necessary to make clear his concrete relation to Christianity, and the meaning of his position from Christianity's viewpoint.

"The sense of the divine," Unamuno writes, "makes us wish and believe that everything is animate, that consciousness, in greater or less degree, extends to everything. We long not only to save ourselves, but to save the world from nothingness. This is what God is for. This is His felt purpose.

"Can one imagine a universe without any consciousness to reflect and know it? Can one imagine reason objectivized, without will or feeling? For us, the same as nothingness; a thousand times more fearsome than nothingness.

"If such a supposition should turn out to be true, then our life has no value or meaning.

"What leads us to believe in God is not, then, rational necessity but vital anguish. And to believe in God is, before all and above all, I must repeat, to feel hunger for God, hunger for divinity, to feel His absence and void, to will that God exist. And it means to want to save the human purpose of the Universe. For one could even come to the point of resigning oneself to being absorbed by God, if our consciousness is based on a Consciousness, if consciousness is the aim of the Universe.

" 'The evil man has said in his heart: there is no God.' And that is the truth. For a just man can say in his mind: 'God does not exist!' But only the evil man can say it in his heart. Not to believe that there is a God, or to believe that there is not, is one thing; to resign oneself to His not existing is another, though inhuman and horrible; but not to want Him to exist exceeds every other moral monstrosity. Although in fact those who deny God do so through despair at not finding Him.

"And now the rational question comes again, a Sphinxlike question —for the Sphinx is in fact reason: 'Does God exist?' That eternal and eternalizing Person who gives meaning—and I will not add 'human,' for there is no other—to the Universe. Is He something substantial outside our own consciousness, outside our own yearnings? Here is an insoluble problem, and it is better it should be so. Let it suffice that reason cannot prove the impossibility of His existence.

"To believe in God is to long for Him to exist, and further it is to act as though He existed; it is to live by that desire and make of it our private mainspring of action." *

As we see here, Unamuno bases himself almost exclusively on the need or hunger for God, to the point of identifying it with belief in Him, which is, at the very least, excessive. In the second place, his idea of God is, for the present, that of an eternal consciousness which at the same time eternalizes us; at the moment no other divine attribute interests him, no other relation between man and Divinity. The theme of creation does not appear, nor do those of justification or sanctification, nor even the intense desire of the vision of God for the sake of God Himself, not as a simple guarantee of survival. In the third place, Unamuno declares the problem of the existence of God to be rationally insoluble, without even making a serious effort to prove his own assertion; he mistrusts the capacity of reason and at the same time fears that the result of its exercise may not be positive; his faith is not sufficiently firm, and therefore he says that it would be better if the question could not be resolved rationally. This insecurity of his faith is understandable, since he finds no other basis for it except in his sense of lack, his hunger, his deprivation of God. This is something, of course; but only enough to begin the search. Does Unamuno find no positive reference to God? Has he no fulcrum?

* *Del sentimiento trágico de la vida,* end of chapter VIII.

A few pages before, Unamuno had written: "As I sank deeper and deeper into rational skepticism on the one hand and my heart's despair on the other, the hunger for God flamed up in me and my oppression of spirit made me feel His reality through lack of Him. And God does not exist, but rather superexists, and He sustains our existence by existing us." He specifically points out the sense of deprivation of God as an indication of His reality; and this reality appears to him as sustaining ours, as that which makes us exist, that "exists us," says Unamuno boldly, making the verb transitive—an intuition of tremendous implications, to which we shall have to return later.* In chapter IX he adds: "I believe in God as I believe in my friends, because I feel the breath of His love and His invisible and intangible hand, which draws me hither and thither, and clasps me. . . Again and again in my life I have been suspended over the abyss; again and again I have found myself at a crossroads where a whole network of pathways were spread out before me, and if I took one I would have to renounce the others, for the roads of life are irreversible; and again and again in such exceptional moments I have felt the pressure of a conscious force, mighty and loving. And then the path of the Lord opens out before one." Unamuno speaks here of a contact with God, a personal dealing with Him, and at the same time of His guiding impulse, which sends a person in a certain direction, points out a mission in life. But neither of these perceptions can carry him even so far as an attempt at the knowledge of Divinity; at bottom, Unamuno is firmly fixed in the idealism which dominated European philosophy up to the end of the nineteenth century; for the few doctrines apart from idealism were either little-known attempts to carry the matter further of which he was probably unaware—at least in their true scope—or else they had little to do with philosophy. Thus he can write a few lines later: "What does it mean, in fact, to exist, and when do we say that a thing exists? To exist means that something is placed outside of us in such a way that it preceded our perception of it and can subsist outside of us after we are gone. And can I really be sure that anything preceded me or that anything will survive me? Can my consciousness know that there is anything outside itself? Whatever I know or can know

* See Chapter VIII, "El tema de Dios" [The Theme of God].

resides in my consciousness. Let us not become embroiled in the insoluble problem of an objectivity apart from our perceptions, for whatever acts, exists, and to exist is to act."

This paragraph contains a vivid example of the range of Unamuno's philosophical ideas—or rather, of his convictions. Next to a typical realist's idea of reality as that which is independent of me appears the idealist's concept of knowledge as knowing about my own consciousness and its states. Further, he is strangely precipitate in decreeing that the problem of the objectivity of perceptions is insoluble, and ends with a call to a dynamic and active idea of existence, which has a pragmatist flavor in spite of its echo—which I believe to be purely formal—of Leibnitz. Precisely for this reason Unamuno must abandon rational knowledge of God, because in Him, he says elsewhere, only an *idea* can be grasped. Unamuno's philosophical assumptions, limited by the circumstance of his time, condition his position in regard to the problem of God.

And this God of Unamuno's, who only occasionally appears as the support and real basis of existence, and scarcely as creator or sanctifier, is, almost exclusively, the guarantee of personal immortality. When Unamuno speaks of salvation, he does not understand it primarily as heavenly beatitude, the beatific vision of God as opposed to eternal damnation, but simply survival, salvation from nothingness, from the annihilation beyond death. Frequently, on the other hand, Christians do not concern themselves with the life everlasting, the resurrection of the dead, and the *venturum saeculum,* but think only of the otherworldly reward or punishment, not, naturally, because of lack of faith in that survival, but, on the contrary, because they consider it an obvious assumption—or, which is much the same thing, because they believe in it not with living but with dead faith. There are many ways of forgetting things, and one of them, one of the most serious, is to forget them purely and simply because they are so well known. And it does occur that some Christians—particularly Protestants, who pay attention, as Unamuno so accurately points out, to *justification* more than anything else, and almost convert religion into ethics—believe much more intensely and strongly that they will go to Heaven or Hell than they believe in the life everlasting; which is illogical, but vitally possible. They are able to "realize" the idea of eternal reward or punishment, and they suffer anguish at the thought of their final fate, but they do not feel the living hope of eternal life as such, nor anguish at the fear of annihilation. Unamuno, on the contrary, represents the extreme inverse of this attitude, and for him all religion is reduced to concern for his personal immortality and the consolation of his tormented yearning.

This is why he says at the end of chapter X of the *Sentimiento:* "One must believe in the other life, in the eternal life beyond the tomb, in an individual and personal life in which each one of us will feel his consciousness and will feel it sinking, without being confused with all the other consciousnesses, into the Supreme Consciousness, into God; one must believe in that other life in order to be able to live this one, and bear it, and give it meaning and purpose. And perhaps one must believe in that other life in order to deserve it, to attain it; or perhaps the man who does not desire it above all reason, or even against reason if that were necessary, does not deserve it or attain it." Then he recalls Sénancour's famous phrase, which he repeats so often, from letter XL of his *Obermann: L'homme est périssable. Il se peut; mais périssons en résistant, et, si le néant nous est réservé, ne faisons pas que ce soit une justice.* Clear Kantian traces are to be noted in this position, in accordance with the doctrine that, when life demands to be continued, when it claims prolongation so as to bring its labor to fruition and achieve its true meaning, this postulates immortality, and even proves it up to a point. Unamuno is using this way of approach when he says that the question man cries aloud to God is, "Tell me Thy name!," and adds, "We ask Him His name so that He may save our souls, so that He may save the human soul, so that He may save the human purpose of the universe. . . and there is only one Name which can satisfy our longing, and this name is Saviour: Jesus." * From the very center of his vital agnostic preoccupation with immortality, Unamuno appeals to Christianity.

* *Del sentimiento trágico de la vida,* chapter VIII.

## CHRISTIANITY

But this Christianity of Unamuno's, do not forget, is always vacillating, and therefore heterodox. We have already seen how he recoiled from what he called "being pigeonholed," and took refuge in a vague sentimental and appreciative attachment toward the specifically Christian. In his essay, "Mi religión" (1907), he writes: "I have, yes, with my sentiments, with my heart, with my feelings, a strong tendency toward Christianity, without adhering to special dogmas of this or that Christian confession. I consider Christian everyone who invokes the name of Christ with respect and love, and I am repelled by those orthodox persons, be they Catholics or Protestants—the latter are likely to be as intransigent as the former—who deny Christianity to those who do not interpret the Gospel as they do." But then, in his book *Del sentimiento trágico de la vida* (1912), he reacts against this position and states, as we saw before, that "he who does not believe in the resurrection of Christ in the flesh may be a Christophile, but he is not specifically a Christian." And later he insists at length on the central position of the resurrection of Christ within the Christian religion, and very concretely in Catholicism. With this, though on the one hand he rises above his earlier vague concept of Christianity and approaches its true meaning more closely, on the other hand, when he interprets it more strictly, his deviations also appear even more strongly emphasized. Was Unamuno a true Christian, or did he never get past being a Christophile? Surely neither of the two, for he lacked humility, fundamental seriousness, and in the last instance faith, in the strict sense, to be the former; and he had too much depth and spirituality to go no further than the latter. Unamuno recognizes the contradiction, and defines himself as skeptic, agonic, and polemic (see particularly *La agonía del cristianismo*). He has recourse again and again to the words of the father mentioned in St. Mark (9:24): "I believe; help Thou mine unbelief," and speaks constantly of the will to and even "just wanting" to believe. And in this "wanting to believe," in this agonized doubt, he remains permanently fixed.

Unamuno never made a courageous and implacable effort to

emerge from that doubt. Perhaps he refused to emerge from it, probably from fear of falling back into denial, but this caution of his, comprehensible if he had felt himself rooted in a faith, however weak and vacillating, arises from a situation of restlessness, of intimate unease. "Faith," says Unamuno, "proceeds from grace and not from free will. The man who merely wants to believe does not believe." It proceeds from grace, and he cannot feel that he holds it in his hand; but, since he does not have it, what about reason? We have already seen that he does not trust it, that it seems to him impotent to penetrate the mystery of God and man, of human life and personality, mysteries which appear to him to be summed up and inextricably mingled in his *sole question,* that of death and immortality. But, how can Unamuno believe in the impotence of reason before he has put it sufficiently to the test? And when does a man consider that the impossibility of something on which—in his own words—the meaning of life and the consolation for having been born depend, has been sufficiently demonstrated? When, except in death? One might have expected of Unamuno a desperate intellectual effort to rend the veil of the mystery, if indeed he had felt an urgency to solve the problem which could not be gainsaid. And, in truth, an excessive complacency can be glimpsed in that doubt, in that *agony* he speaks of so much and yet which never resolves itself into a radical attempt to exhaust the possibilities of reason for achieving truth. Unamuno says many times that in his struggle he finds his consolation; but a restlessness which is *able* to turn its back on the attempt to calm itself once and for all is not radical nor ultimate. If Unamuno was able to remain, even with a certain enjoyment, in a state of agonized doubt about God and himself, about whether he must die altogether or not, it means two things: first, that there is in it an element of fiction, of the penultimate and of a lack of ultimate urgency; and in the second place, that beneath that doubt there is a deeper faith in which he is rooted and from which he lives, a faith that permits him to carry out his dialectic exercises—which nevertheless are deeply felt and full of emotion—with his feet firmly planted on this foundation. What is that radical belief? This is the real question which we must clarify.

Unamuno finds himself implanted in a vital Christian tradition, Catholic, maintained and enriched throughout his life by his constant reading, especially by his assiduous recourse to the New Testament, whose Greek original never left his side. And this, united with his profound religious sense, an attitude which always leaned toward God, makes him feel, underneath all his ideas and all his doubts, the presence of God in his life; the Christian God, One and Triune, with His three persons, with the virgin motherhood of Mary, with the entire content of the Catholic liturgy; a God represented and made visible in images, above all in those bloody Spanish Christs he liked so well, and still more in the Christ of Velázquez, which moves him to authentic and pious devotion. In spite of his problematical intellectual attachment, Unamuno actually lives within the spiritual ambit of Catholicism. And this accounts for the fact that an extraordinarily vivid Christian sense flowers in his pages, replete with immediacy and intimate reality.

For example, in chapter XI of *Del sentimiento trágico de la vida,* where he speaks doubtingly, with extreme intellectual insufficiency, and even with verbal irreverence of many Christian dogmas, he writes these words, which reflect keenly and vividly the religious sense of daily labor, of the work of every man, famous or obscure: "Here you have a shoemaker who lives by making shoes, and makes them with the exact amount of care necessary to keep and not lose his customers. Another shoemaker lives on a somewhat higher spiritual plane, for he takes pride in his job, and for pique or a point of honor he does his best to pass for the best shoemaker in the city or the realm, even though this may not give him a larger clientele or greater earnings but merely more renown or prestige. But there is a still higher degree of moral perfection in the trade of shoemaking, and it is to aspire to make oneself for one's customers the unique and irreplaceable shoemaker, the one who makes their shoes in such a way that they will necessarily miss him when he 'goes and dies on them'—'dies on them,' not just 'dies'—and so that they, his customers, will feel that he ought not to have died, and this because he made their shoes with the intention of sparing them any discomfort, so that concern for their feet never kept them from the contemplation of the highest truths; he made their shoes for love of them and for love of God in them; he did it out of religious feeling."

In an even more extensive and lively manner, Unamuno expresses his Christian sense of prayer and of everyday life in its entirety, with deep and moving fervor, in chapter VII of *La tía Tula:* "No, prayer is not so much something one must carry out at this hour or that, in a private and quiet place and in a particular posture, as it is a way of doing everything as an offering, with all one's soul and living in God. Prayer should be eating, drinking, walking, playing, reading, writing, conversing, and even sleeping, and all formal prayers, and our life a constant and silent 'Thy will be done' and a ceaseless 'Thy kingdom come!,' not pronounced, nor even thought, but lived."

This life immersed in the religious atmosphere of Christianity, this proximity of God in his mind and all his work, give rise in Unamuno, underneath his conceptual doubts and the interesting spectacle into which he turns himself at times, to a peculiar *confidence* in God—this is the form faith takes in him—which we would do well to examine with care. In his essay "La fe" [Faith] he says: "Faith, our word *fe,* is inherited, together with the idea it expresses, from the Latin, which was *fides,* from which were derived *fidelis,* faithful, *fidelitas,* fidelity, *confidere,* to confide, etc. Its root *fid* is the same Greek root πιθ— (labial for labial and dental for dental) of the verb πείθειν, to persuade, in the active voice, and πεὺθεϛθαι, to obey, in the middle voice; and to obey is an act of confidence and love. And from the root πιθ comes πίϛευϛ, a very different thing from γνῶϛιϛ or knowledge." Then he adds: "Faith or confidence, religious rather than theological faith, pure and yet free from dogmas." "To confide in the kingdom of eternal life: *pistis,* that is, to believe in what they did not see." And finally he adds: "Because, after all, what is Christian faith? Either it is confidence in Christ or it is nothing; in the historical person and in the historical revelation of His life, let each one hold that faith as he may. Many of those who say they deny Him have it; they would discover that as soon as they dug down a little. Faith in Christ, in the divinity of Christ, in the divinity of man revealed by Christ, in which we move and live and have our being in God; faith which is not founded on His ideas, but on Him; faith not in any doctrine He represents, but in the historical person, in the spirit who lived and gave life and loved. Ideas do not live nor give life nor love." *

The expression noted before fits well here: "I believe in God as I believe in my friends." Unamuno feels himself in God's hand, confides in Him, counts on Him—maybe that is the most accurate expression—and, therefore, *hopes*. Perhaps to excess; rather than despair, his sin was what the theologians call presumption, *praesumptio;* and perhaps it was in a certain sense this presumption, this excess of hope, which undermined his faith, and consequently in the last instance his hope itself, of which faith is the foundation.

This personal and friendly confidence in God, in a God who was directly concerned with him, is the deepest stratum of Unamuno's beliefs. He counts on the fact that God knows him, loves him, and at last will save him from nothingness, will cause him to live, will make him eternal. At the same time he believes that, in order to achieve this immortality, to merit it, he must long for it fervently, live in anguish, even doubt it; at bottom he makes efforts to have a singular and unique personality so that God will not forget him. When Unamuno turns himself into a bit of a spectacle, and even delights in it, underneath it all he is performing exaggerated gestures before the countenance of God, so that He will take notice of him, not mistake him for anyone else, and so, eventually, will call him by his name and give him life.

Proof of the fact that, in the last instance, he did not take seriously his doubts or his moments of unbelief and that these all rested on and were sustained by an implicit and deeper belief can be found in some of his statements, especially those of his latter years, in which the subsoil of his life is made plain. Thus, in *San Manuel Bueno, mártir*—his most intimate and truthful novel—when Angela says of Don Manuel and of Lázaro, the characters whom Unamuno created with inner fear and trembling, projecting himself outward through them: "I believe that. . . they died believing they did not believe what we are most interested in knowing, but believing it without belief, believing it in an active and resigned sense of desola-

* *Ensayos,* III, 224–227, 228.

tion." And later: "I believed, and believe still, that God our Lord, for I know not what sacred and inscrutable designs, made them believe themselves unbelievers. And perhaps at the end of their passing the blindfold fell from their eyes." This is still more evident in the poem dedicated to his dead wife which he wrote in 1934, beside the sea, during the only period I was associated with him.

> "She lived day by day and waited for me
> and she awaits me still in another sphere;
> death is another waiting.
> That calm suffused with resignation;
> her eyes of silence; and that heavy weight
> of God's silence to my question,
> while He, with His all-powerful hand
> yoked us to plow the field of life together;
> this so-precious life, in which
> I thought not to believe,
> for her faith sufficed for me.
> Her faith, hers, her faith suffused
> with holy not-knowing, faith from which she drew
> her simple and pure seeing.
>
> . . . . . . . . . . . . . . . .
>
> Ah, her eyes, with the light
> of a modest star,
> rooted in infinity of love,
> in which I felt the traces
> of the footsteps of the Lord!
> She is here, she is here, ever with me,
> naked at last to all mere seeming;
> she is here, forever sheltered
> from destiny and doubt."

I cannot know whether Unamuno ever came to a final accounting with himself; certainly he did not in his public writings, and these are the only source I can abide by. But the principal function of hermeneutics is to come to a final accounting with the *writings* commented upon; and that constitutes what is called their assumptions. Very well then; if we go deeply into the assumptions which effectually support Unamuno's speculation about religion, we discover this radical confidence in God as the guarantor of immortality, which permits Unamuno to give up the attempt to *know* and to dedicate himself to making ingenious mental and ideological constructions. Just as Unamuno exaggeratedly identifies the being of the fictional person with that of the real man, in the same way, though in the opposite sense, he reduces all *truth*—intellectual, religious, scientific—to the sphere of fantasy, what he calls phantasmagoria or poetry, and he changes himself as a thinking being into a character of a novel, a protagonist who agonizes before the eyes of others, before himself, and before God. But he can do so only because he is firmly rooted in belief—not intellectual but vital—in the author of the novel of his life, in the consistency of his *I* that feels itself real when it rests on a *Thou* who is God and who believes eternally in him.

# VIII.

## *UNAMUNO AND PHILOSOPHY*

After this long examination of Unamuno's work we come at last to the real question: what has Unamuno to do with philosophy? We have seen that his concern had a basis coincident with the philosophical problem, especially in the manner in which he conceives this problem. We saw also that in spite of this his work is not *sensu stricto* philosophical; however, we have interpreted the most substantive part of his work as an oddly shaped effort to achieve a kind of knowledge akin to philosophy. But with all this we cannot know for certain whether Unamuno has philosophical significance or not, whether, in short, he has something to say to philosophy.

The question divides itself into two different, if closely linked, aspects: on the one hand, it is important to know Unamuno's relation to philosophy as he encountered it in his time, the mode of participation in it of which he was capable, and the position he took in respect to it; on the other, we must determine the results of Unamuno's personal preoccupation with philosophical themes, what we might call, without committing ourselves in advance, his contribution to philosophy, even though that contribution may have taken the form of a guess or conjecture and consequently have had an essential immaturity. First we must see what idea Unamuno has of philosophy, in order to investigate later his attitude in respect to its central themes.

## THE IDEA OF PHILOSOPHY

*Philosophy in its ambiance.* Unamuno begins by separating philosophy from science in order to bring it closer to other human activities. Even in his youth he asserted that philosophy and poetry are "twin sisters." * A little later he dwelt on the relation of philosophy, especially in Spain, to literature, ethics, and mysticism: "It is useless to belabor the point. Our gift is above all a literary gift, and everything here [in Spain], philosophy included, is therefore converted into literature. Our philosophers, from Seneca on, are what the French call moralists. And if we have any Spanish metaphysics it is mysticism, and mysticism is metaphysics of the imagination and the feelings." Let us remember these two qualifications. Then he adds these revealing words, which throw no little light on the meaning of the literary manipulations to which Unamuno submitted his agony and his religious doubt: "Literature is perhaps the greatest and almost the only consolation for having been born which remains to Spaniards who have had the misfortune of losing religious faith in another life beyond the grave." † He continues to speak of Spanish despair, founded upon hope; and he defines it as a hopeless hope, impatience with hope, and, finally and most profoundly, as hope without faith. This is the other face of that ultimate confidence which earlier I have shown to be the support of his religious position.

On the other hand, Unamuno contrasts philosophy and religion as enemies, at the same time as he finds them mutually necessary; and from the point of view of knowledge in general, he equates philosophical knowledge with poetry, phantasmagoria, and mythology rather than with scientific knowledge. He does not lose sight of Plato, although he fails to cite the passages in Aristotle in which the latter says that the friend of myths (φιλόμυθος) is in a certain sense a philosopher,§ and that when he is most alone, he has made himself most a friend of the myths (φιλομυθόστερος).

This attitude of Unamuno's has its roots partly in his lack of con-

* *Ensayos,* VI, 93.

† *Ibid.,* VII, 207–209.

§ *Metaphysics,* book I, chapter 2, fragment 618.

fidence in reason, so often noted, but still more in the fact that for him philosophy is a reaction to the mystery of reality, and concretely to the mystery of human life and its destiny. And this is why he seeks the affinities of philosophy with all those human attitudes in which a total meaning of existence, lived in whatever of its forms, is shown. Philosophy, as he says in chapter VI of the *Sentimiento,* is an effort to rationalize life and at the same time to vitalize reason; and, even though this rational characteristic brings it into conflict with poetry or literature, its concrete origin in man, that which leads him to philosophize, is that same longing for total explanation, for justification of life in his own eyes, and consequently a "consolation for having been born," as Unamuno's favorite expression has it.

All this becomes even clearer if we recall another passage* in which Unamuno contrasts science and *sabiduría*—what the French call *sagesse,* the English *wisdom,* and the Germans *Klugheit* or *Weisheit;* in short, *sapientia.* The object of science, says Unamuno, is life, and science tries to prolong it, make it easy and pleasant; wisdom deals with death, and tries to prepare us to die well. Philosophy is knowing about death; and this knowledge, as Unamuno will go on to say, is necessary in order to live. Therefore he considers science something provisional and insufficient, for in the last instance it depends on this knowing about the general meaning of life and death, which brings wisdom or philosophy closer to those other human possibilities.

*Philosophy and life.* All this leads Unamuno to understand philosophy as a way of conceiving the world and life. "Philosophy," he writes in the first few pages of the *Sentimiento,* "responds to our need of forming a unitary and total conception of the world and life, and as a consequence of this conception a feeling which will engender an inward attitude and even an outward action. But the fact is that this feeling, instead of being a consequence of that conception, is the cause of it. Our philosophy, that is, our mode of understanding or not understanding the world and life, springs from our feeling in respect to life itself." And therefore he also says that the intimate

* *Ensayos,* VII, 162–165.

biography of philosophers is what explains most about the history of philosophy.

Man philosophizes in order to live, he is to say later on. That is, the man who takes as a point of departure a certain feeling about life, a certain primary attitude in the face of it, needs to make comprehensible the reality which he encounters, so as to be able to live, to know what to abide by and what to do; therefore he requires that his conception be unitary and total, that it leave nothing out—as the sciences do—and that it be the foundation of a confident and congruent conviction. Unamuno interprets philosophy as a vital and necessary function, for man needs to justify himself to himself, know what to abide by, what is to become of him, to console himself for or despair of having been born. Actually it is not enough for man to live; or, in other words, he cannot merely live because he is in life, but he must make life for himself, invent it, find a final purpose: Unamuno suggests all these types of realities with his constant recourse to the idea that each one of us is a character in a novel.

This is why Unamuno says, at the beginning of this same book, that man is at once subject and supreme object of all philosophy. It is man who makes philosophy; and the theme of his meditation, says Unamuno, is man himself. But this must not be understood in a theoretical way; it does not mean that the reality "man" is the thematic object of philosophy as plants are of botany. Unamuno expressly states that the question is not that of the species "man" but of each man, the concrete man of flesh and blood: *the* man is the source of philosophy's concern, that which must be made clear, the problem which each human being is to himself. In what way?

*The point of departure of the philosophical task.* Unamuno frequently recalls Spinoza's thesis according to which the essence of a thing consists in its endeavor or tendency to persevere in its being indefinitely. This appetite or endeavor to survive, this longing for immortality, is what makes our existence problematical in the extreme. To be is to want to keep on being forever; knowledge of man has as its motive force the longing to know himself everlasting. The yearning for immortality, then, is for Unamuno the true point of departure of all philosophy. Anxiety for one's own existence is manifested in concern for one's permanent being; what is not eternal is not real, says Unamuno; death brings man's being into question, and that being can be affirmed and assured only in its survival; therefore life is related to death and the comprehension of the one is possible only in the light of the other. Traditionally, philosophy has grown out of the fugacity or disappearance of things; its origin among the Greeks is the perishableness of all things, the movement or change which affects them all and brings them into being only to cease to be at last; in the face of this essential mobility of the real, the Greek man seeks what remains forever, what truly is, and he calls this, for the moment, principle or *nature;* and, at the same time that he investigates this permanent entity, he tries to understand what the movement itself is—do not forget this. With the advent of Christianity, philosophy turns to an even more radical idea of perishableness, that which consists not only in change but in annihilation; not mobility but contingency. While for the Greek things cease to be what they are only to become something else, because of mobility, from the Christian point of view what threatens entities by their very constitution is nothingness. Very well then, in Unamuno this intimate experience comes to life in a different form, for he reduces the problem to man; thus mortality and the search for the true being—personal immortality—are for him the authentic motive force of philosophy. But we must examine this a little more closely.

Death cannot be interpreted from the point of view of movement, of change; to die—for man—is not to pass from being one thing to being something else, but is the actual suppression of the subject or principle; this is why the Greeks tended to suppress the reality of death by the specious reasoning that, when death arrives, I no longer exist. On the other hand, the reality of death is not exhausted in the simple idea of contingency either. We are not dealing with the fact that it is possible for man not to be, and that one day, in fact, he simply ceases to be. In that case life would *terminate,* as the trajectory of a projectile or the biological process of a plant terminates. But reality is otherwise: the end of life is not something alien and extrinsic to it, for life is not ready-made, nor do I simply possess it, nor is it realized eventually in time by itself. I have to make it, with a project, directing it toward some end, adjusting it to a vital plan which I have had to invent or imagine previously; each act in my life has to be decided in accordance with that plan, without which no one can live. Very well then; for man, to live is to know that he must die, to know his days are numbered; life is closed off by the horizon of death, an uncertain but sure boundary, the frontier of living. Yet this boundary, this frontier, is not something outside of life, but something which defines it by limiting it, and gives life its true being. And comprehension of life—which is essential to it—includes the comprehension of its boundary or frontier as one of its essential moments. What is the other side, the "over there" of that frontier? Is it nothingness? Is it life everlasting? Is it another temporal life, also transitory and also closed off by another death? The very meaning of the verb "to live" depends on the response given to these questions. The plan on which the meaning and possibility of the most insignificant acts of my life depend changes essentially according to the way I understand death, according to what I am looking forward to. Life acquires a totally different reality according to whether I live in order to die and cease to be or whether I live in order to survive. Therefore—and this is something Unamuno saw with great clarity—the radical certainty which I need is that which relates to my own survival. In this concrete sense, the interpretation of death is the key to my conception of the world and life, and hence the longing for immortality becomes the effective motive force—if not the only one—of the philosophical task.

But let us not forget that Unamuno takes an irrational position without sufficient justification, and let us not expect too many precise definitions from him about what philosophy is, about what man does once the desire to know himself immortal has moved him to investigate the question. Unamuno resorts from the outset to what he calls mythologizing, to poetic or novelesque procedures which are extraphilosophical; therefore, strictly speaking, he does not philosophize, because he considers rational knowledge impossible, and this produces a curious attitude in respect to the philosophy of his day and to his own work, one which it is important to clarify.

If philosophy as an effort to rationalize life is a contradictory and frustrated attempt, this carries as a consequence a devaluation of the whole history of thought from the point of view of its success and efficacy. Unamuno does not in fact adhere in any way to anybody else's philosophical system, nor does he attempt to have one of his own; he does not even take up a clear position relative to the philosophical past, from the point of view of truth. What Unamuno appreciates in philosophy, what seems to him necessary and valuable, is its origin, its vital source, its very effort, that of philosophizing, and therefore, the reality of the lives of the men who have dedicated themselves to philosophy. This is why he constantly quotes the philosophers, not to utilize their doctrines or take over the content of their thought, but to give himself company, to comfort himself even, with the presence of other men concerned with the great question; we have already seen that his quotations were not sources of authority but of personality. This is why he says: "There is no profounder philosophy than the contemplation of how a man philosophizes. The history of philosophy is the perennial philosophy." * That is, the true reality of philosophy lies in the reality of the philosophizing process itself, not in its ideal content nor in the rational propositions which make up philosophical systems. For Unamuno philosophy is a way of life; and its relation to science is based on philosophy's desperate need, its fruitless and agonized effort to achieve it.

And what does Unamuno retain of philosophy in his own work? Naturally he is not going to philosophize; we have seen that he warns the reader that what he writes is *perhaps* no more than "poetry or phantasmagoria, mythology in any case." Therefore he writes literary books, dramas, novels, and poems. But he does retain the *purpose* itself of philosophy, that is, a desire to state clearly the problem of immortality; and he tries to carry it out, quite properly, not by a philosophical route in the strict and rational sense, which seems impracticable to him, but by an imaginative route, employing the only faculty which he considers capable of penetrating the intimate and substantial reality of things and of life. Unamuno's work, therefore, is not philosophy, precisely because he believes that through it he can achieve the permanent and living goal of all philosophy.

* *Del sentimiento trágico de la vida,* chapter VIII.

## THE PROBLEM OF BEING

It is not easy to determine the doctrine in regard to being, nucleus of metaphysics, held by Don Miguel de Unamuno. Strictly speaking he had none, for he was very far from being an authentic philosopher, nor did he even seriously propose to be one. Is there any point, then, in our asking ourselves about his idea of being? Yes, because the verb "to be" is the general assumption which underlies all saying, and man moves from the beginning in the sphere of comprehension of being. Whether or not he arrives at an adequate ontological notion of it is another matter, but every man, according to his personal and historical situation, already has a previous idea of being which makes possible his reference to things through language; and obviously a minimal kind of ontology is apparent in language itself. Unamuno makes use of the philosophical elements of his circumstance, especially those of Kantian origin, somewhat tinged with pragmatism. Thus, at the end of chapter VIII of the *Sentimiento,* he alludes to the problem of existence, and says: "To exist, in the etymological sense of its meaning, is to be outside ourselves, outside our own mind, *existere*. But is there anything outside our own mind, outside our consciousness, which takes in all that is known? Surely there is. The matter of knowledge comes to us from without. And what is this matter like? It is impossible to know, for to know is to clothe matter with form, and hence we cannot know the unformed as unformed. It would be equivalent to having chaos ordered." There is an echo here of the Kantian theory of the phenomenon and the thing in itself *(Ding an sich),* inaccessible by definition, and of the ordering function of knowledge, which brings things out of the chaos of the sensations.

But this is not all. Quite apart from the philosophical assumptions he has acquired, Unamuno reacts in a rather primary and elementary way to reality, and especially to the peculiar realities—concrete man, the fictional being, and God—which are the subject of his liveliest concern. And his vision of these realities compels him to construct a vacillating and minimal, almost germinal and allusive, idea of being, which is worth detaching from its confused surroundings and putting in a proper light.

*Substance.* Perhaps the most original and acute facet of Unamuno's thought in reference to this group of problems is the interpretation of the notion of substance. In the first place, he attempts to vitalize it, to give it a content which is not abstract and logical but related to my life, my experience of reality. As far back as 1906 he wrote in an essay, "When we make use of a general idea, say that of force, its core, its living content, is the dark mass of concrete sensations awakened in us by the vague recollection of felt efforts, the crowd of impressions which arose from that abstract concept. The other part, the logical concept of force, as defined in a treatise on physics or metaphysics, is only an empty shell which can be submitted, among other ideas, to logical games of solitaire, to dialectical combinations." * That is, Unamuno attempts to find the immediate reality of force, as it is encountered in my life in the form of effort; and he reacts against the tendency to substitute conceptual realities for vital ones, for he sees very well that vital realities are the primary and most important ones; to the point that only they can impel us to seek concepts, precisely so as to understand or manipulate—technically or mentally—those realities which are immediately lived. And Unamuno immediately gives a first approximation of the idea of substance: "When I hear substance talked of, vague memories of concrete substances arise in my mind, the substance of a broth, the substantiality of a stew, the insubstantiality of a piece of writing, the substance of meat, etc." He relates the notion of substance to a vital circumstance, within which it acquires *meaning* for the first time. It is only then that its nature as a problem arises, and leads us to ask in a necessary and authentic way: "What is substance?" Why do I call —in a living and immediate sense—such diverse realities full of substance, substantial, or insubstantial? How can the term substance be applied to a broth, a piece of writing, a person, or a stone? What is its origin, that is, its primary meaning, that which establishes this presumed analogy of substance?

Contrary to what might be believed, when Unamuno thinks of substance he does not think first of all of a permanent reality, one which is unalterable or difficult to change or solid, of a *thing*. Rather he takes note of the range of capacities or energies natural to a thing:

* *Ensayos,* VII, 92.

the nutritive power of a broth, the inner capabilities of a person, the richness and fruitfulness of a piece of writing. Up to this point Unamuno avoids the interpretation of substance as *sub-stantia,* as the subject or support of attributes, to approach more closely the Aristotelian notion of *ousia* (οὐσία). But this is not all; while it has traditionally been thought that the prototype of substantial being is things, and that man, at least insofar as he is a living mental or spiritual reality, is opposed to that prototype, Unamuno, in two passages in chapter VII of the *Sentimiento,* finds the origin of the notion of substance in the idea of *consciousness,* in the most subjective area of all, in the *personal* being of man. "And what is the notion itself of substance," he writes, "but objectivation of the most subjective, that is, will or consciousness? For consciousness, even before it recognizes itself as reason, feels itself and touches itself, exists, rather, as will, and as the will not to die." The primary reality I encounter, says Unamuno, is that of my own self, as the will not to die; here Spinoza's thesis, so many times repeated, reappears: that everything, insofar as it is at all, tends to persevere in its being *(Unaquaeque res, quantum in se est, in suo esse perseverare conatur),* and that this endeavor is nothing less than the actual essence of the thing, and includes an indefinite space of time.* Then Spinoza explains how in man this endeavor is conscious, how man knows that he desires to keep on being forever, and he calls this conscious appetite desire, *cupiditas,* and says of it that it is the very essence of man *(Cupiditas est ipsa hominis essentia).* Duration or survival appears, then, primarily related to me, as temporal reality; I, because I make myself—not simply *am*—in time, therefore *endure;* the intemporal—the triangle or the number 5, for example—has no duration and seems insubstantial to me; material inanimate things—stone or metal—resist time, which envelops them, and in that sense they endure; but it must be noted that their identity appears only from my point of view, from my successive—and therefore temporal—contacts with them. Thus the duration of a block of granite appears only in relation to my own duration and permanence; when I, who endure, see that I find the same block again and again along the whole span of my

* *Ethics,* part III, propositions vi-viii.

persistence or subsistence, I project this duration of mine upon it and attribute to it the everlasting character, persistent or substantial, in short, which I find in myself. Therefore, the foundation of substantiality, its primary mode, is that of my own human reality, mental and living. The substantiality of things is based on that of man, and not of biological man but of the *human person,* on what Unamuno calls, perhaps improperly, subjectivity.

Thus, at the end of the same chapter, Unamuno says that the only substantial thing is consciousness—eternal consciousness—and that the rest is only appearance. "What is not consciousness and eternal consciousness, conscious of its eternity and eternally conscious, is nothing more than appearance. The only truly real thing is that which feels, suffers, pities, loves, and desires; the only substantial thing is consciousness." This notion of substance as essentially changing and temporal, barely sketched out conceptually in Unamuno, has very great scope, and lies at the base of his total idea of reality. We must see how it conditions the meaning of his whole work.

*Being as activity.* Using these assumptions as a point of departure, Unamuno rejects traditional "substantialism," which makes reality consist in what is there, outside of me, and which endures or subsists. In chapter IX of the *Sentimiento* there is an extremely instructive passage, to which I have alluded before. "What does it mean, in fact, to exist, and when do we say that a thing exists? To exist means that something is placed outside of us in such a way that it preceded our perception of it and can subsist outside of us after we are gone. And can I really be sure that anything preceded me or that anything will survive me? Can my consciousness know that there is anything outside itself? Whatever I know or can know resides in my consciousness. Let us not become embroiled in the insoluble problem of an objectivity apart from our perceptions, for whatever acts, exists, and to exist is to act."

We must consider four distinct points here: (1) a formulation of the notion of existence—that which is there, independent of me—as it appears in realism; (2) the traditional criticism which the idealists make of realism: the impossibility of knowing anything about the behavior of things apart from myself, and therefore the necessity of my testimony if the verb "to be" is to acquire any meaning; (3) the necessity, guessed at rather than known, of rising above subjective idealism and justifying the objectivity of the real; though Unamuno hastily rejects this as impossible, from the point of view of the idealist assumptions themselves; (4) the attempt to escape the difficulty by means of transition to an "antisubstantial"—in the usual sense of the word—and dynamic idea of being: to exist is to act.

Earlier, in chapter VII, he had written: "The old adage of *operare sequitur esse,* acting succeeds being, must be modified to say that to be is to act, and only that which acts, that is, the active, exists, and this to the degree that it acts." This active interpretation of being will lead him, on the one hand, to affirm the primary reality of what is most active, life itself and human consciousness; and, on the other, to recognize the reality of *all* of that which acts. This leads him in its turn to complete his theory of the substantiality of the conscious person and to proceed from that to the affirmation of the reality of the fictional being. Let us examine the first point, leaving the problem of the being of fiction for later on.

"Nothing is lost, nothing passes away altogether," Unamuno writes in chapter IX of the *Sentimiento trágico de la vida,* "since everything is perpetuated in one way or another and everything, after passing through time, returns to eternity. The temporal world has roots in eternity, and there yesterday is side by side with today and tomorrow. The scenes pass before us as in the cinema, but the film stays one and entire on the other side of time.

"The physicists say that not a single piece of matter nor a tiny bit of energy is lost, but that both are transformed and continue to persist. And is any form ever lost, no matter how fleeting it may be? We must believe—believe and expect!—that forms are not lost either, that somewhere all are laid away and perpetuated, that there is a mirror of eternity in which all the images which parade through time are gathered up, and that none are confused with others. Every impression that reaches me stays stored up in my brain, although it may be so profound or so feeble that it sinks into the depths of my subconscious; but it quickens my life even from there, and if all my spirit, the total content of my life, should become conscious for me, all the fugitive forgotten impressions that I did not completely perceive, and even the ones I never noticed, would rise up in me. I carry within myself everything which has passed before me, and I perpetuate it in myself, and perhaps all of it goes in my genes, and all of my ancestors live fully in me, and will live, along with me, in my descendants. And perhaps I, all of me, with all this universe of mine, go into each of my works, or at least the essential part of me goes into them, what makes me be myself, my individual essence."

Here Unamuno arrives at an almost monadic perception of the individual, although explicit references to Leibnitz do not appear in his work. The person appears integrated by all which is, acts—has been real—in him, and the principle of the conservation of matter and energy is postulated as extending to an entire reality. The important point here is that Unamuno recognizes the peculiar irreducible reality of each being, and understands that the conservation of matter cannot take the place of that of form; if only matter persists, form is destroyed, because the survival of something different is of no use to him. This idea will be one of the capital elements in his conception of personal immortality.

*Real being and apparential being.* This permits us at last to understand the sense in which Unamuno sometimes says that man is a thing, *res,* although it appears to contradict his idea of nonrealism. Man's reality—*substantial* reality—is active, dynamic, temporal, and capable of being turned into a narrative; it is at the same time an active reality in the sense of acting and producing: therefore he calls it a thing [*cosa*], in its etymological sense of *causa.* And he contrasts to this real mode of being the *apparential*—an excellent word—being, which is precisely the being in the sense of things, of what is substantial only in the second degree by means of the projection of the consciousness. In the prologue to *Tres novelas ejemplares,* Unamuno says: "The realest man, *realis,* most *res,* most thing [*cosa*], that is, most *causa*—only that which acts exists—is the one who wants to be or the one who does not want to be, the creator. Only this man, whom we might call noumenal in the Kantian sense, this man of will or idea—idea-will or strength—has to live in an apparential, rational, phenomenalistic world, the world of the so-called realists. And he must dream life, which is a dream." In this way, contrary to what might be supposed, Unamuno considers apparential the static and exterior being of things, and only truly real and substantial the dynamic and intimate being of human life and personality. This explains his understanding of being from the point of view of temporal consciousness, and at the same time permits us to understand his theory about human reality and the reality of the fictional creature. When Unamuno says that the creature of the novel is "of the reality of fiction, which is the fiction of reality," he means, as we have seen, that the mode of reality imagined in him is the true reality—the human one—and not just the apparential one of things. With these bases we find the way open for the understanding of life and its forms in Unamuno's thought, so disperse and so difficult to grasp.

## HUMAN LIFE

*Life and dream.* We have observed repeatedly that Unamuno makes use of the metaphor of the dream in order to consider life; the type of reality to which vital reality belongs is subtle, shifting, and temporal, and from the point of view of things is no more than a quasi-reality. Life is something whose being consists in being made, temporally, at the same time that it is being unmade. "Life," writes Unamuno, "is continuous creation and continuous consumption, and is, therefore, unceasing death. Can you possibly believe that you would be living if you were not dying at every moment?" * This is the very character of time; time does not endure, but only the now comes to pass and becomes the hollow of the past instant, immediately made preterite. Life is only, is only made, at the price of continual loss, of leaving its moments behind, leaving behind precisely that in which it has consisted. In contrast to things, which exist because they resist time, because they defend their persistence against it, life comes

* *Ensayos,* III, 221.

to be only by basing itself on the unstable mobility of the temporal, following its flow, consuming itself as it creates itself, with time. Elsewhere, Unamuno says: "Life, which is everything, and being everything becomes nothing, is a dream, or perhaps the shadow of a dream, and maybe Cassou is right when he says it is not worth being dreamed in a systematic form. Of course! System—which is consistency—destroys the essence of the dream and with it the essence of life." * Here Unamuno formally contrasts life and dream with that which is consistent, contrasts the plastic and mobile form of being with the fixed and stable one. But it is obvious that, if dream and life are anything, they also have some consistency, even though of a different kind, and it is precisely that of aspiring to be always, and to be always the same reality, within its constant and constituent variation; this mode of being we call "life."

This life must be made, created by man, imagined or invented by him; life, because it is a dream or temporal narrative, is a novel, a poetic, imaginative fiction. When Unamuno says, "the novel of our life," he is not setting down a cliché but expressing a formal characteristic of human life. And this creative task of our life presupposes freedom; but freedom is closely related to temporality itself. The past is what it is, already made; the present is already in being, and its reality becomes fixed as it is taking place. Only the future remains, that which is not yet. "Only the future," says Unamuno, "is the domain of freedom, for once something is given over to time, it becomes subject to time's chains. Nor can the past be more than it was, nor is it possible for the present to be more than what it is; the 'may be' is always future." † As life is essentially creation, realization of the possible, it moves toward the future, toward which it is oriented, and its prime reality is not present, a thing of the moment, but future: the imaginative expectation of what is going to be, its project or novel. This has a deep-rooted affinity with Spinoza's idea which defines the being as an endeavor to survive, an idea which Unamuno took up and used as the nucleus of his ontology. Strictly speaking, to be is not—as traditional substantialism believed—to be in actuality,

* *Cómo se hace una novela,* page 53.

† *Ensayos,* III, 189–190.

now, but is wanting to continue being, in the future, to have the possibility of doing so. And the most profound and deepseated reality, that of human life, displays this essential attribute of being to the maximum degree.

*The I and the world.* Now a new question arises: what is the structure of this peculiar temporal reality of life or dream? Unamuno has laid great stress on the active, dynamic, and mental character of living. The favorite term to which he has recourse is consciousness —the residue no doubt of some idealist assumptions, at odds with his profoundest conjectures, yet which he cannot wholly rid himself of. He particularly fixes his attention on the creative or imaginative nature of life. All this probably tended to bring him to a clearly idealist conception of existence, to consider the world as something purely phenomenical, "apparential," as he prefers to say, based on the reality of the living I, on human consciousness. In fact, expressions informed by this conviction frequently appear in his works; but they are far from showing the most individual and authentic part of his thought. In one of his first essays, entitled "Civilización y cultura" [Civilization and Culture], Unamuno expounds on the structure of human life, though not without some descriptive errors, and in an extremely sketchy manner.*

He begins by distinguishing two ambiances, one exterior, that of phenomena accessible to the senses, and the other interior, that of consciousness; and he warns at once that it is not easy to draw a clear dividing line between them. But it would be well to note the term he uses: "ambiances," that is, something which surrounds us, which encompasses us, which therefore cannot be confused with us. The world of the senses and that of consciousness are ambits in which I am placed, but they are not *I* myself. But, immediately after this and without drawing any careful distinctions, Unamuno begins to speak of the "I," deriving it from the idea of "mine." *"Mine* precedes *I;* I is made in virtue of being a possessor, then it considers itself as a consumer, and ends by becoming a true *I* when it succeeds in directly adjusting its production to its consumption." Here Una-

* *Ensayos,* II, 65–67.

muno is dealing, naturally, only with the discovery of the I by itself; the terms which he uses for his description—production, consumption—are a little unpolished and deficient; the most interesting feature is that Unamuno singles out as the original idea of mine its possessive quality; and the possessive is precisely the point at which the I and the other converge; what is mine is different from me but related to me; only in the relation of the I with the other is what is mine established.

Afterwards, among many impressions and inaccuracies, effective descriptions begin to appear. After speaking of the mutual reactions between the exterior and interior ambiances, Unamuno writes: "There is a continual decisive ebb and flow between my consciousness and the nature which surrounds me, which is mine too, my nature; and in the same degree that my spirit becomes naturalized by saturating itself in external reality, I spiritualize nature by saturating it in internal ideality." There is a first glimpse here of what I have called the world of man—the world of the characters, in the novel—which is not just the world of things but is related to the man who is at their center; conversely, the spirit is not a reality cloistered in the consciousness, but is realized by becoming saturated in exterior reality. And now Unamuno adds the most important point: "The world and I make ourselves mutually. And from this interplay of actions and reactions the consciousness of an "I" arises in me, "my I" before it has become purely and simply I, a pure I. Consciousness of myself is the nucleus of the reciprocal play between my exterior and my interior world. The personal arises from the possessive." The reality of life appears as defined by the interaction of the I and the world; this is the decisive point. The I, far from being shut away and isolated, finds itself among other things, phenomena of the senses, ideas, desires, the whole variety of the spiritual and natural ambit which surrounds it; thus it is apprehended as *my I,* in a possessive way, and only later, after it has attained a *full* possession of itself, does it recognize itself as the only center, *I,* and turn to face all the rest. It is clear that once again Unamuno starts from an assumption which is not particularly compatible with the profoundest meaning of his discovery: the radical and primary independence of the I and the world; while he strongly emphasizes the interaction between the world and the I, which make themselves mutually, he treats them as two ultimately autonomous realities, and considers that *therefore* they can act upon each other. But, in spite of these limitations, perhaps no more could be asked at the end of the nineteenth century.

And then, as an example of his theory, he makes use with surprising exactitude of the interpretation of the tool, from a strictly vital point of view, in a way which reveals his understanding of the articulation of human life. "Nature," he writes, "caused us to have hands, and with our hands we manufacture tools in our exterior world and have use and comprehension of them in our interior world: tools and their use enriched our minds, and our minds, thus enriched, enriched in turn the world we had taken them out of. Tools are simultaneously my two worlds, the inside one and the outside one." The tool is a typically human creation; it is a thing, something belonging to the exterior world, made from it; but at the same time it possesses comprehension and use, for apart from these it does not have being as a tool; and these, naturally, are vital determinations which relate it to man, and without which it does not strictly speaking exist. The mode of being of the tool qua tool involves and implicates that of human life, understood as a reciprocal making of the I and the world.

This interpretation of life appears even more clearly in a somewhat later essay (1904), entitled "Intelectualidad y espiritualidad" [Intellectuality and Spirituality]. "My acts," writes Unamuno, "are never exclusively mine: if I speak I must make use of an air which is not mine so that my voice can be produced; not even my vocal cords are properly speaking mine, nor is mine the language which I must use if I am to be understood, and the same happens if I write, if I strike a blow, if I kiss, if I kill myself." * In this brief paragraph Unamuno establishes with complete precision the distinction between what is I and what is alien to my vital acts. In the first place, the physical world—the air—which surrounds me; in the second place, my own body, the portion of the exterior world primarily and intimately related to me; in the third place, the social realities—language,

* *Ensayos,* IV, 201–202.

for example—which make up another world into which I find myself necessarily inserted. And all my acts, which constitute my own life, require the presence of the other, that which is alien to me, yet inextricably entwined with my own I.

And it is here that the problem of authenticity arises. "I," he adds, "want to make the world mine, make it I, and the world tries to make me belong to it, to make me it; I struggle to personalize it, and it struggles to depersonalize me. And in this tragic combat, for indeed such combat is tragic, I must make use of my enemy in order to master him, and my enemy must make use of me to master me. Whatever I say, write, and do, I must say and write and do it through him; and then he instantly depersonalizes it for me and makes it his, and I appear as other than what I am." The person, to realize himself, that is, in order to live, needs to act and to do, and he can accomplish this only with things; therefore his acts are not his alone, nor his life either for that matter, and the realization is simultaneously an alienation. When man lives, when he makes himself, he *loses* himself in the environment, in the natural and social world around him. The reality of any human act is interpreted by Unamuno as a result of the interaction of the I and the world. When I say something, it is I, naturally, who say it, yet not only I, but I together with the air which vibrates, stirred by my vocal cords, in alien words which I did not invent—that is why they can be understood—and with thoughts that proceed from my spiritual circumstance. Therefore, I alone am not the subject of my acts, and living is consequently a task which I undertake together with my world, making myself in that task.

And this world with which we must make our life is a temporal world, not only physical or social, but existing in the dimension of time. However, this in its turn can be understood in two senses: on the one hand, as we have already seen, the reality of life is temporal because it consists in something which is formed in duration, instant after instant, in time; but, on the other hand, this time, insofar as it is the world or environment in which one is placed, is not an undifferentiated and indifferent continuum but a qualified temporality, a "when," a historical time. Man lives in the instants, the hours, the years which make up his life; but those years are certain specific years and not others. Thus, Unamuno says that it is possible for a soul to find its idea or not, that the idea may have passed or may not have come to pass; that is, that the historical time in which a man is called upon to live may or may not correspond with his own inwardness, his private vocation, what Unamuno calls his "secret." "For each soul there is an idea which belongs to it and which is, as it were, its formula, and souls and ideas are always in the process of seeking each other out. There are souls which go through life without ever finding their own idea, and they are the majority; and there are ideas which, revealing themselves in some souls or others, nevertheless fail to find their own souls, the ones which would reveal them in all their perfection. And here again the terrible mystery of time confronts us, the most terrible of all mysteries, the father of them all. And it is that souls and ideas come into the world either too soon or too late; when a soul is born its idea has already passed, or the soul dies without the idea's having come down into the world." *

*The shape of life.* We have already seen the general characteristics of that peculiar reality which is human life. Now we must dwell with a little more precision on the internal structure of life. Unamuno was insistent on the role of the future, the only domain of freedom, in human life; as he discovers the basis of man in his will, and will refers to the future, the future is what primarily defines human life.† Elsewhere Unamuno returns to the theme more strictly. He speaks of the man whom "one wants to be," and says: "This one, the one a man wants to be, is in him, in his bosom; he is the creator, and he is the truly real one. And we will be saved or damned by the man we wanted to be, not the one we may have been. God will reward or punish throughout eternity the man one wished to be." § That is, Unamuno places the root of life in futurity, in the imaginative and voluntary anticipation of what one wishes to be in one's

* *Ensayos,* VII, 54–55.

† *Del sentimiento trágico de la vida,* chapter IX.

§ Prologue to *Tres novelas ejemplares.*

vital project. And he distinguishes this man who deeply wishes to be from the one which he in fact is, the one who actually comes into existence. We have seen already how he insists on the fact that the world—that which is other than I—with which I have to make my life, depersonalizes me, alters me, makes me be other. Other than whom? Not other than the man I *am,* for I can be only the one who came to be, but other than the one I *wish to be.* My radical vital project, the man I am called to be by my intimate vocation, is the vantage point from which I can judge the man I actually come to be, the self that comes to pass in the world and with it.

Closely related to this, Unamuno contrasts two strata of human reality, which he calls the everyday, shadowy, apparential man and the real, tragic, substantial man. In the prologue mentioned he writes: "Those poor fellows who fear tragedy, those shadows of men who read so as not to learn, or to kill time—they will have to kill eternity—on finding themselves in a tragedy or a comedy or a novel or a 'nivola,' if you will; when they find themselves in the presence of a man, neither more nor less than a man, or a woman, neither more nor less than a woman, ask themselves, 'Where in the world has the author got this from?' The only adequate reply would be, 'Obviously not from you!' And as nobody has got it from him, from the everyday and shadowy man, it is useless to show it to him, because he will not recognize him as a man. And he will even go so far as to call it symbol or allegory.

"And this everyday and apparential person, who flees from tragedy, is not even the dream of a shadow, which is what Pindar called man. At most he may be the shadow of a dream, as Tasso said. But he who, being the dream of a shadow, and having consciousness of being just that, suffers because of this, and wishes either to be that or not to be, can be a tragic figure."

Two radical possibilities of life are being dealt with: everyday or trivial life and authentic life, or, as Unamuno usually puts it, "tragic" life. But these terms may lead to error. Everyday life does not mean, of course, simply commonplace life with no great unusual events in it; everyday life in this inferior sense means the life of the man who pays no heed to his own being and the problem of his survival, the man who evades anguish or grief, and thus becomes a hollow cast of himself; he does not live out of his own depths, and therefore he is insubstantial and has only an apparential reality. The man who lives out of his own self, who takes care for his being, who has what Unamuno calls the tragic sense of life, the yearning for survival, is real, substantial, authentic; he is the true man. This is why the most commonplace life, everyday in the sense of being the life of every day, can be authentic when it is made personal, when man accepts himself and others as persons, and vitally feels anguish for his being. But on this point I refer you to what I said in Chapter V of this book, in the interpretation of Unamuno's narratives.

When Unamuno analyzes the modes or forms in which authentic and personal life comes to be and manifests itself, its very substance, he points out two dimensions of living, different but essentially linked together, although he does not indicate their relationship very precisely: they are pain and grief, which in other places he also calls tribulation.

Pain, suffering, is for Unamuno the highest form of consciousness. Reality is fully felt in suffering. Just as Maine de Biran discovered the reality of the existing thing in its resistance, Unamuno, using a similar intuition as his point of departure, interprets this discovery as pain. "Suffering," he says, "is to feel the flesh of reality, to sense the bulk and weight of the spirit, to touch oneself; it is immediate reality." And he adds, "Pain is the substance of life and the root of personality, for one is only a person when one suffers. And it is universal, and what unites all us human beings is pain, the universal or divine blood that circulates through all. That which we call will, what is it but pain?" But, what sort of pain is being considered? Can Unamuno be thinking, like Schopenhauer, of the pain that accompanies will when it can never be satisfied nor sated? No, Unamuno is not thinking of the impossibility of achieving the various contents of volition; he is dealing with the pain provoked by finitude, by imperfection, by the impermanent being, by not being more than "this" and "now" and wanting to be everything and forever. He does not say that will is accompanied by pain, but that will *is* pain. And the painful link which unites all things, according to Unamuno, could easily be interpreted as their limited nature as imperfect creatures who are all united by their sense of need.

Secondly, there is tribulation or grief. In an essay entitled "El secreto de la vida" [The Secret of Life], Unamuno speaks of the mystery of the human soul and relates it to tribulation. "The mystery is a secret for each one of us. God plants a secret in the soul of each man, the more deeply the more He loves each man; that is, the more of a man He makes him. And in order to plant it He tills our souls with the sharp-pronged tool of tribulation. Those who know little of tribulation have the secret of life very near the surface of the soil, and the secret runs the risk of not seeding down well and not taking root, and, because it has not taken root, giving neither fruit nor flowers." * It is a new vision of the difference between the apparential man and the substantial man; the former is at the same time the uprooted one, and the latter the man who has been tilled by deep tribulation; later we shall see what this tribulation is. Then, after stating that "nothing unites men more truly than the secret," Unamuno adds: "And the secret of human life, the common one, the secret root from which all others spring, is the longing for more life, the ravening and insatiable yearning to be everything else without ceasing to be ourselves, to make ourselves master of the whole universe without the universe's becoming our master and absorbing us; it is the desire to be other without ceasing to be oneself, and continuing to be oneself but being at the same time other; it is, in a word, the appetite for divinity, the hunger for God." And then: "What you want is that life, and this, and the other, and all lives." Finally he concludes: "The mainspring of life is the longing to survive in time and space; human beings begin to live when they wish to be other than who they are, and yet to keep on being the same."

Tribulation, then, is the superior form of pain, more than superior, *radical*. When it refers not so much to what one wants as to what one wants to be, pain afflicts the soul and makes it take possession of itself, touching its limitations, feeling its ultimate neediness, and seeing "the bulk of itself," as Unamuno says in a vivid and graphic expression. Tribulation consists in man's turning back into himself

* *Ensayos*, VII, 43–61.

and knowing himself as what he is: something finite, limited, and indigent, who necessarily aspires to the infinite and the eternal, to everything. Because of this, because tribulation consists in living the deepest being of man, Unamuno can say that it is the secret of human life.

Elsewhere Unamuno refers to the same human possibility and gives it the name of "grief." First he also considers it as a culmination or radicalization of pain ("from that pain which floats on the sea of appearances, to the eternal grief, the source of the tragic sense of life, which settles in the depths of the eternal and there awakes consolation"), but then he immediately and forcefully distinguishes it from pain: "Grief is something much deeper, more intimate, and spiritual than pain. One often feels grief even in the midst of what we call happiness and because of the happiness itself, for grief is not resigned to happiness and trembles before it. Of happy men who resign themselves to their apparent joy, a passing joy, it might be said that they are men without substance, or at least that they have not discovered substance in themselves, that they have not touched it within them." * In these words, vague but strangely acute, a reader of today might tend to see something akin to Heidegger's doctrine of anguish *(Angst)* and of care or *cura (Sorge)*. But we must proceed with extreme caution, and not confuse in any way the indecisive conjectures glimpsed in these lines with Heidegger's ontology. However, the first impression is not totally incorrect or unfounded; there is a certain relationship between the intuition which is glimpsed in Unamuno and Heidegger's analysis, for both proceed from a common ancestor: Kierkegaard. In *The Concept of Anguish,* whose influence on Heidegger is so obvious (especially in *Was ist Metaphysik?),* Kierkegaard points out that the object of anguish is *nothingness,* that I feel anguish of *nothing,* and adds that the spirit feels anguish for itself; man feels anguish because the psychic and the corporeal are united in him by the spirit; an animal cannot feel anguish. Then, referring to original sin, Kierkegaard adds: "After the words of prohibition come the words of judgment: thou shalt die. Naturally Adam does not understand in the least what this having to die means; but there is

* *Del sentimiento trágico de la vida,* chapter IX.

nothing to prevent us from thinking that he must have had a picture of something frightful when he was told this. . . Fright is simply turned into anguish, for Adam has not understood what he was being told; so in this case too there exists no more than the ambiguity of anguish." * Kierkegaard places anguish in relation to death, but it is not fear of death—this is not even understood—but rather the threat of it, the feeling of its essential possibility. Elsewhere (chapters I and II) Kierkegaard refers to one of St. Paul's terms, the *αποκαραδοχία τῆς κτίσεως*, the *expectatio creaturae* of the Vulgate, the expectation or longing of the creature who awaits the manifestation of the sons of God.† And he adds: "If it is licit to speak of a longing, this of course means that creation must be in a state of imperfection. . . The expression of such a longing is anguish, for in anguish one denounces the state from which he longs to emerge and does so by means of anguish, for longing alone does not suffice to save him."

We see how the presence of nothingness, inherent to the creature as such, appears here. The essential imperfection of man, his finiteness, which reveals itself in the fact that he fades away, in the threat of death, and which has nothing to do with his *states* and naturally does not exclude "happiness," is what brings about this radical situation which is not fear (fear is always fear of something specific) nor pain, but anguish—tribulation, or grief, as Unamuno prefers to say. He rediscovers in grief the possessing of man by himself, the characteristic of authenticity of life as opposed to triviality; in other words, the characteristic of the true human being as opposed to the insubstantial one, as opposed to *annihilation*. "Satisfied men, happy men, do not love; they lull themselves to sleep in custom, so near to annihilation. To become accustomed is already to begin not to be. The more that man is man, that is, the more he is divine, the more capacity he has for suffering, or better still, for grief." § Custom, the "everyday"—in this concrete sense—the "trivial," is the beginning of man's not-being, of his annihilation. At bottom, then, it is a question

* *The Concept of Anguish*, chapters I and V.

† Romans 8:19.

§ *Del sentimiento trágico de la vida*, chapter IX.

of man's being, which consists primarily in his capacity for grief or tribulation.

We have seen how far Unamuno's fleeting and unsystematic analysis of human life carries us; and, guided by it, we have reached the ultimate question, that of man's being. One can be more or less a man, more or less authentic, true. What does this mean? Man as a thing, as an entity in the world, simply *is;* his life qua life *is* also, at least as long as it lasts, and possesses a reality of its own. Who is affected then by that *more* and that *less?* This is precisely the problem. If not man as an entity *simpliciter,* and not his life qua life, must it not be in the measure that it is *his* life? That is, must not the more and the less affect the relation of life to its own subject? But this in turn refers us to one last question: Who is that subject? Who is the man who lives? Do not the more and the less which show up in the authenticity or triviality of life affect in the last instance the who of existence? The problem of human life refers us inexorably to the problem of personality.

## THE PERSON

*Mihi quaestio factus sum.* Man is a problem to himself; more explicitly stated, *I* am a problem to *myself.* With this expression I am trying to eliminate the false impression involved in interpreting this problem as a question about the reality of man as any sort of entity, or even about the reality of his life. There is a moment in the history of philosophy when the mind turns back on itself for the first time and sees itself as a problem. *Mihi quaestio factus sum,* I have become a question to myself, St. Augustine says.* Here the first person indicates at once the subject and the object of the *quaestio;* I, I myself—not that universal object we call man—I am problematical. This must have been for Unamuno, although he never says so, the most accurate and condensed philosophical formula of all, since he affirms that philosophy's subject and supreme object is man himself, he who is born and dies, the *I* who is each and every man.

* *Confessions,* book X, chapter XXXIII.

Unamuno picks up this Augustinian quotation, though he scarcely makes use of it.* But I have taken pains to emphasize it because it clarifies the meaning of the question which concerns us at the moment. While up till now the questions have been referring to nouns —man, life— and the basis from which they have been asked was the category of substance in the sense of the *quid,* what—"What is man?," for example—here we are dealing with personal pronouns, and therefore with circumstantial concepts, which acquire their meaning only in the concrete circumstance in which they are expressed; the meaning of the question itself depends on the reality and the situation of the one who inquires. The question "What is man?" has—at least in principle and as a first approach—a single and universal meaning, no matter who formulates it. But if I say "Who am I?," the question and answer include the being of the person who asks, and only he can give meaning to what is asked. When the *person* is asked about, we are therefore dealing, not with another question but with a question of another type.

*Individual and person.* The very first thing revealed to us by the question expressed in the form of a pronoun is that no universal reality is being referred to, for the personal pronoun substitutes for the name of a person, a proper name. One may think that, instead of referring to the universal, the species, it refers to an individual. Unamuno opposes this possible belief, but considers it already established that the difference between an individual and a person is recognized, and he distinguishes them only allusively. "The idea of person," he says, "refers rather to the content, and that of the individual to the spiritual container. Even though a man may have a great deal of individuality, and may stand out very strongly and definitely from other analogous individuals, he may have very little of the self and the personal. And it could even be said that, in a certain sense, individuality and personality are in opposition, although in another, broader, and more exact sense it could be said that they offer each other mutual support. Strong individuality without a respectable dose of personality can hardly be conceived, nor can

* *Cómo se hace una novela,* p. 151.

there be a strong and rich personality without a certain eminent degree of individuality which holds its various elements together; but it is quite possible to imagine a vigorous individuality possessing the least possible degree of personality within its vigor, and an extremely rich personality with the slightest possible degree of individuality enclosing its richness." * Then, after indicating several metaphoric explanations—states of molecular grouping, crustaceans with rigid and external skeletons and vertebrates with internal skeletons, vegetable or animal cells with strong or delicate membranes—he adds, "Individuality is concerned with our outside limits, it presents our finiteness; personality refers principally to our inside limits, or better still our lack of limits; it presents our infiniteness."

The individual, in these vague explanations, appears as that which is differentiated, separated, within a whole—the species—that which is homogeneous, externally limited. The attribute which Unamuno insistently assigns to personality, on the other hand, is that of richness, and sometimes that of ownership; these are, obviously, substantial attributes, not in the sense of fixity and permanence, but in the sense of possessions or property, the sense of the Aristotelian *ousia*. The person refers to the contents; it is an innerness, an *intus* of its own, which possesses itself and has a certain richness, a certain property which it can utilize. Unamuno thus leaves out the personalities of nonindividual entities, such as the angels according to St. Thomas, or God Himself. This is the result of Unamuno's first contact with the problem of personality.

*Person and life*. In Chapter III of this book, under the subhead "Existence and Person," we have seen the philosophical problems raised by the relationship of these two terms, more strictly stated than we find them in Unamuno, and at the same time not dwelling on his thematic contribution to the solution of the question. Now we must approach it from another point of view. This time we are not trying to sketch an ontological linkage of human life with personality in order to clarify the assumptions, and therefore the meaning, of Unamuno's novels, but primarily to find out to what extent

* *Ensayos*, IV, 69–71.

Unamuno achieves clarity in regard to the problem and what his mode of looking at it is. Stated in other words, earlier we were dealing with gaining the necessary philosophical elements for understanding the reality of Unamuno's novel; now we must clarify Unamuno's thought in regard to the philosophical problem of personality.

In an old essay of 1900 entitled "¡Adentro!" [Inward], Unamuno confronts, perhaps for the first time, the question of the relation between the person who lives and the life of that person. "You gradually emerge from yourself," he writes, "revealing yourself to yourself; your finished personality is at the end and not the beginning of your life; only in death is it completed and crowned. The man of today is not the man of yesterday nor tomorrow, and as you change, so the ideal of yourself that you are forging changes too. Your life, in the face of your own consciousness, is constant revelation, in time, of your eternity, the development of your symbol; you keep on discovering yourself in the measure that you act. Advance, then, into the depths of your spirit, and every day you will discover new horizons, virgin lands, rivers of spotless purity, heavens not seen before, new stars and new constellations. When life is deeply felt it is a poem with a constant and flowing rhythm. Do not chain your eternal depth, which develops in time, to a few fugitive reflections of it. Live day by day, in the waves of time, but resting on your living rock, within the sea of eternity; day by day in eternity—that is how you should live." *

Two points of view appear here, which show a certain contrast, and which in their opposition stir up the very nucleus of the problem, two points of view which will continue to be contrasted and oppose each other in his later work. On the one hand, Unamuno alludes to a depth or starting point from which one lives, a depth which is made manifest or reveals itself: "You gradually emerge from yourself, revealing yourself to yourself"; "your life is. . . constant revelation, in time, of your eternity"; "you keep on discovering yourself in the measure that you act." Life in this view could be an *explicatio* or unfolding of an intimate root, an individual depth, in time; and it seems that this interior nucleus, this depth of the soul, is the *who* of each man, that is, the *person*. But, on the other hand, Unamuno

* *Ensayos,* III, 186.

places the personality at the end of life, as a result, crowned by death: "your finished personality is at the end and not the beginning of your life; only in death is it completed and crowned." That is to say, the person appears as a life finished, consummated, concluded in death; man would make his personality at the same time as his life was being made. The person would be the precipitate of the temporal process of events which is human life. At the end of this passage Unamuno attempts to overcome the discrepancy of its two points of view in formulas pregnant with meaning but insufficiently clear, or at least insufficiently explicit: he speaks of the eternal depth, which develops in time, and finally sums up his doctrines in a single imperative: *live day by day in eternity*. Unamuno attempts to escape from the bare temporality of life to what we might call, in a very fashionable term, "historicism." To do so he appeals to eternity, but perhaps the appeal is a little precipitate.

The question reappears later. In chapter XI of *Del sentimiento trágico de la vida* Unamuno writes: "Each man is in fact unique and irreplaceable; there can be no other I; each one of us—our soul, not our life—is worth the whole Universe. . . For life has value only inasmuch as its lord and master the spirit has value, and if the master perishes with the servant neither one is worth much." Here it is affirmed that each man, irreplaceable, is his soul—his person—and that the person is what gives value to life. Life is at the service of the soul, of the person, and therefore depends on it; consequently the soul is the root of living, the primary and substantive reality. But in *La agonía del cristianismo,* Unamuno again insists on the opposite point of view: "The purpose of life is to make a soul, an immortal soul. A soul which is one's own handiwork. For when we die we leave a skeleton to the earth, a soul and a work to history. This when we have lived, when we have done battle with the life which passes for the life which remains." * Again the soul appears as a result, and, moreover, identified with work and related to history. What has become of that longing to escape to historicism, to the flow of time? It is of interest to pick up one phrase from this paragraph: the contrast of the life which passes with the life which remains. What

* "Introducción," page 25.

does this mean? If we place this last phrase in relation to the expression "immortal soul" used earlier, we see that Unamuno thinks of the concepts soul and life as united; the immortal soul is that which does not die, which lives therefore, and the life which remains is eternal life. This is the final meaning of Unamuno's formulas in his old essay. There he said: Live day by day in eternity; live the life that remains, everlasting life, eternal life, he says in the book of his maturity. The permanent conflict of the soul or person with life is the one revealed in the disquieting expression "eternal life." What does it mean to live—for the moment, a temporal task, in the measure in which the verb "to live" has a meaning we can grasp—in eternity? How can eternity and time be reconciled? But, notwithstanding, the fundamental question of the person arises again. Unamuno repeats over and over: "Your life passes and you will remain." And it is fair to ask: "Who am I?" Who is it who lives life, whether temporal or eternal? And that who—the person—whether or not he makes himself in a certain measure and in a certain sense as he lives, is essential to life, for my life is mine, the life of each his own, and life is not given without that who, which is its subject, and as Unamuno says, its lord and master.

*Personal substantiality.* Apart from the question of the person's relation to the realities closely connected with it, Unamuno at last must face the question of what the personal self consists. The question of "What is man?" in its radical form of "Who is man?" brings us finally to the problem of the person's being. In an essay of 1904, "¡Plenitud de plenitudes y todo plenitud!" [Plenitude of plenitudes and all is plenitude], Unamuno sketches a theory of personal substantiality and of the sense in which this is revealed to us. In the first place, he speaks of "one's feeling for his own body and the life in it." Then he says: "I do not know how to express myself when I enter into these hiding-places and dark corners of the life of the spirit, and I foresee that adequate words are going to fail me." *

Unamuno is alluding to a certain sense of the reality of the world, of himself and of God, and in these pages one can make out a remote

* *Ensayos,* V, 67–68.

and imprecise echo of the doctrine of *sense* of Father Gratry, whom Unamuno probably did not know, however, since he cites him only twice so far as I am aware, and then very much in passing and by indirect references.* "It is a bad thing," he says in the abovementioned essay, "when one puts a hand on his leg, for the leg not to feel the hand nor the hand the leg; but it is worse when you fix your attention on yourself and do not *feel* yourself spiritually. It is a bad thing, when you stretch out on the ground, not to feel the touch of the earth the whole length of your body, and that it is firm and solid; but it is worse when you receive the world in your spirit and do not feel the touch of the world, and feel that it is firm and solid and full, with plenitude of plenitudes and all is plenitude." He then speaks of one's fellow man who "does not touch his soul with his very soul, does not have full possession of himself, lacks the intuition of his own substantiality." This is the most exact expression for Unamuno: *the intuition of his own substantiality,* what he also calls *spiritual touch,* revealed in the necessity for survival. When this is lacking, the world seems apparential or phenomenical, and man feels himself to be the dream of an hour. The apparentiality of the world corresponds to the insubstantiality of the person. When, on the other hand, one has the sense of one's own substantiality, the soul, the person, feels itself as the true reality, realer than the body. "Your body can come to seem like a function of your soul."

Unamuno immediately equates this intimate sense, with which the person touches and possesses itself, with love. He says that, "we do not love our fellow man more because we do not believe more in his substantial existence," and, "we do not believe in the existence of our fellow men because we do not believe in our own existence, I mean in our substantial existence." What does this mean? Love cannot be related, as we saw elsewhere, to the body, nor to psychic acts or qualities, nor even to the life of one's fellow man, but only to himself, to his person. It is a strictly personal relationship, and there-

* In *Del sentimiento trágico de la vida,* chapter X. See also Unamuno's *La agonía del cristianismo,* chapter X; Alphonse Joseph Gratry, *De la connaissance de l'âme* (Paris, 1857), book III; and my book *La filosofía del Padre Gratry* (Madrid: Revista de Occidente, 1959) (*Obras,* volume IV).

fore shows the reality of its object, the person himself. Love presupposes the feeling of substantiality—in the sense in which, as we have seen, Unamuno understands this term—of the loved fellow being. Thus, if this feeling is absent or deficient, love is equally affected; this is what Unamuno emphasizes. And lack of self-love arises, according to him, from insufficient belief in our own personality or substantiality, from our not always looking upon ourselves as persons; and, when this primary intuition of personality fails us in ourselves, we cannot through imagination—the most substantial faculty, Unamuno says—experience that same intuition toward others, see them as persons and consequently love them. Father Gratry said, and Unamuno seems to glimpse it, that I feel my fellow man with the same sense I feel myself, with *intimate sense,* rather than external sense which is what I use to enter into contact with my own body and the world.

But let us not forget the significance which Unamuno gives to the word "substance." It is a question, as we have observed at length, of something active, related to activity and even to the human task, and therefore to the future; and it is manifested—as in Spinoza—in the yearning for survival. Thus Unamuno must define the idea of person in a positive way.

"One must distinguish first of all," he writes in *La agonía del cristianismo,* "between the reality and the personality of the historical figure. Reality derives from *res* (thing), and personality from person. The Jewish Sadducee, Karl Marx, believed that it is things which make and influence men, and hence his materialist concept of history, his historical materialism—we might call it realism. But those of us who would rather believe that it is men, who are persons, who make and influence things, we nourish with doubt and in agony faith in the historical concept of history and the personal or spiritual concept.

"The *persona,* in Latin, was the tragic or comic actor, the one who played a role on the stage. Personality is the achievement in which history is fulfilled." *

Note that Unamuno makes the terms personal concept and historical concept synonymous; that is, there is no possibility of history

* *La agonía del cristianismo,* IV, 60–61.

without persons, and they are its only authentic subject. *Things* have no history; for history presupposes an action, a role which is played or carried out; but the person *sensu stricto* is the actor, the one who plays the role, not the role itself.

Finally, at the beginning of his book *Del sentimiento trágico de la vida,* Unamuno achieves the greatest precision in his theory of the personality. "What makes up a man," he writes, "what makes him one man, one and not another, the man he is and not the man he is not, is a principle of unity and a principle of continuity. A principle of unity, first in space, thanks to the body, and then in action and in purpose. . . At every moment of our life we have a purpose, and the synergy of our actions combines toward it. Although our purpose may change the next moment. And in a certain sense a man is the more a man the more unitary his action. . . And a principle of continuity in time. . . Memory is the basis of the individual personality, as tradition is the basis of the collective personality of a people. We live in memory and for memory, and our spiritual life, at bottom, is no more than the effort of our memory to persevere, to take hope, the effort of our past to make itself our future."

Apparently Unamuno is seeking a principle of spatio-temporal individuation; but basically it is something else. Apart from the local reference to the body—which brings up a delicate problem—Unamuno emphasizes the relation with time. Time in two forms: purpose, which is aimed at the future, and memory, in which the past survives; a man is one man, he is who he is, because he unites *in a present* which is that of his current life, constantly coming into being and ceasing to be, a past recalled in memory, and a future anticipated in a vital purpose or project. But one could ask again: What is the principle of that union? What is the link which joins that past of the memory to the future of the project? In other words, why am I myself the one who remembers and anticipates? Does the past which lives in my memory condition my vital project? And, especially, how and in what measure do I, the person I am, possess that past and that future, that is, my life? It would be vain to try to find in Unamuno an adequate answer to these questions; we find in him only an obscure reference to "the effort of memory to persevere," the "effort of the past to make itself future," in which we find a new allusion to the dynamic principle of persistence in the being and a clear reference to everlasting life. For Unamuno, in the last instance, to be a person is to be—or want to be—immortal and everlasting. All this brings us back to the "sole question," the question of death, key to the problem of the person and of life.

*The discovery of the person.* Unamuno relates personality to the most authentic, and therefore most personal, human modes of being; love and grief. Within these, bound together, the discovery of the personality takes place, the taking possession of oneself as a person, as what one is; and, at the same time, in this discovered reality the essential mortality of man and the relationship to God appear.

In chapter VII of the *Sentimiento* ("Love, pain, compassion and personality"), Unamuno writes: "To love in spirit is to pity, and he who pities most loves most. Men afire with burning charity for their fellows were so because they had reached the depths of their own misery, their own apparentiality, their own nothingness; and turning their eyes, thus opened, on their fellow creatures, they saw them as also miserable, apparential, and annihilable, and so pitied and loved them." Then he adds, with more precision: "In the measure that you turn in upon yourself and go deeper into yourself, you discover your own soullessness, that you are not everything which you are not, that you are not what you would like to be, that you are not, in short, anything but nothingness. And in touching your own nothingness, in not feeling your permanent depths nor reaching your own infinitude, still less your own eternity, you have a heartfelt pity for yourself, and you are on fire with painful love for yourself. . ." Finally, he adds: "The consciousness of oneself is only the consciousness of one's own limitation. I feel myself when I feel that I am not others, when I know and feel the point at which I cease to be, beyond which I no longer am."

This deals, then, with the consciousness of man's contingency, felt in oneself. When man feels himself to be nothingness, when he touches his limits, his finite and passing reality, his lack of a permanent depth, he knows himself as a person and loves himself. Is there not a contradiction between these statements in which Unamuno places the root of love in the consciousness of "nothingness," and his doctrine that love arises from belief in the substantial reality of man? No. We have already observed the nature of Unamuno's substance, identified with the dynamic personal being of the consciousness; to believe in the substantiality of man is to take him as a person and not as a thing; but this person is affected by nothingness, by contingency, and by misery. And this provokes compassion in its most fundamental form, not in reference to what is *happening* to someone, but to what he *is*. Then, as we saw before, it is called "grief," tribulation, or concern for the limited and perishable being of the person.

In chapter IX of the same book, Unamuno confronts this question directly. He speaks of "the painful yearning to survive and be eternal," the longing to escape the most radical limitation, to evade contingency, and he says that grief discovers God to us, for He is precisely the full reality, the only possible savior of contingency, of the essential human misery and nothingness. Afterwards Unamuno adds these essential words, which sum up the densest and most closely reasoned part of his thought on the subject.

"It is grief which makes consciousness turn back on itself. He who is not grief-stricken knows what he does and what he thinks, but he does not truly know that he does it and thinks it. He thinks, but he does not think about what he thinks, and his thoughts are as if they were not his. Nor does he belong to himself. And it is solely through grief, through the passionate desire never to die, that a human spirit becomes master of itself.

"Pain, which is an undoing, makes us discover our own inwardness, and in the supreme undoing, that of death, we shall reach through the pain of annihilation the very bowels of our temporal inwardness, shall reach God, whom we breathe and learn to love in spiritual grief."

Grief, then, makes man enter into himself, possess himself, and therefore become a person; strictly speaking, personality is constituted in suffering and simultaneously discovers itself. But this is not all; it is the discovery of an irreducible reality, substantial but contingent, with a limited and finite being which struggles to survive, never to die. Unamuno interprets death as a *supreme undoing,* as the radical culmination of grief, which is equivalent in its turn to interpreting grief as an anticipation or prefiguration of death. Death is present in life in the concrete form of grief; and, since grief consists in knowing oneself mortal and believing oneself everlasting, immortality is also postulated in it. And there is yet more: this intimate contact with one's own being leads to God, whom Unamuno calls *the very bowels of our temporal inwardness,* that is, the foundation or support of our intimate personal reality; consequently God also shows himself in grief.

The reality of the person as such, revealed in grief as anticipation of death, makes clear its essential mortality, its mortal destiny, and its demand for survival, and finally brings us to God as the radical support of the person and guarantor of personal immortality. This is the internal structure of these problems, as they can be seen in the mind—so perspicacious, yet so lacking in continuity—of Unamuno.

## DEATH AND SURVIVAL

*The urge for survival.* Unamuno's intellectual point of departure is the oft-cited doctrine of Spinoza that everything tends to persevere indefinitely in its being, that this urge or appetite is its very essence, and that, in the case of man, this appetite is accompanied by consciousness. No other philosophical statement was shared more deeply and sincerely by Unamuno, who discovered in the sober Latin propositions of Spinoza's *Ethics* the expression of his agonized yearning for immortality.

At times he calls this the "appetite for divinity"; but, as we have seen, it is not a longing to attain God for His own sake but to achieve the guarantee of immortality, which is necessary in order to live this passing life. "I need the immortality of my soul; I need the indefinite survival of my individual consciousness; without it, without faith in it, I cannot live, and doubt, the lack of belief that I will achieve it, torments me." * As we have seen, a horizon is essential to life, and its whole meaning, its very possibility, depends on that

* *Ensayos,* VII, 182.

horizon's being either a frontier of the hereafter or of nothingness. As Unamuno's religious faith is vacillating and insufficient, and, on the other hand, man is rational and struggles to know even that which he believes *(fides quaerens intellectum),* he must try to think about this theme of death and the hope of everlasting life so as to calm himself and be able to live this life with confidence in the other. This is why Unamuno says that it is "the only true vital problem, the one which strikes into us most deeply, the problem of our individual and personal destiny, of the immortality of the soul." * What does Unamuno do with this problem, with the "sole question," at which we have finally arrived?

*The problem lived.* We cannot expect, here less perhaps than in any other area, a rational elaboration of the question at Unamuno's hands. We have already seen, reserving the right to investigate it more deeply later, that Unamuno's point of departure is a radical lack of confidence in reason, which leads him to consider it incapable of penetrating the mystery of life and consequently of death, and still more of immortality. In the book most directly concerned with this theme, *Del sentimiento trágico de la vida,* he embraces the thesis, with some few exceptions, that the immortality of the soul cannot be proved rationally and that, on the other hand, reason finds its mortality more probable (see the beginning of chapter V). But, as in the case of the existence of God, Unamuno does not go to any great lengths to try to prove immortality, not even to prove that it cannot be proved; and so his arguments about both questions are intellectually inoperative, which makes them in the last analysis ineffectual.

But what Unamuno does do is to *live* the problem with an intensity and a keenness to which we are unfortunately unaccustomed. As a general rule, immortality and life everlasting—even death itself—are talked about at a distance, without direct contact with the reality being thought about, without "significant realization," as Husserl would say. No attempt is made to think to the very depths—or, if you like, to feel or imagine—just what this inescapable and

* *Del Sentimiento trágico de la vida,* chapter I.

obligatory human possibility we call death really is; what it would be like to cease to be, to be annihilated; what it might mean to survive death, to live, after having died, a life which is *other,* an *everlasting* or *eternal* life. Not even in the lives of other men does the mortal horizon of man appear in full consciousness—and hence its triviality; one lives "counting on" death and at the same time ignoring it, or using it as a pretext not to live life fully, to deny and evade it. Unamuno, on the contrary, scarcely has eyes for anything else; thus he places before our own eyes, with the highest degree of vigor, the reality and problematical nature of death, and obliges us to take it into account whether we want to or not. *In this sense,* Unamuno's work is for the reader a powerful and effective call to himself, and consequently to the essential assumptions of all religion.

At the beginning of chapter III of the *Sentimiento,* in a first attempt to bring us close to the reality of death, Unamuno writes: "It is in fact impossible for us to conceive of ourselves as nonexistent, and no effort is sufficient for the consciousness to realize absolute unconsciousness, its own annihilation. Try to imagine, reader, when you are wide awake, the state of your soul in the deepest sleep; try to fill your consciousness with the image of nonconsciousness and you will see. The effort to comprehend it causes a terribly painful vertigo. We cannot conceive of ourselves as not existing." A little later he adds: "Withdraw into yourself, reader, and imagine a slow unmaking of yourself, in which the light is extinguished, things fall dumb and give no sound, wrapping you around with silence; palpable objects melt in your hands, the ground slips out from under your feet, memories vanish as in a swoon, everything melts into nothingness, and you melt away too, and not even consciousness of nothingness remains, not even the ghostly handhold of a shadow." *We cannot conceive of ourselves as not existing,* says Unamuno. This is what we are dealing with, the mind's resistance to imagining its own annihilation, and the reason is clear: to imagine presupposes that I am imagining, presupposes my presence, and the imagination of *my* annihilation is a contradiction in terms. This is why we must make note of the leap Unamuno takes in his previous description, when he passes from the dissolution of all that is outside me to my own dissolution, which cannot be reconciled with what precedes. He describes it all in vital terms, in reference to my life; no matter what its type of reality may be per se, the *vital* reality of the shades, or of silence, or the nothingness into which, for example, one may fall is undeniable; they are tremendous realities which occur in my life and which I must take into account. The destruction of things, even in principle of my own body, is quite thinkable or imaginable; but the picture changes if I proceed to imagine the annihilation of my own "I"; and, naturally, this is what is being dealt with if we are to speak of an effective annihilation. After this attempt, Unamuno says: "If we die altogether, what is it all about? What is it for?" Life, this life which we possess and know, has no interest, is no use, if it is not forever, if the annihilation of my consciousness is going to follow it, if after death nothing happens. And he says that what is not eternal is not real either. Unamuno, seeming to recall the Greek doctrine of *ἀεὶ ὄν*, the being which eternally is, denies true reality to what is perishable.

Moved by fear of nothingness, of the destruction of the personality, Unamuno clings to hope; the arguments in favor of mortality do not suffice to destroy his hope, which stands firm in spite of them. "These reasonings," he says, "make no impression on me, for they are arguments and nothing more than arguments, and not by them is the heart appeased. I do not wish to die, no, I neither wish it nor wish to wish it; I want to live forever, forever, and *I* want to live, this poor self which I am and feel myself to be here and now, and that is why I am tortured by the problem of the survival of my soul, my own soul." This long cry of yearning extends throughout Unamuno's life and, like a fresh and lively sap, makes his whole work live. And he recalls Plato's hopeful doubt in the *Phaedo,* when he says that the risk (*καλὸς γὰρ ὁ δκίνυνος*) of the soul's immortality is a glorious one. Unamuno vigorously restates the need not to die altogether, and refuses to mistake personal survival *sensu stricto* for any substitute, whether it be called fame or works or posterity or annihilation or dissolution in the great Whole. After discovering and having fully experienced the irreducible reality of the person, he understands that it is the person, in the strictest sense of the word, who dies and does not want to die altogether, who can, therefore, survive or revive to live again in eternal life. Unamuno states the problem as a problem with a fullness rarely known before; he places it in front of our eyes, forces us to concern ourselves with it; evasion becomes impossible.

With this Unamuno brings us face to face with the authenticity of living; I repeat, he calls us to ourselves. But at the same time he is committed to grappling radically with the problem. To what point and in what measure does he do so? That is to say, to what point, after *living* the problem, does he face up to it intellectually? This is another question.

*Immortality and Resurrection.* There are two forms of survival: one consists in not dying, at least in not dying altogether, in being —totally or partially—immortal; the other, which supposes a previous death, is resurrection. In the first, survival has only a spiritual value, for the body dies and it is a question of the immortality of the soul, not the whole man; in the second, which supposes the previous immortality of the person, life is reestablished in the complete man and he lives again in his body, which has been dead but is now on the other side of death. In his moments of agnosticism Unamuno sometimes refers to the immortality of the soul "à la Hellenic," as he usually says, to the survival of name and fame, to glory, even to vanity; and, on the other hand, he finds in paternity a reflection of the survival of the flesh. But most of the time he feels fully the real meaning of life everlasting, and affirms his longing for it.

"I tremble at the idea of having to tear myself out of my flesh," he says in chapter III of the *Sentimiento.* "I tremble still more at the idea of having to tear myself away from all which is sensible and material, from all substance. If perhaps this merits the name of materialism and if I cling to God with all my strength and all my senses, it is so that He may bear me in His arms to the other side of death, looking me in the eyes with His heaven when those eyes are about to close forever." Further on he emphasizes the whole Pauline preaching about the central dogma of the resurrection of the flesh. And then he speaks of the opinion of Brother Pedro Malón de Chaide, according to which the blessed lament in heaven because they are not whole, with their bodies, until the Resurrection, although they cannot suffer since they enjoy the beatific vision. Unamuno affirms the necessity man feels, not only to have an immortal soul but to rise again with his own body.

And he interprets the desire for name and fame, from the point of view of survival, as a yearning to retain one's apparential immortality when one does not have faith in true immortality. In connection with this idea we might note the fact that in the Middle Ages, during which European man lived immersed in a firm belief in the other life, the sense of intellectual or artistic originality almost disappears, and there is an extraordinary abundance of anonymous works and those others which proceed from a collective task, from Scholasticism to the cathedrals. Conversely, a lively desire for notoriety, for fame, awakened with the Renaissance, and concern about plagiarism appears, the desire for linking the name with the work, however unimportant the work may be; today the last note or newspaper cartoon is signed, while we do not know who planned the majority of the Romanesque or Gothic cathedrals, nor who wrote the *Poema del Cid,* the *Chanson de Roland* or the *Theologia Deutsch.*

In the same way, vanity appears in Unamuno as a reflection of the longing for survival, the yearning to outlive oneself. Even more: vanity is an inversion—like avarice—of means and ends. The miser takes money as an end, when it is only a means, and clings to it; the vain man clings to appearance for its own sake, not as a simple indication of reality. "To seem to be something," writes Unamuno, "leads to being it, ends by being our objective. We need to have others believe we are superior to them in order to feel so ourselves, and to base our faith in our own survival on that belief, at least as concerns the survival of fame." And, he interprets from the same point of view, envy, the hunger for personality, which feels jealous of the value and glory of others because it feels that its own self and its own fame are diminished thereby. But Unamuno takes care to emphasize the negative and timorous nature, born out of indigence, of these apparently petulant and aggressive passions. "Is it pride to aspire to leave an undying name? Pride. . . ? That is not pride but terror of nothingness. We aspire to be everything because we see in this the only hope of escaping nothingness. We want to preserve our memory, if only our memory. How long will it last? At most, as long as humankind lasts. And what if we preserve our memory in God?"

Unamuno feels, then, that the only authentic survival, able to satisfy man and lull him in his hope, is life everlasting as affirmed in Catholicism: guaranteed by God, exemplified in the resurrection of Christ, with the complete reality of the immortal soul and the body restored at the last day: *expecto resurrectionem mortuorum et vitam venturi saeculi,* according to the Credo. This is the question; the rest are only substitutes which man seeks in darkness, when the true faith fails him. Realizing this, Unamuno adds: "many, especially the simple, slake that thirst for eternal life in the fountain of religious faith; but it is not given to everyone to drink of it." * And his intellectual or, especially, imaginative efforts are attempts to supply faith, or rather to seek it or affirm it.

*Death as solitude.* Unamuno considers that the very problem of immortality, as such, is irrational, apart from its solutions.† Naturally, he does not justify this opinion, merely enunciating it, but it necessarily conditions the treatment of the theme in his work. He tackles it poetically, imaginatively, attempting to penetrate through fantasy the inaccessible redoubt of death, and therefore the meaning of survival, of otherworldly life. We have to see, then, how far Unamuno carries the imagination of that strange reality which is death.

Probably Unamuno's profoundest insight in regard to death is his interpretation of it as *solitude,* an idea scarcely grasped, nowhere formulated thematically, and referred to only rarely, but one which lies at the base of all his imaginative intuitions of the mortal process. Only in *La agonía del cristianismo* does he say: "We men live together, but each one dies alone and death is the supreme solitude." § The meaning of this isolated sentence, lacking any ulterior explanation or development, is problematical. For the moment, it is focused

* *Del sentimiento trágico de la vida,* end of chapter III.

† *Ibid.,* chapter VI.

§ *La agonía del cristianismo,* III, 53.

on the obvious fact, which I pointed out elsewhere, that it is not possible to be, to *coexist* with the one who dies, because this represents a contradiction; each man must face death alone, with no possible companionship, because this ceases just where life ends, where death arrives therefore. But this alone would not justify the second clause of Unamuno's sentence, "death is the supreme solitude." At most it could be said that death "occurs" in supreme solitude, but not that it "consists" in it. But could not this be imagined also? Unamuno does not say so, of course; nowhere in his writings does he even attempt to answer the fundamental question: What is death? Nevertheless, it would be possible to discover in his less directly intellectual works, in his novels, where he presents death in its immediacy, where he tries, if not to imagine it, to *live* it, traces of a perhaps unrecognized presence of this interpretation. Let us see how Unamuno shows imaginatively the reality of dying, in what modes he exemplifies this human possibility whose essence we should like to apprehend.

The two novels in which he presents the reality of death in a most emphatic and vivid manner are *Paz en la guerra,* his first, and *La tía Tula,* and these are the ones I prefer to concentrate upon.* In the first of these narratives he refers to the preoccupation with death felt by Pachico Zabalbide, and says: "To have to pass from yesterday to tomorrow without being able to live in the whole continuum of time at once! The emotion of death in the solitary darkness of night brought him these reflections, a vivid emotion which made him tremble at the idea of the moment when sleep would clutch him; he was overwhelmed by the thought that one day he would fall asleep never to wake. It was *a mad terror of nothingness, of finding himself alone in empty time,* a mad terror which shook his heart and made him dream that he was choking for lack of air, that he was falling constantly and unceasingly into the eternal void in a terrible fall. He was more terrified of nothingness than of hell, for it was a dead and cold image for him; but an image of life, after all" (pages 54–55). For Pachico the image of death is nothingness, but nothingness

*Austral edition (1940) quoted. The italics in the quoted passages which follow are my own.

which can be encountered, nothingness as vital reality, not the annihilation of himself, but of everything else; absolute solitude, therefore. He speaks of finding himself alone, and both terms of this expression are equally interesting; the solitude as well as the finding himself. Death is not a simple ceasing to be, but rather a radical finding oneself alone. How is this possible?

And after this anticipation in expectation (pages 54–55), the presence of death fulfilled and consummated takes place in *Paz en la guerra*. The death of Doña Micaela is everyday death, death which breaks into the family's trivial life, in the troubled days of the siege of Bilbao. The explosion of a bomb is expected momentarily, and an anguished quiet has been produced in the house around the mother, who is eking out her last few moments of life. "A supreme silence followed, in whose emptiness could be heard the labored breathing of the sick woman. Her mind was filled with last farewells to be said, but she was unable to remember any of them, full of sleep. 'When will this end?,' she thought. After the moment of anguished silence came a great quaking explosion that seemed to make the whole house shudder. The sick woman, terrified, stretched out her arms, and giving a cry, her last, fell back on the pillow. . . Her heart had broken, *the world had died for her,* and with it there vanished from her poor battered head all the fears and anxieties, the ghosts which haunted the unquiet dream of her life, and so *she could rest at last* in the eternal reality of unending sleep" (page 168). The disappearance of the surroundings, of the circumstance, is stressed again; death is interpreted as the world's dying for the one who dies; the world, interpreted here in its turn as a *task,* as tormenting movement, which is replaced by *rest,* also a vital reality, which presupposes the survival of the one who rests.

Later the timid and melancholy old bachelor Don Miguel dies, and evokes in his last moments the life he might have lived and has not known. "He began to shudder as he felt an immense sadness for not having lived, and a belated repentance for that fear of happiness which had made him lose it. He wanted to relive life, *feeling himself alone in the middle of a sea*" (page 194).

And violent, dramatic death, infrequent in Unamuno, appears

when Ignacio dies, wounded by a bullet in Somorrostro. "Just at dusk, Ignacio was looking out of the entrance of the trench for pure curiosity, when he felt a blow under the Sacred Heart of Jesus embroidered by his mother; he put his hand on it, his sight dimmed, and he fell. He felt himself failing very rapidly, that his head was swimming, that *the sight of present things was vanishing,* and then came immersion in a great sleep. At last his senses closed to the present, his memory collapsed, his soul gathered itself together, and a closely knit vision of his childhood arose in it for the briefest space of time. . . His dying life concentrated itself in his eyes and then was lost, leaving mother earth to suck the blood from his almost bloodless body. An expression of quiet calm was left on his face, as if he had rested, when *he conquered life,* in the peace of the earth, that peace in which not a moment passes. Near him the noises of combat sounded, while the waves of time beat in upon eternity" (pages 213–214). Once more the same intuitions appear: the dissolution of the present world, solitude, concentration on the self; then rest—which requires a subject, not the annihilation of the subject—and active expressions are stressed, such as the one in which Unamuno says, "he conquered life," that is, he died. "Who died?," one might ask. Exactly the one who dies, the one who is different from his life, the one who is alone—what we have called the person.

This death, seen from outside, from the point of view of the parents, points out clearly to Unamuno two dimensions of the death of a fellow creature: loss and death itself, in which its irreducible reality is felt and lived. Pedro Antonio the chocolate-maker, Ignacio's father, "could not succeed in changing the cold 'I have lost my son!' into the mysterious 'My son has died!' His son had gone away, naturally, as others went; he had not come back yet, also naturally, but he might return any day, and the only thing that stood between that memory and this hope, equally alive, as a present reality was a piece of news, a mere piece of news, something someone said" (page 226). Only much later, during a ceremony which moves him profoundly (page 255), does he go from one position to the other and discover in himself the reality of his son's death; and then he becomes conscious of the grief he has slowly incubated for many long days, not for the lost son—that is, for his relationship with him —but for the son himself, for his dead son.

In *La tía Tula,* written twenty-three years after *Paz en la guerra,* there is another long series of deaths in the bosom of Gertrudis' family. And, along with the persistence of the same imaginative interpretations, some new elements appear, which we would do well to emphasize. The two most interesting and moving examples are the deaths of Ramiro's two wives, that of Rosa, his first, Gertrudis' sister, and that of Manuela, the orphan servant girl. In the first, already cited, Unamuno says: "Speech and strength failed her, and holding the hand of her man, the father of her children, she looked at him as the sailor who sets forth *to lose himself on shoreless seas* looks at the far-off promontory, the tongue of native land, which little by little is lost in the distance and merges with the sky; during the choking spells her eyes looked into the eyes of her Ramiro from the edge of eternity. And that look seemed to be *a despairing and supreme question,* as if, on the point of departing never more to return to earth, she were asking him what the hidden meaning of life was. . . It was an abysmal afternoon. . . " And then: "At last the supreme moment came upon her, the moment of *transition,* and it seemed as though, on the threshold of the eternal shades, *suspended over the abyss,* she clung to him, to her man, who trembled as he felt drawn in too. The poor thing tried to tear open her throat with her nails, she looked at him terrified, her eyes begging for air; then, with her eyes seeming to plumb the depths of his soul, she let go of his hand and fell back on the bed where she had conceived and borne her three children" (pages 56–57). What is new in this moving description, or better, this intimate narrative? Unamuno emphasizes the moment of solitude, using the same metaphors of the shoreless sea, the shades, and the abyss; but here it is not a question of pure solitude without any other characteristics, but is a whither, a journey, a solitude in respect to all this, so as to *go*—where? This is why solitude is problematical as well; this is why death puts life itself in question and turns into a query, a radical interrogation; this is why death is transition. And this transition, this passing, presupposes a passenger, a traveler who passes, and who feels anguish at the tearing away which departure means, the separation from all the circumstance in which he has lived and the uncertainty of the other end of the transition. Solitude troubles us with its mystery; man, when he finds himself in its void, is given over to another where. Pure solitude contradicts the essential characteristic of existence, and its presence shows us a radical otherness, another latent reality. And, in regard to this, note how Unamuno changes his point of view when he narrates Rosa's last agony: first he tells it from hers, but at the end, when death arrives and the great solitude breaks in, when coexistence is impossible, he sees her from outside, with the eyes of a spectator who watches her fall back, beaten, on the bed.

But Unamuno takes one further step in divining death's meaning when he tells us—and in this case, rather, interprets for us—the death of Manuela, the poor orphan girl. "She died," he says, "as she had lived, like a submissive and patient beast, like a chattel even. And it was this death, such a natural one, which struck deepest into the spirit of Gertrudis, who had been present at three deathbeds already. In this death she felt even more the meaning of the enigma. . . Eva brought her a card with the story of Genesis, which she had read not long before, about how God breathed the breath of life into man's nostrils, and she imagined that He took away life in a similar way. And then she fancied that *God had taken with a kiss* the life of that poor orphan, the meaning of whose life she could not understand, putting His infinite invisible lips, those lips that close and form the blue sky, on the lips, turned blue in death, of that poor girl, and so drawing out her breath" (pages 104–105).

Here the explicit allusion to God as the background of death appears for the first time. God intervenes in dying. Now it is not a question of simple solitude, nor even of a vague transition toward an unknown and problematical destination. Life appears related to God, and the great solitude which is death is made by God, Who receives the life He previously breathed into man. Over the dark question mark of death the great presence of God is drawn, giving meaning to solitude in relation to things, of every thing. And this death, thus understood, is for Unamuno—let us not forget his words—

that in which the meaning of the mortal enigma is best divined. The reference to God is what makes death more comprehensible.

Unamuno reaches this point; it would be useless to seek for greater detail in him, not even a translation of these guesses into strict conceptual terms. However, it is possible to attempt to see in these conjectures the ultimate content of his imaginative experience of death. This would mean—if, I repeat, we carry to its extreme what is merely insinuated in Unamuno—radical solitude, the suppression of all that is *other* than the man who dies, the disappearance of the world around him. Since I am related to the exterior world through my body, its biological death would mean the absolute solitude of my person, separation from all of my circumstance. This corporeal death would bring with it a partial destruction of my life, of all that which is not strictly personal; but, in the same manner, up to this point nothing would affect the irreducible reality of the person *sensu stricto*. Therefore for him there would exist that solitude which supposes that someone is alone, not the annihilation of the person, for then there would not be solitude either; because of this, in the last instance man could truly die, not merely cease to exist. But there is still more. This absolute suppression of the circumstance, this solitude of the man himself, of the *who* of each one, would uncover what is by definition latent in man: the very foundation of his existence and his personal being, that which, because it has made me to be, cannot be given in my life, but transcends me and is inaccessible to me—God. In radical solitude the ontological assumption of his own reality would be revealed to man.

Now we must ask ourselves, What is the role of God in Unamuno's thought?

## THE THEME OF GOD

*Similarity and contrast.* In his meditation about Divinity, Unamuno usually skims capriciously through the theme, and in that zigzag course he frequently *errs*. His attitude of distrust in reason, pointed out so many times in this book, prevents him even from grappling seriously with the problem, and he accepts uncritically his own agnostic position. Therefore, as soon as he deals with the theme directly and explicitly, he disqualifies himself to take it up in any fruitful way; and this to the extreme that the main bulk of his heterodoxy does not result from his statements themselves, but rather from his denial that anything can be affirmed or known in relation to God. Unamuno's fundamental error lies not so much in launching himself on a misguided path as in closing off any possibility of access to the theme of Divinity.

In spite of this, when Unamuno, without having taken up the question previously—and therefore, almost always, *in modo obliquo* —thinks about the urgent problem of God, he at times attains extremely accurate and perceptive insights. "The greatest novelty of Christianity, in the religious sphere," he writes in his *Ensayos,* "is to have discovered the filial relation between man and his God. God is the Father of Jesus and Jesus is the Son of Man. In his *Confessions,* St. Augustine has a marvelous passage in which he says, speaking of God: 'Who can understand, who can express God? What is it that shines at moments in the eyes of my soul and makes my heart beat with terror and love? It is something very different from myself, and so I am frozen with fear; it is something identical to myself, and so I am inflamed with love.' The origin of the fear of God and love for Him could not be better expressed." Then he adds: "God becomes ourself projected into infinity. This projection makes Him, at the same time that he is something like ourselves, something in which we can trust, because His ways and acts are like our own, an anthropomorphic power, something also entirely different from ourselves, as different as the infinite can be from the finite, something before which we must tremble, for He can surprise us when we least expect it with some unlooked-for thing." *

Aside from some minor inaccuracies of expression, this paragraph clearly expresses the traditional Christian attitude in regard to the knowledge of God and man's relation to Him. In the first place, it is a matter of filiation; more concretely, man resembles God in that both are persons, but man is infinitely different from Him in that one is finite and imperfect and the other perfect and in-

* *Ensayos,* IV, 96–97.

finite; similarity and contrast are, therefore, essentially linked; hence prayer arises, the impulse to raise oneself toward God, and the possibility of knowing him *per ea quae facta sunt,* through created reality—and above all human reality—using the similarity as a point of departure and denying all that is negative and all limitation, so as to carry to the infinite the affirmation of all that is positive and real. This is the foundation of the traditional approaches to knowing God, that is, together with the *via causalitatis,* the *via excellentiae,* and the *via negationis.* Once again, it might have been thought that Unamuno, after having grasped so accurately the point of view in which Christian thought has placed itself, would have employed these approaches in order to achieve, or attempt at least, an effective knowledge of God, even though *in speculo et aenigmate.* But, instead of this, he arbitrarily rejects the possibility of knowing rationally, and thus exposes himself to all the risks of a hazardous imaginative inquiry.

*Personal and eternalizing God.* For Unamuno, God, in whom he sees above all his own self raised to the infinite, is necessarily a person. He seeks in God the guarantee of immortality, of survival; but as it is a personal immortality, a survival of my own self and not of any thing, no "preservation" in an impersonal totality will be of use to him. To assure the immortality of the person, God must be one also. Therefore Unamuno rejects any pantheism, from this point of view equivalent to atheism for him. "To say that everything is God, and that when we die we return to God, or rather that we continue in Him, does not serve our yearning at all; for, if this is so, we were in God before we were born, and, if after death we return to where we were before we were born, the human soul, the individual consciousness, is perishable. And, as we know very well that God, the personal and conscious God of Christian monotheism, is no less than the provider and above all the guarantor of our immortality, it follows that it is said, and well said, that pantheism is nothing but a disguised atheism. And I would even say an undisguised one."* Unamuno understands that the foundation of my everlasting existence must be a person, and further that it must be

* *Del sentimiento trágico de la vida,* chapter V.

transcendent, other than I, the support of my perishable reality; that is, the God which Unamuno yearns for and thinks about, the only one who seems conceivable to him as the true God, is the Christian God. This point is worth emphasizing: for Unamuno any idea of God which is not strictly that of a God who is indivisible, personal, immortal, Father of men, who saves them from nothingness, brings them to life, and makes them His sons in Christ, is inadmissible and useless.

Unamuno understands this becoming eternal as a consequence of God's being eternal and at the same time personal, an imperishable mind. What God thinks does not pass away, does not cease to be. God's Word is creative, and in God there is no eventual forgetting, for He is eternal. The survival of consciousness seems to Unamuno to be a salvation in the divine mind, in His eternally present consciousness, superior to time, and consequently to memory and forgetting. "Is it not said in Scripture," he asks, "that God creates with His Word, that is, with His thought, and that He through His Word made all that exists? And does God forget anything He has thought at its proper season? May it not be that in the Supreme Consciousness thoughts that once pass through it continue to exist? In Him, who is eternal, is not all existence made eternal?" *

These ideas appear in an even clearer and more forceful way in chapter VIII of this book, where Unamuno especially emphasizes the personal relationship of man with God and the divine personality, which permits the love of God for Himself and for man. "The God we hunger for," he says, "is the God to whom we pray, the God of the Pater Noster, of the Lord's Prayer; the God of whom we ask, before all and above all, whether or not we realize it, that He give us faith, faith in Himself, that He make us believe in Him, that He make Himself in us, the God to whom we pray that His name be hallowed and that His will be done—His will, not His reason—on earth as it is in Heaven; but feeling that His will can only be the essence of our will, the desire to live on eternally." Then he adds: "And if you believe in God, God believes in you, and believing in you He continually creates you. For at bottom you are

* *Del sentimiento trágico de la vida,* end of chapter VII.

nothing more than the idea of yourself that God has." Salvation through faith, God's making eternal the man who believes, is interpreted by Unamuno in a directly personal way, in terms of "coexistence": God believes in the believer and so in eternity He creates him continually, that is, preserves him and makes him to be forever.

Shortly before this Unamuno had interpreted the Trinity as a condition of the authentic divine personality: "The God of faith is personal; He is a person because He is three persons, for personality does not feel itself in isolation. *An isolated person ceases to be a person.* Whom could that person, in fact, love? And if he does not love, he is not a person. It is not possible to love oneself being only one, without love's splitting one in two." (The italics are mine.) Now we shall examine the scope of this thought.

*The foundation of personal existence.* "God," says Unamuno, "does not exist, but rather superexists, and He sustains our existence by existing us." As usual, he does not add a single word to this serious and interesting statement. And as always we are left in doubt about the implications this thesis may have had in his own thought, about the extent to which it was really possessed and rigorously thought out by him. Its meaning is not even univocal and explicit. However, we can make an attempt to understand it, even at the risk of exceeding the precise limits of what this detached phrase meant for him.

In it Unamuno distinguishes between two different things: existing, and another superior mode of reality he calls superexisting, employing a shrewd neologism which was very much to his taste. Strictly speaking, we are dealing here with an application of the method of the *viae remotionis et excellentiae:* Unamuno denies existence to God, not because He lacks it, but because existence in the sense of things or of men is not applicable to Him except in another higher and more excellent mode, which Unamuno calls superexisting. Very well then, what is this superexistence? With an even bolder neologism, Unamuno makes the verb "to exist" transitive, and says that God *exists us.* It seems, then, that God, still more than existing, *causes to exist.* But perhaps this is not sufficient either. If Unamuno is referring solely to this, to causing to exist, that is to say, to the creating and preserving action, why does he not employ the usual terms? Is it for the pure pleasure of inventing a new word or of doing violence to the grammatical structure of the verb "to exist"? Possibly, but there may be a more profound reason.

In the first place, Unamuno is referring in this context to men, not to things, not to creation in general; it might be thought, then, that he is alluding to something exclusive to the human being, and in fact we find the expression "to sustain our existence," in which the last word seems to refer not to pure existence, but to existence in the sense of human life. But, on the other hand, if we compare that passage with another, found in *Cómo se hace una novela,* in which he speaks of the ways of approaching God, we find something which may help us to understand. Here Unamuno says: "There is that which is already made and that which is being made. One arrives at the invisibility of God through that which is already made—*per ea quae facta sunt,* according to the Latin canonical version, which is not very close to the Greek original, in a passage from St. Paul*—but this is the way of nature, and nature is dead. There is the way of history, and history is alive; and to take the way of history is to reach the invisibility of God through what is being made, *per ea quae fiunt.*" Then he adds: "Hugo de San Victor, the twelfth-century mystic, said that to ascend to God was to enter into oneself and not only into oneself but to pass out of oneself, into the innermost depths—*in intimis etiam seipsum transire*—in a certain ineffable manner, and that the most intimate is the closest, the supreme, and the eternal." †

What does this mean? What do the passages, so far apart in time, which we have assembled here show us? When Unamuno proposes the expression *per ea quae fiunt* as more precise and alive than the one which reads *per ea quae facta sunt,* he merely affirms, after Augustine, that the point of departure for attaining God, rather than natural things, is man himself, the soul and life of man, *imago Dei.* The point of departure for raising himself to Divinity is man him-

* Romans 1:20.
† *Cómo se hace una novela,* pp. 150–152.

self, in what is most himself, in that which is being made, in his own personal existence; according to Hugo de San Victor's expression, which Unamuno accepts, one ascends to God by transcending oneself, going beyond one's own intimacy. Why? Because God—and here we return to our starting point—is continually sustaining our existence in addition to having created it; not only does He make us exist, but He *exists us*. This is the most profound and radical point Unamuno sees, or at least glimpses, in his uncertain inquiry into God.

And now the deepest sense of his interpretation of death is made clearer for us. When man dies he is in absolute isolation, in radical solitude; it is precisely on this fact that the seriousness of death is founded, not on an annihilation in which the very reality of completed and consummated death would disappear. But, Unamuno says, an *isolated person ceases to be one,* stops being a person; very well: for man, as Unamuno always saw plainly, to cease to be a person is the same as ceasing to be *simpliciter*. Therefore only the presence of God saves man from death. The most radical and absolute way of transcending oneself, of going beyond one's own intimacy, is to be left totally alone, detached from the world and one's own body, from all vital circumstance; and in this total nakedness would be found the all-embracing reality of God, the foundation of one's own existence. Thus we can also understand the words of Scripture which tell us that no man has yet seen God and that no man will see God and live.*

## UNAMUNO AND THE HISTORY OF PHILOSOPHY

Having arrived at this point, after examining throughout the length of this book the different dimensions of Don Miguel de Unamuno's work, we are in a position to answer the questions formulated earlier in regard to the relation in which that work stands to philosophic

* It is clear that any direct knowledge of God, as ontologism incorrectly held, is impossible. Knowledge of God, while man lives, is indirect and reflected; man, in his mundane circumstance, can know God only as reflected in it or in his own intimate reality. Only the dead man, already in everlasting life, can have the vision of Divinity *facie ad faciem*.

thinking. We have seen what Unamuno's "sole question" is, the question which motivates all his thought, and the structure assumed by the fundamental themes of metaphysics in the workings of that thought. We have also seen, in the nature of that question and in the idea Unamuno has of reason, an idea conditioned by the period in the history of philosophy within which he was formed intellectually, why his work contains that strange mixture of philosophical concerns and themes, in molds and modes which are typically literary. We have also seen by what fundamental traits we can consider his novel as the culmination of all his work. This has revealed to us also the unity that is to be found among all these elements, apparently so diverse, and how all of his thought depends on the same point of departure and remains faithful to the same sole purpose.

The relation of Unamuno's work to philosophy seems, therefore, to be as indubitable as it is intimate and essential. But, saying this, I have implied that it is not philosophy in the strict sense. And this is true, as has been shown by noting the conditions which the personal novel satisfies and those which it does not, insofar as concerns the demands of an authentically philosophical knowledge and the substantial formal deficiencies of Unamuno's inquiry into the great themes of philosophy. What is indeed fully present in Unamuno is concern for the problem of philosophy. His entire work is motivated by this concern. He combines an extraordinary sensitivity to the urgency of the metaphysical problem with a sure sense of the true dimensions in which it takes place and the method necessary to confront it. This is true to the point that his thought, as we have seen, keeps abreast of the most fundamental steps of the progress of philosophy in the twentieth century, and in a certain sense he can be considered as a precursor of it. Probably there will be some delay in recognizing the implications of his creation of that novel which I have called personal or existential, and in giving it its full value; but it is undeniable—as I believe I have shown—that his novel is a decisive step forward and one of fruitful consequences.

Unamuno is a characteristic example of the thinker who has a lively sense of a newly discovered reality, but who lacks the intellectual resources necessary to enter into it with the maturity of philosophy. His intuitions, motivated by his anguish in the face of the problem, lived with rare completeness, are of a profound perspicacity, but they go no further. Unamuno shows us the dramatic and profoundly instructive spectacle of a man who confronts in an extra-philosophical, or, if you will, a prephilosophical, manner the problem *itself* of philosophy. This example, which is repeated not infrequently in history, can serve to cast a decisive light on the nature of philosophy itself, and its relationship with the minds which undertake it on this earth. It is the problem of the *history of philosophy,* which is tantamount to being the philosophical problem.

And it poses the question of Unamuno's inclusion or exclusion, when we think of the ambit of the history of philosophy. Does he belong within it or not? To what extent is he incorporated in the reality of the philosophical movement? This is a problem which we cannot solve here; the decision belongs to the future. Human reality is not concluded in itself; it is historical, and therefore only in history does it achieve the wholeness of its being; the present reacts on the past and essentially modifies it. One might say, to use an extreme expression more comprehensible because of its very extremeness, that what is, if indeed it is conditioned by what was, depends equally on what it will become. The past, the present, and the future are given in an indestructible unity and cannot be conceived as isolated moments. What Unamuno *may be* depends on what happens subsequently in the history of philosophy. It is possible that his posthumous action, because of the force of his intuitions, if it is given to these to be realized and to take on metaphysical consistency at any time, may gain a place for him in that history. Otherwise he will remain on the fringe of it, like so many others whose minds have only been open to the problems of philosophy, but in whom philosophy has not taken definite form and achieved forward movement.

This cannot be decided today. The only way of solving the problem is to philosophize: the history of philosophy itself must make the final judgment. And that judgment depends, in the first place, on the *possibilities* existent in Unamuno's work; but these possibilities can be shown only from the viewpoint of reality, that is to say, after actually having philosophized. Therefore the sloth of men enters the picture here also, and with it the element of chance which belongs inexorably to history. It is important for us Spaniards, who until now have not been rich in philosophical substance, to salvage the metaphysical possibilities contained in Unamuno's thought. It is what has led me to write this book.

# *SELECTED BIBLIOGRAPHY OF UNAMUNO'S WORKS*


## COLLECTIONS

*Ensayos*, 7 vols. Madrid: Publicaciones de la Residencia de Estudiantes. 1916–1918. A collection of the articles published by Unamuno, 1895–1916. (This is the edition referred to throughout by Marías.)
*Ensayos*, 2 vols. Madrid: Aguilar, 1942. A collection of all the essays published in book form before Unamuno's death.
*Obras completas*, 5 vols. Madrid: Afrodisio Aguado, 1950–1952.

## WORKS

*En torno al casticismo* (essays). Madrid: La España Moderna, 1895.
*Paz en la guerra* (novel). Madrid: Fernando Fe, 1897.
*Tres ensayos* (essays: "¡Adentro!"; "La ideocracia"; "La fe"). Madrid: Rodríguez Serra, 1900.
*Amor y pedagogía* (novel). Barcelona: Henrich y Cía., 1902.
*Paisajes* (travel). Salamanca: Colección Calón. 1902.
*De mi país* (travel). Madrid: Fernando Fe, 1903.
*Vida de Don Quijote y Sancho, según Miguel de Cervantes Saavedra, explicada y comentada por Miguel de Unamuno* (essays). Madrid: Renacimiento, 1905.
*Poesías* (poetry). Bilbao: J. Rojas, 1907.
*Recuerdos de niñez y de mocedad* (memoirs). Madrid: V. Suárez, 1908.
*Mi religión y otros ensayos breves* (essays). Madrid: Renacimiento, 1910.

*Soliloquios y conversaciones* (essays). Madrid: Renacimiento, 1911.
*Por tierras de Portugal y de España* (travel). Madrid: Renacimiento, 1911.
*Rosario de sonetos líricos* (poetry). Madrid: Fernando Fe, Victoriano Suárez, 1911.
*Contra esto y aquello* (essays). Madrid: Renacimiento, 1912.
*El porvenir de España* (essays). Madrid: Renacimiento, 1912.
*Del sentimiento trágico de la vida* (essays). Madrid: Renacimiento, 1913.
*El espejo de la muerte* (short story). Madrid: Renacimiento, 1913.
*Niebla* (novel). Madrid: Renacimiento, 1914.
*Ensayos*, 7 vols. (essays). Madrid: Publicaciones de la Residencia de Estudiantes, 1916–1918.
*Abel Sánchez. Una historia de pasión* (novel). Madrid: Renacimiento, 1917.
*El Cristo de Velázquez* (poetry). Madrid: Calpe, 1920.
*Tres novelas ejemplares y un prólogo* (novels: *Dos madres; El marqués de Lumbría; Nada menos que todo un hombre)*. Madrid: Calpe, 1920.
*La tía Tula* (novel). Madrid: Renacimiento, 1921.
*Andanzas y visiones españolas* (travel). Madrid: Renacimiento, 1922.
*Teresa* (poetry). Madrid: Renacimiento, 1924.
*Fedra* (drama). Madrid: 1924.
*De Fuerteventura a París* (poetry). Paris: Excelsior, 1925.
*La agonía del cristianismo* (essays). Paris: Rieder, 1925. (This book first appeared in French, translated by Jean Cassou.) First Spanish ed. Madrid: 1931.
*Cómo se hace una novela* (essays). Paris: Rieder, 1927. (This book first appeared in French, translated by Jean Cassou.) First Spanish ed. Buenos Aires: Editorial Alba, 1928.
*Romancero del destierro* (poetry). Buenos Aires: Editorial Alba, 1928.
*El otro* (drama). Madrid: Espasa-Calpe, 1932.
*San Manuel Bueno, mártir, y tres historias más* (novels). Madrid: Espasa-Calpe, 1933.
*Raquel* (drama). Madrid: 1933.
*El hermano Juan* (drama). Madrid: Espasa-Calpe, 1934.
*La esfinge* (drama). Madrid: 1934.

## POSTHUMOUS COLLECTIONS OF POEMS

*Antología poética*, ed. by Luis-Felipe Vivanco. Madrid: Ediciones Escorial, 1942.

*Antología poética*, ed. by Agustín Esclasans. Barcelona: Editorial Fama, 1944.
*Antología poética*. Buenos Aires: Espasa-Calpe, 1946.
*Cancionero* (collected poems, 1928–1936). Buenos Aires: Losada, 1953.

TRANSLATIONS

*Abel Sánchez, and Other Stories (Abel Sánchez; The Madness of Dr. Monarco; St. Emmanuel the Good, Martyr)*, translated and with an introduction by Anthony Kerrigan. Chicago: Regnery, 1958.
*The Agony of Christianity*, translated by Pierre Loving with an introduction by Ernest Boyd. New York: Payson and Clark, 1928.
*The Agony of Christianity*, translated and with an introduction by Kurt F. Reinhardt. New York: Ungar, 1960.
*The Christ of Velazquez*, translated by Eleanor L. Turnbull. Baltimore: Johns Hopkins Press, 1951.
*Essays and Soliloquies*, translated and with an introduction by J. E. Crawford Flitch. New York: Knopf, 1925.
*The Life of Don Quixote and Sancho according to Miguel de Cervantes Saavedra, expounded with comment by Miguel de Unamuno*, translated by Homer P. Earle. New York and London: Knopf, 1927.
*Perplexities and Paradoxes*, translated by Stuart Gross. New York: Philosophical Library, 1945.
*Poems*, translated by Eleanor L. Turnbull, foreword by John Mackay. Baltimore: Johns Hopkins Press, 1952.
*Three Exemplary Novels and a Prologue*, translated by Angel Flores. New York: A. and C. Boni, 1930.
*The Tragic Sense of Life in Men and in Peoples*, translated by J. E. Crawford Flitch, introductory essay by Salvador de Madariaga. London: Macmillan, 1921.

# INDEX